I got on the radio. "Big Ten, this is Long Rifle. We just lost two minutes. If you can't get here in five minutes, we'll be in a world of hurt! Over."

I glanced over to see Lightfoot shaking his head. "We don't have five minutes. The gooks have already set up two machine guns and two mortars."

"No sweat," I told him, while inside I had my own doubts. Lightfoot and I had never tangled head-on with that many enemy troops. They could overwhelm us by sheer numbers. The whole thing depended on split-second timing between us and two jets miles away.

I looked at my watch and back at Charlie. The lead man was six hundred yards away. Lightfoot whispered as loud as he dared, "Ward!"

"Shuu!" I was listening for something, and just then I heard it; we all heard it—a sound like distant thunder. Charlie stopped and started looking skyward. They knew something was up.

"Now!" I shouted at Lightfoot. He began firing, and at the same moment, I shot a machine gunner between the eyes.

DEAR MOM:

*

A Sniper's Vietnam

Joseph T. Ward

IVY BOOKS • NEW YORK

An Ivy Book
Published by The Ballantine Publishing Group
Copyright © 1991 by Joseph T. Ward

http://www.randomhouse.com

Library of Congress Catalog Card Number: 91-91988

ISBN 0-8041-0853-6

Manufactured in the United States of America

Drawings by Rita Hanner

First Edition: October 1991

OPM   29   28   27   26   25   24   23   22   21

Dedicated to my mother who lived with the anguish of never knowing. I would not have traded places.

A sign at the Marine Corps Scout Sniper School, Quantico, Virginia, reads: "The average rounds expended per kill with the M-16 in Vietnam was 50,000. Snipers averaged 1.3 rounds. The cost difference was $2,300 vs. 27 cents."

Acknowledgements

I would like to give thanks to the following for their invaluable assistance:

The personnel at the Marine Corps Recruit Depot, San Diego, CA;
The Belmar Museum, Lakewood, CO;
Foothills Photo Lab, Longmont, CA
The Marine Corps Historical Center and Museum, Washington, DC;
The Military Records Division of the Pentagon, Washington, DC;
The National Archives, Washington, DC;
The Naval Museum, Washington, DC;
The National Oceanic and Atmospheric Administration, National Ocean Survey, Riverdale, MD;
The Records Branch, USMC, Quantico, VA.
Star Enterprises, Louisville, CO

A very special thanks to the following:

Winnie Ferrill
Rita Hanner
Jen Karber
Nancy Leach
Maj. Charles Melson, USMC
Mary Rodriguez
Bertram Rothschild
Sgt. Jeffrey Schinker, USMC-RS
Jan Sword
Trudy Ward

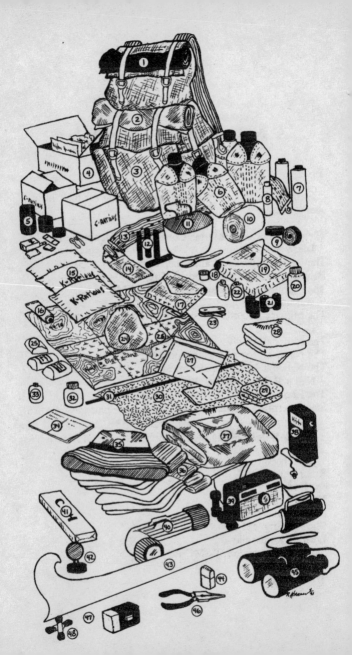

Scout Sniper's pack and contents
J. T. Ward's typical load for a minimum
72-hour assignment

Poncho (1), poncho liner (2), pack (3), package from home: cookies, hard candy, Kool-Aid, dried soups (4), three boxes C rations (5), minimum four canteens (6), two cans foot powder (7), BFI powder, a blood coagulant (8), two rolls black tape (9), toilet paper (10), cooking cup (11), grease paint–black, brown, dark green, and light green (12), web belt (13), tool kit for minor adjustments to scope (14), three K rations (15), zinc oxide ointment (16), first aid kit (17), halazone water purification tablets (18), ammo pouch—holds 80 rounds 7.62mm match ammo (19), vitamins (20), extra batteries for scope, flashlight, strobe light (21), insect repellent (22), Swiss Army knife (23), personal items—shaving gear, soap, toothbrush and toothpaste (24), extra battle dressings (25), tactical maps (26), writing gear (27), three T-shirts (28), two washcloths (29), two towels (30), rifle cleaning rod (31), gun oil (32), linseed oil (33), kill sheets (34), bush hat (35), six pairs white cotton socks (36), jungle fatigues (37), transistor radio (38), camera and film (39), flashlight (40), C-4 plastic explosive (41), compass (42), Turkish battle axe (43), Zippo lighter (44), field glasses (45), wire cutters (46), strobe light (47), two extra boot laces (48).

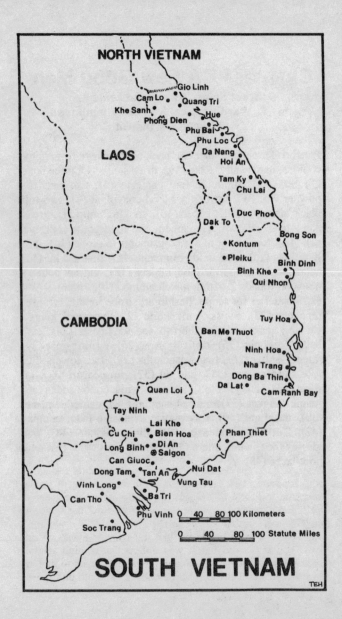

Chapter I ★ A Few Good Men

★

1st Division
Okinawa
April 5th, 1969

Dear Mom,

Well, I'm almost there. I'm in Okinawa and should be leaving for Da Nang today. It doesn't seem like home is halfway around the world. We've been here a couple of days. I was feeling pretty blue when I got here, so I went to the EM club and got drunk.

In some sense, my involvement with the U.S. Marine Corps began with the summer of 1967, high school graduation, and four young men: Dave Young, Mike O'Grady, Nick Herrera, and myself.

Nick was quiet, short, stocky, and strong as a horse. Mike, an average, all-around nice guy, and state wrestling champ. Dave, tall and lanky, with the fastest hands in a fight I've ever seen. Me? I was into sports like Mike, except I liked basketball and track. Oh, yeah, my name's Joseph T. Ward, J.T. to my friends. These differences didn't keep us from becoming best friends in high school. If one of us did something off-the-wall, it was likely the other three were in on it, too. I've got to admit, we were pushing the limits of our manhood further all the time.

Graduation came and went like most major events in our lives, one big party, but it was different after high school. Suddenly we were faced with being separated, each to find his own way in life. Dave and I tried college and both quit in less

1

than a year. We worked odd jobs, and the four of us partied together.

Longmont, Colorado, where we lived, was a small farming community of about thirteen thousand people. Its main industries were a sugar factory and a turkey processing plant, and its main claims to fame were quiet, tree-lined streets and an immense variety of birds. As teenagers, our primary pastimes were cruising Main Street, woodsy parties, and lots of rock and roll.

My mom was in her mid-forties and a single parent who worked long hours as a secretary in the oil business. My friends liked her because they knew they could count on her for a meal or a place to stay when needed; she treated them as one of her own.

Early 1968 found Mike, Nick, Dave, and me sitting on the hoods of our cars on one of the lonely back country roads we knew so well. Bolstered by beer, the conversation wasn't the usual talk about girls, cars, or parties. We were wondering what the hell we were going to do with the rest of our lives, when the talk turned to the military.

I'm from a family with a long, and honorable military history, but there hadn't been a Marine in the family yet. I decided to be the first. When I brought the subject up, Mike, Nick, and I were surprised to learn that Dave had already joined the navy. Our discussion continued, along with the demise of several more cans of beer. Mike and Nick decided to go into the Marine Corps with me on the buddy plan. Dave was hesitant, but to keep us together he switched to the Marines. We sealed the pact with a toast.

Joining on the delayed entry program gave us a couple extra months at home before we were standing in a crowded room at the Customs building, being sworn into the Marine Corps. We were then flown to the MCRD (Marine Corps Recruit Depot) in San Diego. Mike was seventeen years old. Nick, Dave, and I were eighteen.

Our first taste of the Marine Corps came as we got off the bus at the staging area and were greeted by a vision straight from hell with a name to match—Drill Instructor Sergeant Graves. I can't think of too many things more depressing than having a DI named Graves. He closely eyed each of us when we stepped from the bus.

He gathered us into a platoon-size formation, walked back

and forth, looking mostly at the ground, shaking his head. He stopped pacing, spread his feet, put his hands on his hips, and stared. He was silent for a moment, and then began with, "So you candy ass mama's boys want to be Marines, huh?"

"Yes, sir."

"I can't hear you."

"Yes, sir."

"I still can't hear you."

"Yes, sir!"

"Well you can forget your mamas, I'm your mama now and the proper response will be: sir, yes, sir or sir, no, sir. Do you understand me, you sorry, hippie-looking bastards?"

A mixture of "yes, sirs" and "sir, yes, sirs" came from the ranks. Graves looked at the ground and shook his head again. We came to know this as his usual gesture when the platoon screwed up. When only one man made a mistake, he used a more personal, savage, nose-to-nose, eye-to-eye stare.

He strolled back and forth for the next fifteen minutes, using a steady flow of swear words with an occasional comment on what was expected of us. He stopped pacing and became quiet again. Slowly, methodically, he lit a cigarette and strolled upwind of us. I caught a light whiff of smoke and thought how much I wanted one. Graves walked back to the center of his latest platoon and casually said, "The smoking lamp is lit for one cigarette."

There was a rustle as we reached for our cigarettes, but before anyone could light up, he said, "And I'm gonna smoke it." A low groan swept through the platoon. Graves walked upwind of us again, and I began to wonder where a guy like him came from. He stood in front of eighty confused boys and blew smoke in the air for everyone to see. He didn't look at us when he finally said, "Light up, and I don't want to see one single butt on the deck."

Graves was six feet two and 220 pounds of pure mean, but he was one of the best DIs at MCRD. I had no idea at the time that he and I would later develop a strange friendship. He stood motionless, legs spread, hands on his hips and staring, constantly staring.

"They send me worse-looking peckerheads each time." He moved toward a recruit, grabbed him by the shirt collar, pulled him face to face and shouted. "Why the fuck you want to be in my Marine Corps, boy?" He shoved him back in line before he could answer. He did the same thing to several people, but when he got to a small guy, he lifted him right off the ground.

"How in the hell did you get in my Marine Corps? I have bigger wet dreams than you!"

"Sir, I wanted in, sir."

Pretty soon he was there, in front of me, looking as though he expected me to say something. I was still holding the manila envelope with my orders in it, which a sergeant had given me at the airport. I handed Graves the envelope, and he opened it without taking his eyes off mine.

"What's your name, boy?"

"Sir, Ward, sir."

"You're a squad leader now."

He quickly worked his way through the platoon and picked his three other squad leaders: Dave Young, a streetwise guy by the name of Johnson, and a gung ho dude named Perry. We were then marched to the barber shop. To say we marched is giving us too much credit. Half of us were out of step, and the other half stumbled into those trying to keep some kind of rhythm. We were a sad looking lot, especially with Graves swearing at us constantly.

I was in charge of 4th Squad, and we had to stand by as the men of the other three squads entered one end of the barber shop, looking fine, only to emerge from the other side rubbing the tops of their heads. Some were swearing, and a few were bleeding, either from a sliced-off wart in their hairline or from scratches made by what I would more liken to sheep shears than something used to cut human hair. After my turn, I walked down the steps doing the same thing, trying to find hair on my head, and that's the way it would stay all through boot camp.

While we got our hair cut, Graves chose his "house mice," the smallest man in each squad. House mice kept the DI's hut clean and made sure Graves had freshly starched uniforms and spit-shined shoes. If a DI wanted an errand run, the call went out for a specific house mouse. They would be replaced from time to time by someone on punishment detail.

Our next stop was a building with rows of semiprivate booths. A cardboard box, an envelope, a pencil, and one sheet of paper were set neatly on each wooden table. We took off our civilian clothes, put them in the box, and addressed it home. We sat naked on that cold cement floor and wrote a very quick letter home to say we were doing fine. Man, that was some line. We were eighty cold, scared kids.

*

Company B, MCRD
San Diego, California
August 23, 1968

Dearest Mom, Grandma and Laura,

This letter will have to do for all of you. We're only allowed one letter so far. All I can say for this outfit is that it's rough.

I have ten minutes to write this and address it, so I'll have to make it short. I miss everyone very much. Hope you're missing me, too. Well, I've got to close this and get it addressed or I'll be in trouble. I love you all very much. Please take care.

Love, Joe

Our training platoon was part of a larger training battalion, commanded by Lt. Col. D. R. Walker, but the officers we would see the most of when we saw them at all were our company commander, Capt. J. A. Ruffer; our platoon commander, G. Sgt. H. W. McKinney; and our two drill instructors, Sgt. D. J. Thomas and, of course, Sergeant Graves.

By the time we were issued uniforms and toiletries it was nearly 2:30 A.M. When Graves marched us to our billets, we were separated by squad to four Quonset huts strategically located on each side of the DI's hut. Each billet was exactly the same, a waxed cement floor, a small gas furnace set in the middle, and green painted "racks" (bunks) lined against both walls.

I picked a bottom rack at the front of the billet. I was so tired all I could think of was sleep, but before I could unfold my mattress, the call went out for all squad leaders to assemble in front of the DI's hut on the double. I ran to the hut and stood with the other squad leaders in what we hoped was a straight line. Several minutes passed before the hatch (door) was flung open, and there was Graves, fists on his hips, legs stiffly spread.

"I want to see each of you inside, one at a time. This is my home and you will treat it with utmost respect. You will knock on the hatch three times and in a loud clear voice say, 'Sir, private so-and-so requests permission to enter, sir,' or 'sir, private so-and-so is reporting as ordered, sir.' You will stand at attention, eyes forward. I don't want you eye-fucking me or the area. You will not speak unless spoken to."

He turned and slammed the hatch closed, and in a few seconds he bellowed for the first of us.

"Johnson!"

Johnson knocked three times and said, "Private Johnson reporting as ordered, sir."

Graves's voice roared from inside of the hut. "You dumb nigger, get back in line till you learn how to enter my house properly! Young!"

Dave slowly walked to the hut. He rapped three times swallowed hard and said, "Sir, Private Young reporting as ordered, sir."

"I can't hear you."

Dave raised his voice and went through the routine again.

"I still can't hear you."

Dave was shouting as loud as he could when he requested permission a third time.

"Enter!" A few minutes later he left the hut at a dead run to his billet. Perry went through the same drill. Then came my turn. I stepped inside and stood as still as I could. Graves was seated at a large wooden desk; his hat lay near his right hand. Behind him were two military blankets neatly attached to a rod, separating the office from the living quarters. On one side was an American flag, on the other was our platoon banner. I looked back at Graves.

"Quit eye-fucking me, boy. Get those eyes forward and keep 'em there."

"Sir, yes, sir."

"You're in charge of 4th Squad. They fuck up, everyone pays. You fuck up, you pay. Am I making myself clear, boy?"

"Sir, yes, sir."

"Orders and instructions will be given to you, and I expect every swinging dick in your squad to get it right. How you do it is up to you. If you piss me off or I get tired of looking at your ugly face I'll replace you. Still want squad leader, Ward?"

"Sir, yes, sir."

"I can't hear you."

I wanted to rub my throat, but I dared not move. "Sir, yes, sir."

"It is now oh-three-hundred. Reveille is at oh-four-hundred, chow oh-five-hundred. You don't leave this hut, cross the path of a drill instructor or officer without coming to attention and saying, 'Sir, by your leave, sir!' "

He stopped talking, and I think his stare was actually causing me physical pain.

"Sir, by your leave, sir?"

"Go!" I turned and ran from the hut to my billet, much like Dave had done. When I got there everyone was sound asleep. Most had just flopped on their cots in exhaustion. I unrolled my mattress and sat down. In the dim light I looked from rack to rack. I saw nineteen young men of every race from all parts of the country and I wondered how I was going to do it. I fell asleep sitting up, leaning against the wall. At exactly 4:30 A.M. the hatch burst open and Graves entered.

"Reveille, reveille, reveille! Drop your cocks and grab your socks. Now! Ward, you have ten minutes to get these slimes lined up in front of the hut." He was gone as quickly as he'd come.

Thus began the Marine Corps way of training, two months of nearly unending agony. Many wouldn't make it. With the constant lack of sleep, intense physical training, classes, inspections, punishment, hikes, and drills, we would be broken until we were running on sheer guts. The Corps then rebuilt us the way it wanted.

By midday of the twenty-fifth, a plan to handle my squad had come together in my mind. Most of our training called for total cooperation. A big part of the program put us in competition, man against man, squad against squad, and our platoon against three other platoons in our series. DIs collected series banners and used them as bargaining chips to get promotions. High school athletics had prepared me for the competition. I just had to keep it to a minimum between the men in my squad and make it our squad against the others. We had to be a team in every respect. We had to be number one. When we returned from chow, I called everyone together.

"Listen up, people! I'm already spending too much time in Graves's hut taking instructions to pass on to the rest of you. I won't take too much punishment on your behalf, so from now on we're a team, no hotdoggers and no shitbirds. Each man will be responsible for every other man and that includes me. I need two men to help me keep up with things when Graves screws with me."

They all raised their hands, and I began to have some hope that it just might work. I couldn't miss the guy with the big toothy smile standing in the front row. "You, what's your name?" He answered with a slight southern drawl.

"Herald Parker Tyner II, sir."

"Don't call me 'sir,' I'm a private just like the rest of you. How did you come by a name like that?"

"My daddy's a preacher, just call me Parker."

"Okay, Parker, you're number one aide." I looked into the eyes of each man for that unexplainable, something different. I pointed to a small bespectacled figure at the rear of the squad. "Your name's Teams, isn't it?"

"Tennies."

"Graves almost picked you for a house mouse. If he hadn't found Waggoner here, you'd've been it. You're number two aide. Your job will be to lag behind, make sure everyone has cleared out of the billet, and check for anything that might catch Graves's attention." I turned to Waggoner. "You'll be spending a lot of time in the DI's hut. I want to know everything you overhear and can find out from the other house mice."

"You got it," he said.

I called for quiet again. "All disputes come immediately to me. I don't want Graves catching this squad fighting among itself."

By coincidence Nick Herrera was in my squad. I hurried over and asked him if he wanted to be a fire-team leader.

"Might as well," he replied. "It can't get much worse."

"Thanks, Nick. Quiet down people! I need three more men to be fire-team leaders, who wants it?" Six hands went up, and I zeroed in on a freckle-faced guy about my size. "What's your name?"

"Private Bird."

"You're in charge of second fire team." I heard Graves calling assembly and knew I was running out of time. Two more team leaders. I sped up my search. One man let his hand down, and that left four.

"You." I pointed to a wiry, dark-skinned guy. "What's your name?"

He puffed up like a banty rooster. "Cruze, Private Cruze."

"Where you from?"

"LA, I'm Puerto Rican."

I found myself making important, spur-of-the-moment decisions with men of very different ethnic and racial backgrounds. I knew that blacks didn't get along well with Hispanics; neither got along with Puerto Ricans, and whites often had trouble with all three. Of the three remaining men, two were Caucasian and the other a Mexican named Caudillo.

I knew one thing for sure, the way Graves was running me ragged, racial friction in my squad would be a heavy burden.

I looked at Cruze again. He was cocky for sure, but there was something about him. I put him in charge of the third fire team. There was a black trainee in third team by the name of Benham, a touchy situation, but one that in the long run might prove beneficial. Caudillo got the fourth fire team.

"Everyone but Private Parker, fall out on the double!"

As the men scrambled to leave the billet, I took hold of the nearest rack and leaned against it. Sleep, all I could think of was sleep. Parker came up to me.

"You all right?"

"Yeah, I just need some rest. Preacher's kid, huh?"

"That's right, Baptist. By the way, what do you want me to call you?"

"I don't care." I sat down. "Anything but sir."

"Okay, Heathen."

When I looked up at him, he was giving me that big smile I would draw strength from so many times.

"You got an inside line to the Lord, Parker? We may all need it before this is over."

"Sure thing, Heathen."

"Say, Parker, do you want to be a spiritual advisor to the men? What I mean is, I want all problems in this squad settled in this squad."

"Sure, Heathen. I think I can help some of these sinners. What approach do you want me to use?"

"What's your old man preach?"

"Hellfire and brimstone."

"Well, as you can see we've got everything here. Jews, Catholics, Protestants, atheists, and at least one Baptist. Use whatever works." Parker's smile broadened, and I knew I had done well choosing him as an aide. It would be hellfire and brimstone, and it worked. Men did go to Parker with personal problems, and he took care of them. If it was serious, it came to me. I could always count on Parker to keep me up on the mental health of my squad.

I could hear Graves working his way toward us. While Parker gathered the men together, I had a few seconds to think about the others I had selected. Tennies seemed a good choice, a guy that had to fight extra hard all his life and still hadn't overcome the tag of "nerd." Nick was no problem, neither were Bird or Caudillo. I felt I could trust Waggoner. It was

Cruze who was on my mind as I fell out for assembly. Parker handed me the clipboard. "All present and accounted for, Heathen."

"Thanks, Parker, fall in." Out of the corner of my eye I saw Graves grab men at random by the collar and yank them face-to-face, swearing ferociously. The pace of training would steadily increase with each new day, right up to the hour of graduation.

*

> Plt. 1067
> 1st RTB
> Company B, MCRD
> San Diego, Calif.
> August 26, 1968

Dear Mom,

My letters will have to be short. Things move fast here. I'm finally getting to where I can sleep. I have a bad cold, and it doesn't help things a bit. We've had some shots, and I guess we get more tomorrow. So far, they haven't hurt too bad, but I hear the one we get tomorrow does. We have physical tests tomorrow, too. Like they say, you do things you never thought you could. How are things there?

Breakfast is the worst. The other two meals aren't so bad. When you're hungry, anything tastes good.

Later! We had to go to class. I know these letters don't make much sense, but I just don't have time to think. Better close.

> Love, Joe

By the twenty-sixth, I had a bad cold which soon turned into bronchitis. We were barely getting four hours' sleep, and Graves often interrupted that by making us fall out in the middle of the night. As squad leader, I was doing well to get two or three.

I had to sleep sitting up to keep mucus from draining into my throat and lungs. There weren't enough handkerchiefs to handle the flow of mucus and sputum, so I began using spare pillow cases and soiled a new one every night. I didn't know it then, but that wouldn't be the only use I'd find for pillow cases.

★

Plt. 1067, 1st RTB
Company B, MCRD
San Diego, Calif.
September 7, 1968

Dear Mom,

I am writing this after lights out. I'm using a flashlight, so it won't be very neat. There's five of us under this one blanket, trying to study and write letters.

Like I told Laura, the sergeant made me squad leader. It means I'm in charge of nineteen guys, and I march at the front of the platoon. I didn't want the job, but I'll try to do my best. If these guys mess up, I catch "H" for it. Guess we get another haircut tomorrow. It was just getting long enough to feel, too. By the way, don't send me anything I really don't need. If Laura puts anything mushy on the outside of the envelope I'd have to lick it off.

Wow! Just had an interruption. The platoon commander came in and wanted to know who was standing watch. Good thing I was up.

One thing that really bugs me is that they only give us two minutes each time we go to the head. Things can get pretty strenuous. Well, Mom, guess I better close and do a little studying. I'm a little slow in a couple areas. Take care.

Love, Joe

Our first white-glove inspection came on 7 September. Graves made an elaborate production of putting a clean, white cotton glove on his hand and checked the four billets. All four squads failed. We weren't meant to pass, and Graves looked until he found something. My squad failed over an incorrectly folded pair of socks. Graves went berserk. He pulled the mattresses from every bunk and tipped half a dozen racks over. He dumped the contents from each footlocker and kicked the gear everywhere. The hut looked like a bomb had gone off.

"Private Ward, front and center!"

"Sir, Private Ward reporting as ordered, sir."

"You have twenty minutes to clean this pigpen up and be ready for another inspection."

Somehow we managed. Young's squad didn't pass the second inspection. Graves tore up their billet again and after another inspection they had to clean the head spotless with toothbrushes—their own.

★

Plt. 1067, 1st RTB
Company B, MCRD
San Diego, Calif.
September 8, 1968

Dear Mom,

A quick note while I'm waiting to go to church. I get to make a phone call today. I sure hope I catch you at home.

19 years old today, doesn't seem like my birthday. Thanks for the card and the money. I can't wait to get home.

Next week our platoon starts mess hall detail. Then the following week we go to the rifle range. This coming Friday we take our X-1 test and we have initial drill. To fail the X-1 could set a guy back two weeks. It's got me worried. After this Friday we get to blouse our trousers. That'll be a real relief. Still have that cold.

Someone goofed and we didn't get any mail yesterday so I don't know what's going on there. I haven't seen O'Grady, and with 13,000 guys around here the chances are slim that I'll run into him. Dave and Nick are still with me.

Later—Mom, just tried to call a few minutes ago and you weren't home. I was so disappointed I could have cried. Dave talked to his mom and she said she would try to get a hold of you. We only got 40 minutes to make a call in. I'm pretty blue cuz it's Sunday. Doesn't look like I'll make it home for Christmas. Got to go now, we have drill. Tell all hi.

Love, Joe

The huge asphalt parade area, affectionately known as the "Grinder," was at the dead center of the base, but still close enough to the San Diego airport to make it nearly impossible to hear Graves when he gave a command. We spent three hours every day on the Grinder, learning how to march, especially close-order drill. Some guys actually couldn't tell left from right, and we were all clumsy. Graves shouted orders to the squad leaders, and we in turn gave the instructions to our squads. On 2 September, we were in close-order drill when Graves gave a command, and his voice was drowned out by a jet taking off. Dave and I brought our squads to a halt while the other two made a right turn. Graves instantly flew off the handle, stomped up to us, threw his hat on the pavement, and slugged us both in the chest. We were ordered to wait for him in front of his house at attention. Nothing like this had happened before, and we nervously discussed the possibilities as we walked to the DI's hut. We knew that whatever was in store for us wasn't going to be pleasant.

The "Rack" and the "Invisible Chair" had only been rumors until then. With the Rack, a trainee had to place his forehead on the narrow edge of a metal bunk, set four or five feet from the wall. He then had to span the distance from the bunk to the base of the wall at attention, arms to the side. Nearly all the body weight was concentrated at the edge of the bunk and forehead. The pain and physical exertion were excruciating. The Rack was all I could think about as Graves looked at us with clenched teeth when he passed by and held the hatch to his billet open.

"Come on in, boys."

"Sir, yes, sir."

He put his hat on the desk and talked as he spread the blankets to reveal the living quarters of the DIs in our platoon. Although we had two other DIs, Graves was number one. I nervously glanced at the metal wardrobes along the right wall and the row of racks along the left.

"It's a hot day, and I can understand you boys might be a little tired. As a matter of fact, I think your fucking ears have gone to sleep, so I want you to get some rest. See those nice, soft chairs there?"

"Sir, yes, sir."

"Well, go make yourselves comfortable—oh, yeah, there's one condition to be met if you use my chairs. I don't want your filthy asses touching the deck. Sit!"

"Sir, yes, sir." Of course there weren't any chairs, but we took up a sitting position, backs flat against the wardrobes. Graves strolled over to his desk and took a black leather, fur-lined glove from a drawer. He slipped it on his right hand and stood in front of us, smacking his gloved fist into the palm of his left hand.

"I want you to get plenty of rest, but remember your asses better not touch the deck." After ten minutes our legs began to give out, and we started to slowly slide down the wardrobes.

"Oh, no, motherfuckers, keep those asses up!"

Out of the corner of my eye, I saw him pull Dave back to a

sitting position by the throat and slam his gloved fist into his stomach. Dave doubled up with an "ugh" as Graves knocked the wind out of him. I tried desperately to push myself back up, but my leg muscles had other plans. I slid downward. After Graves hit Dave, he did the same thing to me, then turned on Dave again. Graves was working up quite a sweat as he delivered one blow after another to our bellies. My body was going numb when he finally stopped.

"You two shitbirds have three seconds to get out of my house."

We moved to stand up and both hit the floor, face down. Our legs were useless. As we crawled out of the hut on our forearms, Graves kicked and swore at us like a maniac. I managed to get on my hands and knees when Parker and my fire-team leaders picked me up and carried me to my bunk. My uniform was soaked with sweat, and I was having trouble breathing. Parker furiously massaged my legs as someone held me up, put salt tablets in my mouth, and gave me water. Several hands were removing my uniform, and a wet towel was laid on my stomach.

I could only think, my men, yes, these are my men. I was damned proud of them and swore to do right by them no matter what. I looked up to see the whole squad quietly standing around my bunk. Too hoarse to speak above a whisper, I pulled Parker close.

"Tell the men thanks, I'll be okay, and go back to whatever they were doing. When you're finished, I want to talk to you and the team leaders privately."

"Sure thing, Heathen." Parker quickly returned with the team leaders. I still couldn't get up or talk above a whisper. They all sat on the floor and crowded close to hear me.

"Listen guys, it's getting rough. Graves has a leather glove, and he knows how to use it. I don't want a single man in this squad going through what I just did." They were quick to agree with that.

"The only way I know to do it is to have the best squad in the platoon. In return, I promise to be the best squad leader. We all know how the other squads are being run. Perry and Johnson don't think anything of beating on their men. Young's cool, but I don't think he's tough enough. We've got to stay a step ahead of Graves. Everyone except Tennies, Nick, and Parker fall out and get ready for a surprise inspection. Graves is on a roll, and I know he figures Young and I are in no shape to pass. Nick, slip over to Dave's hut and see how he is. Also tell him there might be an inspection any time. And Nick, don't get caught. Tennies, help me put on a clean uniform. Parker, I know you've been spending a lot of time with the men, and I'm going to ask you to do even more. You have a calming effect on the guys, and you can see how bad things are getting. Go through the squad from A to Z and pick a different man each day to help you keep your gear together. Team leaders and Waggoner are exempt.''

"Do I detect a little horse trader in you, Heathen?"

"Maybe so, Parker, maybe so."

"Sounds fair to me." He winked and went to get ready for an inspection I only had a hunch we were going to have. Thirty minutes later we were more than prepared when Graves burst into the billet for the final kill. He was momentarily taken aback by what he saw.

My legs were still shaky, but I followed him around the squad bay with my clipboard, ready to note any screwups. He checked every bunk and man from top to bottom. He carefully inspected each rifle and dug through footlockers, looking for anything out of order. When he couldn't find a single infraction, he came to my rack, took a quarter from his pocket and threw it on the bunk. It bounced once and landed on the floor. Damn, I thought, I can't make up a rack that tight. Tennies had made my bunk. Graves looked at me funny, but it wasn't anger I saw in his eyes. It was more a sense of his own accomplishment.

"You trying to fuck with my head, Ward?"

"Sir, no, sir. Sir, would Drill Instructor Sergeant Graves like the private to retrieve his quarter, sir?"

"No, Ward, this little show was worth two bits. Your squad has commander's time until chow." With that he left.

I leaned against my rack with a sigh. "Fourth Squad, at ease. You just bought yourselves two hours free time, don't waste it."

I flopped on my bunk. Tennies lagged behind to make sure all the men cleared out. He came up to me.

"Tennies."

"Yeah."

"I want you to show everyone how to make a rack that tight. Most of the guys can't make a quarter bounce at all. I'm a two bouncer myself, but from where you were you couldn't see Graves's face when that quarter jumped off that mattress like it had legs."

"Be glad to," he said as he picked up the coin. "I spend

more time on bedding than any thing else when I sweep." He
stood up and held the quarter out.

"Keep it, the more money we can take from Graves, the
better. Go on outside with the rest of the guys."

I was alone. The barrack was empty, but alive somehow,
and for the first time I felt we were a team.

*

> Plt. 1067, 1st RTB
> Company B, MCRD
> Camp Pendleton, Calif.
> September 13–14, 1968

Dear Mom,

I'm at Camp Pendleton. We got here this morning. We
spend three weeks here and then go back to San Diego. I can
see the ocean about three quarters of a mile away. It sure looks
inviting. Too bad it's on the other side of the fence. This isn't
the California I remember. It's cold here and we have to stay
in tents the first week.

Guess Laura feels bad about me not writing very often.
There's nothing I can do, they make the rules around here.

Later—We got back from chow. The food's pretty good here
and we can have seconds. Lights out, more tomorrow.

Just got through cleaning my rifle. Being this close to the
ocean, they rust fast, and a rusty rifle could send a guy to the
brig. We haven't eaten yet. Will write again soon. Take care.

> Love, Joe

During our last week in San Diego, Mike O'Grady got sick
with pneumonia and was hospitalized, putting him three weeks
behind Dave, Nick and me.

Three days before we were to leave for Camp Pendleton,
Waggoner told me Johnson and Dave had exchanged words
and that Johnson was planning a "blanket party" for him that
evening. A blanket party is no party. A GI blanket is thrown
over a man's head so he can't identify his attackers, and he is
beaten, sometimes to death.

"Like hell he is," I fumed. "Waggoner, go tell Young
what's up. Fourth Squad, hit the deck, now!" I dressed hurriedly as the men rolled out of their racks. I subconsciously
counted the slap of bare feet hitting the floor.

"Fourth Squad, *tinn huhh.* I've just heard that Johnson is

about to give Private Young a blanket party. Round up anything you can use as a weapon, but no rifles or bayonets. Fall
out, on the double!''

Some men put heavy objects in their pillow cases to use as
clubs. I heard a broom handle snap in two. Mop buckets were
snatched up, and several pieces of the furnace were taken.
Most of the men were barefoot, wearing only their underwear
as they hurried outside.

"Fourth Squad, *tinn huhh*, forward *huhh*.'' We were none
too soon. Johnson was already leading his squad towards
Young's billet. I told Dave to get his men behind my squad.
Johnson and I met face to face.

"This is none of your business, Ward.''

"Johnson, I'm a little disappointed. You're going to have a
party and we weren't invited. My people can easily drop your
squad, and then you'll have Young's men to deal with. If you
want to give it a try let's get with it.'' I saw it in his eyes.
Johnson knew he had little choice.

"Ward, you'll be sorry for this.'' With that, he left.
Johnson and I had made so much noise, I was sure Graves
had overheard us and was watching from somewhere in the
darkness.

Two days later, Johnson did get even. During a latrine break
he started roughing up a member of his own squad, Private
Hicks, knowing his actions would anger me. When he kicked
the man, I stepped in.

"That's going too far, Johnson!''

"I told you to stay out of my business, Ward,'' he yelled and
slugged me before I could get my hands up. I fell and tore my
chin open on a commode. I jumped up and tackled him to the
floor. Knowing Johnson had a weak back, I reached around his
neck and started giving him kidney blows. Our little melee was
abruptly interrupted when someone yelled, "Attention!'' As
we awkwardly got to our feet, there was Graves filling the
doorway with his spread-eagle stance.

"Just what the fuck is going on here?''

Everyone was silent except for Hicks, who was curled up on
the floor, moaning. Breathing heavily, Johnson and I said,
"Sir, Drill Instructor Sergeant Graves, it was a misunderstand-
ing, sir.''

"What's wrong with Private Hicks?'' Graves had us. If I
answered, I'd be a squeal, and if Johnson didn't say some-

thing, we were both in trouble. A voice from behind us was my reprieve.

"Sir, Private Johnson kicked Private Hicks, sir." I could see the muscles tighten in Graves's jaws as he looked at Johnson.

"Is that correct, Private Johnson?"

"Sir, yes, sir."

"Why did you do that, Private Johnson?"

"Sir, Private Hicks disobeyed an order, sir."

"So, you just kicked him, huh?"

"Sir, yes, sir."

"What the fuck happened to you, Ward?"

"Sir, I slipped on the wet floor, sir."

"I think I get the picture. The three of you go to sick bay, and I want your Girl Scout asses back in two hours. Move it!" There was a tone in Graves's voice I hadn't heard before, to which I gave a great deal of thought as we walked to sick bay.

This incident ended any further problems between Johnson and myself. The following day we and the rest of the men were packed tightly together in two trucks, headed for Camp Pendleton.

★

> Plt. 1067, 1st RTB
> Company B MCRD
> Camp Pendleton, Calif.
> September 22–23, 1968

Dear Mom,

A quick note. Haven't much time. We just moved into the barracks here and there's a lot of work to do. Went to church this morning. They hold church outside here. We're on free time now, so will try to get off some letters.

Tomorrow we start learning how to shoot the rifle and Wednesday we shoot the .45 caliber pistol. We qualify in three weeks. I'm hoping for Sharpshooter. What a dream, huh?

Well, time's slowly moving me closer to graduation. Just over four weeks left. Guess you don't know if you're going to try to make it. I'm losing some weight. My belt has drawn two inches of slack since I got here. The way I eat, it's a wonder my stomach doesn't drag on the ground.

Well, Mom, I should close. We have rifle inspection later this morning and I haven't cleaned mine yet. Will write soon.

> Your loving son, Joe

The base at San Diego was within the city limits, so we had to temporarily relocate boot camp to Camp Pendleton for weapons training.

The first few days at the rifle range, we lived in unheated tents near some large, mobile trailers designed as latrines. The weather was cold and damp. During reveille we ran to the trailers to clean up and get warm, mainly to get warm. By the end of the week we moved into the permanent barracks, a most welcome break from the cold tents. It was there my frequent encounters of the strangest kind began with Graves.

At 1:00 A.M. I found myself sitting up, yanked forward by the collar of my T-shirt. The smell of gin was a giveaway. Graves had me again. Holy shit, I thought. There's eighty guys in the barracks. Why me?

"Ward, you awake?" How could I not be?

"Sir, yes, sir."

"Cut the crap, Ward, I wanna talk." He pulled me closer. "I wanna know if the men like me."

Oh, man, what a question. Like him? Everyone hated his guts.

"Sure, Sergeant Graves, yeah sure, the men like ya."

"You lying motherfucker!" He slammed me down and jerked me back up.

"Do you like me, Ward?"

"Yeah, I like ya, Sergeant Graves."

"Another goddamn lie!" Down I went and right back up again.

"I want the truth, Ward."

"No, sir, no one likes you." He let go of me, rested his arms on his thighs, and looked at the floor. I barely heard Graves mutter, "Good, good," before he abruptly stood and staggered away into the darkness, only to be the same old Graves at reveille.

Those nightly visits continued throughout our time at the range. Eventually it dawned on me that he was a very lonely man. Sometimes Graves asked about my home or a man in the platoon, but almost never mentioned his own life.

Although classes in other areas continued, the main emphasis at Edson Rifle Range was learning to fire weapons. If you can't hit the target, you're not much of a soldier. In the Marine Corps, if you can't hit the target, you're no soldier at all.

One day we witnessed a suicide at the range when a man in the platoon next to us bent over an M-14, with the muzzle pushed tight against his chest, and pulled the trigger. The dead man still hadn't been carried to the ambulance when Graves called us together to discuss what had just happened.

"In the event any of you shitheads want to do what that turd over there has done, I will explain how to do it properly. He was sloppy, and none of you is worth a single Marine Corps bullet." He rolled his left sleeve up and stuck his arm high in the air.

"If anyone in this platoon has the same idea, you will do it right. You will stand under a hard stream of cold water in the showers, take a razor blade and cut from your wrists to your elbows." He traced an invisible line with his index finger up the inside of his forearm. "Neat and clean. Do you understand?"

"Sir, yes, sir."

"I can't hear you."

"Sir, yes, sir."

"I still can't hear you."

"Sir, yes, sir!"

We were having a hell of a time dealing with the whole thing. A man lay dead not a hundred feet from us, his heart literally blown through his back, and Graves was calmly telling us how to kill ourselves.

*

Plt. 1067, 1st RTB
Company B, MCRD
Camp Pendleton, Calif.
September 29, 1968

Dear Mom,

It's your youngest again. My letters are kind of slow and seldom, but believe me, when they don't have us doing something I'm writing. I got into a fight a few days ago and I have stitches in my left chin. Doesn't look too bad, it's just sore. Since I didn't start the fight I didn't get into trouble.

I just found out that the Sunday before graduation is Visitor's Day, and then we graduate the next Thursday. I've been thinking that if you and Laura come out, you might be able to come on Visitor's Day and then spend a few days at Uncle Ralph's, then come back for graduation. It's just a thought.

I finally found O'Grady. He's in one of the tents across the road from us. I slipped over there this morning during cleanup and talked to him for a couple of minutes. He seems to be doing okay. You can tell Mrs. O'Grady I talked to him. Dave and I both going to try to get over to see him later. Do take care.

Love, Joe

October 2d. Graves took a three-day leave and was replaced by a recent graduate of Drill Instructor School and newly assigned to our platoon, Staff Sergeant D. J. Thomas.

I took an immediate dislike to the man, and he proved my instincts right on his first day there. He made us duck walk to the chow hall via the scenic route, through gullies and sagebrush. The duck walk is done while squatting, with both hands clasped behind the head, and we had to say "quack, quack" the whole time. The duck walk has since been firmly banned in the Corps because of the damage done to cartilage and tendons.

Unlike Graves, Thomas was bent on punishment for punishment's sake, not discipline. He dished out knuckle push-ups on the gravel road and as many as two thousand squat thrusts for no apparent reason. He made us crawl like worms in formation and gave a man in Dave's squad the Rack so long, they had to take him to the hospital. I never thought I'd be glad to see Graves return and Thomas go back to San Diego, but I was.

Competition at the range was intense. I qualified with the .45 caliber pistol, but I really disliked the weapon. Its poor accuracy and weight, along with a lack of knock-down power prompted me not to carry a .45.

We spent a day firing the M-16 to get a feel for the rifle that had replaced the M-14 in Vietnam. The M-16 was light and accurate to five hundred yards, but there were two serious problems with the rifle. The first and most distressing was its tendency to jam, even under the controlled environment at the range. The controversy over the defects in the rifle and the bad gunpowder used in the rounds didn't come to light for some time.

The other problem was immediately apparent. The rifle fired so fast on fully automatic, it could empty a twenty-round magazine before the first shell casing hit the ground. It seemed like a good idea, but the rifle's light weight, combined with a heavy recoil, meant even the strongest man couldn't hold the rifle down. By the end of a magazine, we found ourselves shooting ducks (shooting straight up).

The older M-14 was phased out of active use by all of the services except the Marine Corps Scout Snipers. In many ways it was a loss to the military. A great number of lives were lost by field testing the M-16 in actual combat.

*

Plt. 1067, 1st RTB
Company B, MCRD
San Diego, Calif.
October 6, 1968

Dear Mom,

Bet you didn't think I was around anymore, huh? I'm still here, but they're cramming our time more and more.

We're back at San Diego. I did well at the range. I shot Expert and was the 2nd highest shooter in the series. It's an important factor in getting promotions, so it looks like I'm setting pretty good. I was 6 points from the range record. Not bad, huh? Yes, I'm still squad leader. Sometimes, when the DIs have me in the office punishing me for something my squad did, I wonder if it's worth it. One consolation is that I just have to stand it for three more weeks.

Yes, Dave and Nick are still with me. Dave's a squad leader, too. Like me, he didn't want the job, but is making the best of it. Nick and Dave both shot Marksman at the range. O'Grady will be at the range for two more weeks. If he qualifies he comes back here to graduate.

How are you feeling? I have the stitches out of my chin, but still can't shave that spot. It looks kind of funny.

Well, Mom, I had better close. I have to get these guys on the road for chow in about five minutes. So take care and I'll write as soon as I can. 17 more days.

Love, Joe

Each day at the range brought us closer to qualification. Not to qualify meant going through the range again, a serious setback.

As the day wore on, I noticed a small group of DIs and officers gathering behind me and two other men on the line. I'd qualified Expert, and the word had spread that I was firing against those other two guys for the series record. I was tired, very tired, but I heard Parker yell, "Go for it, Heathen!" The other men in the platoon were shouting encouragements, even Graves. I finished my last magazine and will always remember the shot that gave me second place. Everyone hung around the score board for the final tally, and when it was up, Graves gave me my reward for not placing first. A hefty punch in the stomach.

The racial friction I was worried about between Cruze and Benham started at the range. When it nearly broke out in a fist fight upon our return to San Diego, I took action by replacing Cruze with Benham as team leader. They didn't like it, nor was I sure my solution would work, but it did. After forty-eight hours, I put Cruze back as team leader. Harmony was restored, ending any further racial problems in my squad.

★

> Plt. 1067, 1st RTB
> Company B, MCRD
> San Diego, Calif.
> October 29, 1968

Dear Mom,

A quick note before chow. I'm platoon Honorman. They buy my dress blues for me, and I get to wear them to graduate in. I also have to compete for series Honorman and it's got me worried. Hope I don't mess any of this up. I want you and Laura to be proud of me.

Things are happening pretty fast right now as you might guess. We had our final physical test yesterday and according to the results, I'm twice as fit as when I came in. We have two more real tough inspections and a three mile run, plus final drill, all before graduation. Now you know where my letter writing time is going.

We had another one of our interruptions and I'm having to finish this during fire watch and it's 1:00 A.M. Boy, am I tired.

Well, Mom, I'd better close. I only have ten minutes left on watch. Take care and you'll be hearing from me again soon.

> Love, Joe

When Graves called me to his hut during commander's time on the twelfth, I wondered what he wanted. As far as I knew, no one in my squad had done anything wrong, and I didn't think I had. I knocked three times as usual.

"Sir, Private Ward reporting as ordered, sir."

"Come in, Ward." Come in, I thought. What's going on here?

"Sir, yes, sir." I entered and came to attention, staring as always over Graves's head at the blankets.

"At ease, Ward."

"Sir, yes, sir." I was slightly hesitant. I must have been in that hut a hundred times and never once allowed to stand at ease. I was at last able to look Graves in the eyes in his own house, but my apprehension grew when he got up and walked toward me. Oh, Jesus, I thought, this is it. He's going to knock my head clean off. Why? Instead, he sat on the edge of the desk, his right foot on the floor, hands clasped over his left knee.

"Ward, you've been chosen for platoon Honorman." He looked at me for a moment. "What's the matter, Ward, lose your voice all of a sudden?"

"Sir, no, sir, but I thought, I mean we all thought Johnson would get it. He's been platoon guide all this time and . . ."

"And what, Ward? He's black, like me?"

"Sir, no, sir, it's just that he's worked hard for it."

"You've got a lot to learn, Ward. I recommended you because you have excelled in all areas of training: scholastically, physically, and at the rifle range, even though you didn't take first fucking place. After chow tomorrow morning, take this certificate from *Leatherneck* magazine to clothing issue and get fitted for dress blues. You'll get your promotion to private first class on graduation day. Don't let this go to your head, Ward. We still have a week of training left, and you'll be competing for series Honorman—and, Ward, I want that banner. I'll announce this decision to the platoon tomorrow. Now get out of here."

"Sir, yes, sir." I was in no hurry as I walked back to my billet. When I got there, I called Parker outside to talk.

"What's up, Heathen?"

"Graves just told me I am Honorman."

"Well, well, Heathen, you must have been doing the right things, or maybe it's because you had the Lord in your corner."

"Parker, I don't want the men to know yet. Graves is going to tell everyone tomorrow."

"Whatever you say, Heathen." As soon as we entered the billet, Parker called the squad to attention. "Listen up, you sinners. Private Ward, your squad leader, has been named Honorman." I hardly had time to thank Parker when I was inundated with cheers and hit with a barrage of towels and pillows.

Competition for series Honorman wasn't actually man-to-

man. It was a compilation of points accumulated all through
boot camp. I didn't know the other three platoon Honormen, I
only knew their names. The last inspection and final drill were
tough. My squad was tight, and they went well. For me, the
three-mile run in the intense California heat in combat boots
and sweatshirt was the end of my try at series Honorman. I had
developed viral pneumonia and the cough that went with it. At
the end of the run, I had to hold on to a telephone pole to keep
from passing out. Again, I would have to settle for second
place.

Graves knew I wouldn't place first, and when he came to me
afterward, I expected another punch. Instead, he asked if I was
okay. As I blew snot from my nose and struggled to breathe, I
managed to say, "Sir, yes, sir." As soon as he left, I threw up.

Two days before graduation, Master Gunnery Sergeant
McKinney assembled the platoon for a talk. He was a soft-
spoken man of few words, but what he said that day became
branded in my memory.

"Gentlemen, we are at war, and each of you standing here
today will be involved in this war in some way. The manner in
which you serve your country may decide whether you return
home walking or in a box." With a hand gesture he motioned
toward three card tables with a sergeant seated behind each
one.

"Those men are here to take applications for advanced training when you have finished here: Infantry Training Regiment
(ITR) and Basic Infantry Training Battalion (BIT). You are all
welcome to apply for either language school in Monterey,
Force Reconnaissance Battalion, or Scout Sniper School. Most
of you will be assigned to a regular infantry unit or duty station
in Vietnam. A few of you will qualify for consideration for
entry into one of three schools. One of you has the option to go
to any of the three."

I was that one, and suddenly I was faced with the dilemma
of making a choice that could literally mean life or death. I also
realized the real reason for my extra efforts in boot camp. At
least I had a choice; most of the men didn't. The prospects ran
through my mind. Language school? No, it sounded boring.
Force Recon was a little too gung ho and not really my style.
That left sniper school. I could sure put the bullet where it
belonged. The sergeant read my record and said, "I'll put you
down for Scout Sniper School; sign here. This doesn't consti-

tute automatic entry into the program, but I see no problem."
As I signed the contract, I was beginning to feel some of the
heat from the war.

Graduation day finally arrived, and final preparations were
frantically made. Brass was polished, leather spit-shined, and
uniforms meticulously checked. I donned my dress blues. Although hot and uncomfortable, I was honored that I would be
one of only four in our series allowed to wear them during the
ceremonies.

Two last-minute events had to take place before we would
finally be declared Marines. The first was the exchange of the
platoon banner from Johnson to myself. It was done quite for-
mally with the platoon present and at attention. Johnson had
been such a personal problem all through boot camp that I
looked forward to this final humiliation. Yet, when he handed
me the pole with our banner on it, the crest-fallen look on his
face took away any sense of victory. I actually felt sorry for him.

The second event would make Graves and me unspoken
comrades forever. While inspecting my uniform, Graves noticed I was missing the National Defense Service Medal, required for my dress blues.

"Damn it, Ward, can't you do anything right? Wait here."
Graves returned with a medal. It was slightly frayed, which
betrayed its previous use.

We were soon marched to the Grinder to put boot camp
behind us. It was supposed to be eyes forward, but we each
carefully watched the bleachers out of the corner of our eyes
for a friend or relative who had come. I saw Mom. She had
bought a new red, white, and blue dress just for the occasion.
No doubt, everyone seated around her knew it was her kid at
the front of the platoon, dressed to the hilt.

Graduation was short and to the point. The platoon commander was in the bleachers to answer questions. Graves
handed out certificates as we were called forward one by one.
I walked the few steps in front of the chapel and stood at
attention, facing Graves. His face was expressionless. "Congratulations, Marine." With his left hand, he gave me my
document and simultaneously crossed arms to shake my right
hand. Except for a similar shake of the hands and another
document stating that I was Honorman and a couple of photos
of Lieutenant Walker handing me my promotion to private first
class, it was over. I was officially a Marine. It was a simple
ceremony, but it marked the end of boot camp.

At long last, we were able to greet our relatives and show affection with hugs, kisses, and a few tears. We were allowed to buy pogey bait (pop and candy), our first since entering boot camp.

Four hours visitation put the final touch on graduation and it was back to our billets to begin preparations for the move to Camp Pendleton. Two days later, we boarded the cattle trucks for the cramped ride to ITR.

*

W-Company-16, 3d Bn., 2d ITR
Camp Pendleton, Calif.
October 27, 1968

Dear Mom,

Well, I'm back at Pendleton. We got here Friday morning. We have base liberty today, and we've been eating more junk, as if you couldn't guess.

So far things have been pretty slow, but from what I hear it doesn't last long. I guess this ITR makes boot camp look like kindergarten. Well, I'm in command again. They made me platoon leader and that leaves me with eighty guys to take care of. I thought it was hard keeping twenty guys on track. It should be interesting.

This isn't much of a letter, but I wanted you to know my address. I'd better go, we have formation in twenty minutes. Oh, I'm up for Sniper School, so I'll take it. Dave and Nick are both still with me. Take care. Will write more when I can.

Love, Joe

P.S. I need ten dollars

Camp Pendleton is a sprawling base in the southern hills of California, resplendent with scorpions, tarantulas, and rattlesnakes. During the winter, the weather is as harsh as the terrain. We were usually on bivouac, and all classes were held outside, freezing rain or sun. It was all intended to get us used to being miserable in the bush.

There was another phenomenon peculiar to the training at ITR, the route step (a long quick stride). It was a good way to cover a lot of terrain in a short time, but it was incredibly grueling. A strange thing happened when the company was in route step as it moved over rough ground. The front two platoons were in a steady march, while the 3d platoon was either running to keep up or nearly stopped. The 4th Platoon, my platoon, was constantly running. We ran all over that damned base. The only advantage to being last was that if the front of the column spotted a rattlesnake, we had more warning. Still, we moved so fast when the word ''snake'' reached us, we just had time to take a couple strides and jump to avoid stepping on it.

Except for Parker and three other men, my squad was split up and assigned to other platoons. The DIs were replaced by troop leaders, less harsh in their physical abuse, but with a training schedule that was nearly impossible to maintain. Being in charge again, only this time of a platoon, meant my problems were magnified fourfold. I continued to use the method of cooperation I'd used in boot camp to help keep the platoon tight, but I found I had to pull rank often. Parker proved invaluable again in helping me with tough decisions and separating legitimate grievances from attempts to slack off.

When I was wrong, I took my punishment for it, but by making command decisions immediately, I lessened the number of situations that would place me and my men under the scrutiny of the troop leaders.

*

W-Company-16, 3d Bn., 2d ITR
Camp Pendleton, Calif.
November 7, 1968

Dear Mom,

Don't be too shocked, I'm actually writing. We really have been cramped for time. Since I'm platoon leader, I have less than the others. Last night, I was working in the company office till midnight and had to get up at 4:30 A.M. I'm dragging.

Today we fired the M-16 again. It's a good weapon I guess, but a lot of them did jam. Some of us like the M-14 better. Tomorrow we fire the M-60 machine gun and 60mm grenade launcher.

As for my leave, since it's so close to Christmas, they may send us on our leave the 7th of December. Don't get your hopes up on that early date cuz they change things around here on the spur of the moment.

The spinal meningitis is bad here. They quarantined the whole base at San Diego just after we left. The company next to us is quarantined with it. I'm waiting for it to get to us. That'll mean an extra ten days before I get home.

I got the money you sent, I used it to have the stripes sewn on my uniforms. We have shore liberty this weekend, but I'm broke again. Dave and I may still try to go to Uncle Ralph's. Glad to hear things are going well there. Better go now.

Your Loving Leatherneck,
Joe

I didn't think ITR could be worse than boot camp. That was a mistake. ITR turned out to be the hell boot camp was born from. We trained with live weapons, forced marched for miles from class to class, froze at night, and baked during the day when the sun did shine. Add a platoon to run herd on, and I came closer to giving up at ITR than I ever did in boot camp.

At ITR we were taught to throw a hand grenade, a basic and seemingly simple procedure, but not so. Twenty men at a time were handed an M-30. M-30s are oval-shaped grenades with a thin aluminum casing. They are filled with high explosives wrapped with thick serrated wire that becomes shrapnel upon explosion. We marched down a long trench. Troop leaders were stationed evenly down the line in the event someone dropped his grenade in the trench. The word was given to straighten the pin and pull it while holding the spoon tight with our thumbs. The other arm was stretched straight forward, palm flat, to add balance to our bodies. The order went out to throw the grenade as hard as possible and get down in the trench. Some of us swore as a steady rain of hot shrapnel fell on us, hitting the backs of our hands, occasionally going down a collar, burning much like a bee sting. Pieces steadily bounced off our helmets with a nerve-racking ping.

We also blew up old tanks and personnel carriers with LAWs (Light Antitank Weapon), a disposable rocket launcher which had replaced the bazooka. They were reliable, accurate, and if a man had the target in the sights, he could count on a hit. However, the high explosive round in the early LAWs proved to be of little value in Vietnam. It wasn't until a later version with an anti-personnel round was introduced that the LAW proved its worth in the war.

I was starting to get leery of everything that exploded. There were times when it seemed we were just cutting it too close. I wasn't looking forward to the class on high explosives. As the company was seated in some bleachers, I couldn't take my eyes off the two large tables in front of us, piled high with quarter-pound blocks of TNT. Three of us were picked at a time, taken to a table with fuses, blasting caps, and crimping pliers. We inserted the fuse into the blasting cap, placed the pliers lightly around its base, held it over our helmets, and pinched. We then took a block of TNT and walked seventy-five feet to several pits about three feet deep. We eased the blasting cap into a hole in the block, lit what we hoped was thirty seconds of fuse, gingerly laid it in the pit, and were told to calmly walk back. The impulse to run was agonizing. We had barely returned to the group when the TNT blew up. As I let out a sigh of relief, I realized I was shaking.

After one particularly long and grueling hike, we were again standing in some bleachers, this time for a class on survival. An instructor walked onto a wooden stage, holding a white rabbit. He leisurely strolled from one end of the stage to the other, gently petting the rabbit while he talked.

"People, this class is on survival, in other words staying alive. If you should become separated from your unit, especially in enemy territory, you have two choices. Roll over and die or use your heads and cunning to stay alive. I suggest you listen during this class." He didn't have to tell us. His easy manner and apparent affection for the rabbit had everyone's attention. He reached the center of the stage and became silent, we all were. Suddenly, his right hand slammed down behind the rabbit's head in a karate chop, snapping the animal's neck instantly. As the rabbit went limp, blood streamed from its nose. The trainer held the animal up and allowed a small amount of blood to run into his mouth. He wiped some blood from the side of his face with the back of his hand and let the rabbit continue to bleed on the stage while he reached for his bayonet. He cut and peeled the hide away in one piece and held the carcass in one hand and the hide in the other, high in the air. We were mesmerized.

"Survival, people, means that none of this or any creature you manage to capture will be wasted. Obviously, the meat is edible, but every part of the animal is important: the eyes, brains, bone marrow, and other internal organs. If you are stranded behind enemy lines, building a fire is out of the question. You'll eat these goodies raw, and if you've gone a few days without food, they'll taste better than you realize at present." He threw the carcass down and walked to the front of the stage with the pelt dangling from his hand.

"I want a volunteer." No one moved. He pointed at a man in the first row. "You just volunteered. Get up here and take off your right boot." The reluctant volunteer stepped onto the stage and began unlacing his boot as the trainer prepared the hide.

"On your back, Marine, right leg up." He wrapped the fur side of the hide around the man's bare foot, quickly and deftly pulled the legs of the pelt to specific points, and tied them together. He'd just made a moccasin. As gruesome as the exhibition was, we were all very impressed.

The rest of his lecture was a rundown on how to set snares and which types of vegetation could be safely eaten. "Hair," he said, "isn't digestible, but fingernails are and should be bitten off and swallowed as they grow." I had to wonder how desperate a man would have to be to actually begin consuming himself, starting with the fingernails.

★

W-Co 16, 3d Bn., 2d ITR
Camp Pendleton, Calif.
November 24, 1968

Dearest Mom,

Guess I have everyone mad at me cuz of my writing. I'm not one to complain, but the last two weeks have been the hardest of my life. I won't bore you with the details, but when they want to, they can make you wish you were dead. I really haven't been in the mood to write a sensible letter. Enough of that.

We still don't know when we'll be home. It should be around Christmas. The word is we may not go right to Nam. It seems they have a pile up of Marines and we may get held over for a while.

Well, Mom, I have to get these guys ready to turn in laundry. Take care and tell Grams and Laura hi.

Love, Joe

If there was a graduation from ITR, it was the live-fire course. There was never any joking about it. All we knew was that a man entered the course and came out changed. As we passed the bunker with the machine gun, I saw that it was in an adjustable rack that would put the bullets five or six feet high. I was somewhat relieved; it could be set lower, much lower. My optimism vanished when I saw the course itself. It was about two hundred feet long and one hundred feet wide. Barbed wire was strung across the course at different angles and heights, and shallow craters ringed with sandbags were everywhere.

One of the troop leaders gave us instructions at the entrance to the course. It was so quiet he could have whispered and the whole company would have heard him. As 1st Platoon made ready to enter the course, the rest of us were led well out of sight. I should have clued in more as the morning wore on and the time it took each platoon to get through the course turned out to be much longer than I expected. The troop leaders were also careful not to let the men waiting see anyone who had gone through. My platoon nervously waited four hours as the other three platoons were taken to the course; the only breaks in the sound of explosions and machine-gun fire were the few minutes it took to ready the course again.

As we approached the entrance, the troop leader said, "This is a live-fire course, and you are going to make a frontal assault on the bunker we just passed. In the event any of you think the gun is firing blanks, please observe." He casually signaled the men in the bunker, and they fired several rounds into an earthen berm at the end of the course. Dirt and tracers flew wildly into the air.

"Stay out of the craters, they have charges of TNT and will be detonated at the trainer's discretion. This course will give you a taste of combat, considered as close to actual combat as any in the world. You will crawl low onto, through, and out of the course. Do not, I repeat, do not, for any reason, stand up or crawl into a crater! When you exit the course at the far end, do not stand up until Sergeant Forest slaps you firmly on the ass. This is your signal that you have reached the safety zone. The first man to reach a line of barbed wire must make a passage for the men behind him. If the wire is low, you will crawl on top and stay put until all of the men behind you have crawled over the top of you. If the wire is higher, use your rifle to prop it up, and stay with your rifle until all of the men behind you have passed. Are there any questions?"

"No, sir!"

"I repeat, under no condition are you to stand up or crawl into a crater! Private First Class Ward."

"Yes, sir."

"Get 1st Squad on the deck, now!"

"Yes, sir. First Squad, hit it and assume the low-crawl position!" I went as far as the first line of barbed wire, raised it with my rifle, and the 1st Squad easily crawled under. I had a good view of the course, and as the last man in 3d Squad passed under the wire, I had hopes it wouldn't be that bad. As soon as the last man in 4th Squad passed, the machine-gun fire and explosions in the pits started. I knew bullets were passing overhead, but I nearly forgot about them as one sharp pain after another shot through my body each time a nearby crater blew up. Within a few seconds, everyone was beginning to feel shell shock. There's a limit to the number of times a man can have the wind knocked out of him, his brains rattled inside his skull, and his eardrums assaulted before becoming disoriented. After a minute or two he just might forget up from down.

I had planned to be off the course in five to seven minutes but ended up being out there over twenty because two people got confused and started crawling in circles. I had to go out and get them going in the right direction again.

When I finally reached the exit point and crawled under the orange safety ribbon, I didn't feel the trainer slap me on the butt. I kept crawling until I came to a pair of boots. As I reached out to touch one, I thought I heard Parker calling me in the distance. Reaching higher, I felt a leg in the boot. I rolled onto my back. There was Parker bending over, looking at me upside down, which made sense. Two men lifted me to my feet, and I was suddenly facing Parker right side up, which didn't make sense anymore. Disoriented and confused, I felt somewhat like I did that day in Graves's invisible chair.

When I regained my bearings, I told Parker to lead the platoon back and take it slow because he had a few stragglers. During my long, solitary walk back to the barracks, two things occurred to me. First, don't get shell shock if you could help it. Second, if you did get it, rest was the only cure.

*

BIT Bn., 2d ITR
Rifle Training Co. 3169
Camp Pendleton, Calif.
December 7th, 1968

Dear Mom,

Right now we're sitting on the side of a hill having a class on the M-16. I'm in an awkward position for writing, so I hope you can read this.

I wrote Laura last night and by the time I finished, my hands were too cold to write anymore. We don't have heat in our tents. I should be here at BIT for about three weeks. Boy, am I ready to get out of this place. We start Sniper School when I come back from leave. Afterward, I go to what they call staging, and after staging I go to Vietnam. I'll be in the February rotation, that's all I know right now.

I recommended Dave for PFC and he got it. I picked the seven PFCs from my platoon. There sure were a lot of friendly guys when promotions came around. Dave and Nick are both doing fine. We haven't seen Mike since they put him in his permanent company.

Later—we went to chow and are back on the hill for another class. That about covers the last couple of days. I'll try to get off another letter tomorrow. Take care and tell all hi.

Love, Joe

The transition from ITR to BIT was a short move to different quarters. BIT was a breather, as classes shifted more to tactics, war games, and a general polishing of things we had already learned. Troop leaders were easier on us, and more off-base liberty made a big difference in morale. Even if we were too broke to go to San Diego or Oceanside, we could use the base EM (enlisted men's) club at Del Mar. Three times each week, girls from Oceanside were bussed in, and ten cents would buy a dance.

Most of the time we managed to get to San Diego, and by we, I mean myself, Joe Posey, and Bruce Walters. I knew Joe from boot camp, and I met Walters at ITR. We partied together like there was no tomorrow, and the closer we were getting to leaving for the war, the more real that part of it became. We would often take Parker with us, and to his repeated amazement we always made it back to the base somehow. It was as though something inside of us was saying: "Party down now boys, cuz you might not be able to much longer."

*

BIT Bn., 2d ITR
Rifle Training Co., 3168
Camp Pendleton, Calif.
December 14, 1968

Dear Mom,

I am writing in class again. This one is on offensive combat and I have to do something to keep my eyes open. We only got three hours sleep last night.

Not much news. I've got another cold and as chilly as it gets here, I'll probably have pneumonia again pretty soon. They have a sneaky way to keep too many guys from going to sick bay. They make us pack all our gear and clothes plus rifles and helmet, then carry it all to sick bay. Altogether, it's about 200 pounds of gear and if we miss two training days we get dropped. If I can get in, I may go during liberty tomorrow.

Unless they change it, our outpost is the twenty-ninth. Nick and Dave and I have our tickets for the train. It'll take a little longer, but I'll save about $30.00. Well, Mom, I'd best close now. Tell all hi. Take care and I'll see you before long.

Love, Joe

At the close of BIT, everyone in the battalion was making plans to go home for leave, almost everyone that is. A few guys didn't have a real home to go to in the first place. I asked one man in my platoon why he wasn't getting packed. "Aren't you going home, Olsen?"

"Nah, what for? Hell, I ain't never even had a decent meal till I joined the Corps."

"You can come home with me if you want."

"No, thanks. I'll just kick around here for a while."

"Take care, Olsen."

"Yeah, you too."

I felt bad. I had a nice home, family, friends, and a special girl waiting for me. Olsen, well, he had the Marine Corps. Mark T. Olsen was killed in the Republic of South Vietnam four days before I finished training at Scout Sniper School.

Leave was thirty days of nonstop partying for Dave, Nick, and me. Mike arrived home a week and a half before our leaves were up. The night before we had to return to our units, we went to Smuggler's Mines, a series of old abandoned gold mines in the mountains that we often took refuge in to let some trouble at home die down or to just be alone.

While sitting around a bonfire and sipping suds, we tried to keep the chatter light, but it was hard to put the war out of our minds. We carried out an old military custom. We tore a dollar bill into four equal parts and tucked them safely away in our wallets. The idea being that when the four of us got back, we'd tape the four sections together and use it to buy a beer to celebrate our safe return.

The next day, Laura and I went to a jewelry store and picked out a diamond engagement ring. I made the down payment and agreed to make monthly payments to the store until it was paid off. I flew back to California, expecting not to see my family and friends for at least a year.

I reported to the wrong base and was two days late. No one seemed very worried, the attitude being "better late than never," and there were quite a few nevers. By the time I got to sniper school, I was three days late and still saw little concern about the matter. After the rigors of training, I could easily appreciate a three-day window of slack. The training at Scout Sniper School was much too intense to capitalize on this knowledge, but it was definitely on my mind.

★

ACT Co. 8/69 Sniper School
MCB Camp Pendleton, Calif.
January 21, 1969

Dear Mom,

Finally got here and am pretty settled. The weather is rotten. It's been raining and blowing so hard that last night some of the trees around the barracks came out by the roots.

How ya feeling? Take care so I won't be worried about you. Will close for now, more later.

Me again. This is part of a letter I started six days ago. As you can see by the new address, I'm at Sniper School now.

Later—We've just had time to get our stuff put away and the sergeant got us out to do a "little" running, about three miles and most of it was up. That was the first real exercise I've done since ITR and I'm out of shape. I'm pretty fuzzy right now, so I think I'll find a place to hide and get some sleep. I haven't eaten since yesterday morning, either.

We had mail call. I got the cookies and your letter. I'm saving the cookies for "Hole Watch" Wednesday. That's special guard duty the snipers got stuck with.

Since we're students now, we get better accommodations. It looks like the weather may hold off for a few days. It's colder now though. I wanted to get this off to you with my new address. It sure was good hearing from you. Will write soon.

Love, Homesick

Before school had officially begun we were hard at it. We'd been issued M-14s and infrared scopes with orders to guard the ammo dump at Camp Pendleton, better known to us as hole watch. The dump was a large warehouse surrounded by a steep-sided valley.

Over the years a few break-ins had netted some unsavory customers very lethal weapons, which was an embarrassment to the base commander. Sniper school had a problem, too: how to get us accustomed to staying awake all night. With our barracks close to the dump, it was logical that we should guard it.

There were several camouflaged sniper nests in the wall of the valley. From sundown to sunup week days and from Saturday night to Monday morning, a sniper from the school watched the dump. We were issued live ammo and ordered, "Shoot to kill. No warnings and no questions asked." After the word got around, thefts from the ammo dump stopped. For us, hole watch was one long sleepless night after another.

★

ACT Co 8/69 Sniper School
MCB Camp Pendleton
January 31, 1969

Dear Mom,

We start school Monday, and if I don't have any setbacks, I'll ship to Nam sometime between March 20th and the 30th. I would like to get there sooner. Dave leaves this coming week, Wednesday I think.

Talked to Laura last night. She said you seemed to be getting along okay. Got the package you sent. Thanks for all that stuff, it really will help me out.

I hope I can get off base this weekend. I may go to Camp Las Pogas to see if I can find Dave and Nick. I heard Nick had 30 days of mess duty there.

Later—We just had a surprise inspection by our lieutenant. They just passed down an order that the school only gets twenty-five students and there's thirty-seven trying to get in. They're taking the highest shooters to start with and I'm one. So far they've picked up eleven of us to go to school for sure.

Got to get this in the mail. Take care and Grams, too.

Love, Joe

The atmosphere at the start of sniper school was tense, and the pressure to be accepted meant no screwups would be tolerated. We were being put through finer and finer sifters all the

time. Thirty-seven men wanted in. Twenty-five were initially
accepted. Twenty would eventually graduate.

I never did get to see Dave and Nick, but Parker was at a
base not far from me, and I did manage to spend some time
with him. Posey, Walters, and I continued to party together.
We were an odd combination for sure, yet we loved each other
like brothers.

*

ACT Co 8/69 Sniper School
MCB Camp Pendleton,
February 4, 1969

Dear Mom,

Well, here I am, getting behind on my writing as usual.
Right now I'm waiting to go on hole watch. Yeah, I've got it
again. It's amazing how often I get it.

I'm getting along pretty well. We don't start classes for a
couple of days, so right now we're just getting our gear ready
to start training. They just had an inspection and dropped
eleven more guys wanting to get into school, so there's 25 of
us now.

I got into a little scuffle with one of the troop leaders. He was
drunk and messing around our barracks after taps. Well, he
started giving me a bad time, so I hit him. I've got to admit it
was a pretty good punch cuz it knocked him out for a minute.
A couple of his friends took him away, so there wasn't any
more trouble. I saw him yesterday and he apologized to me. He
said he didn't remember being in our barracks.

My hair is long enough now that I've invested in a comb.
We can have it three inches on top as long as the sides are
"high and tight." That means short.

If I don't get hole watch this weekend, Parker and I are
going to Uncle Ralph's. Just watch, I'll get stuck with it.

Well, Mom, I had best go to chow before I go on duty. Tell
Grams hi and both of you take care. Will write soon.

Love, Joe

On the first day of sniper school, we were issued bush hats,
shooting jackets, and shiny aluminum carrying cases, four and
a half feet long, eighteen inches wide, and eight inches deep.

We had three competent instructors: Sergeant Oron, very
together and two years back from Vietnam; Sergeant Bolstead,
sharp and quiet, one year back from Vietnam; Corporal Hill, a

little looser than Oron and Bolstead, less tolerant of government red tape, four months back from Vietnam. Our instructors wandered around while we opened the cases and seemed amused by the perplexed looks on our faces. The rifle and gear, fitted snugly in foam-rubber slots, was different from anything we'd seen before. Oron did the talking.

"Take the rifle out of the case and hold it in front of you. People, you are holding what we consider to be the best sniper rifle in the world."

The barrel was long and thick, nearly the same diameter at the muzzle as at the chamber. There were no iron sights, just a scope mount and beautiful stock, recently hand-rubbed with linseed oil. Oron continued.

"It comes to us as a Remington model 700 bolt-action rifle with a medium-heavy, free-floating barrel. Modifications to suit our purposes are made here at Camp Pendleton. There will be no dry fire with this rifle. It would cost most of you a week's pay to repair a broken firing pin. The first time you squeeze the trigger, it will be in earnest, and the last time you squeeze the trigger, it will be in earnest. Does everyone understand?"

We were beginning to.

"It fires a 7.62mm, 173 grain, boattail bullet, match (suitable for competition or shooting matches) ammo only. In your carrying case, there is a wooden box with 120 rounds in it. A main requirement to graduate from this school will be that you fire 120 rounds each day except for Sunday. If we miss a training day because of bad weather, it will be made up. The rifle holds five rounds which load into the stock from the bottom. The scope is a 3×9 variable Redfield. Now pick it up and watch closely while Sergeant Bolstead and Corporal Hill mount the scope. You do exactly as shown and wait until one of us has checked it."

We were a little clumsy at first; Bolstead and Hill had made it look so easy. After all our mountings were inspected, we dismantled them and put everything back in the case.

"You will notice that with each cleaning kit, there is a package of lens paper. Anyone caught cleaning the lenses of these scopes with anything but the paper provided will be immediately dropped from the school. Understand?"

"Yes, sir."

"Good! Gear up. We have time before chow to bust some caps (fire rounds)."

Bust caps, we did, well past chow. By the end of that first

day we were exhausted and our shoulders sore as hell. With very little instruction, almost everyone was hitting the target. We didn't know it then, but this was just a small taste of the pace of training yet to come. As expert shots, we understood the basic principles of what Oron had said earlier that day. All aspects of the bolt rifle were intended to put the burden of error on the shooter and not the equipment.

The justification for the use of a bolt-action rifle lay in its reliability and the fact that an automatic weapon, such as the M-14 or M-16, must divert a small amount of gas from the chamber to eject the spent casing and push a new round into place. With the bolt rifle, that gas is used to increase the muzzle velocity of a heavier bullet.

The boattail bullet was shaped somewhat like a boat. It had a slightly tapered base, producing smoother airflow which prevented turbulence that could affect its accuracy in flight. The bullet was further stabilized by the rifle's free-floating barrel. The barrel was secured at the chamber. The precision of the rifle was such that the clearance between the barrel and stock was the thickness of a dollar bill. From the point where the bullet left its casing and started down the rifle bore, the barrel could not touch anything. Any contact between the barrel and the stock would affect the muzzle velocity from one round to the next and make constant scope adjustments necessary. The medium-heavy barrel distributed the heat from the burning powder and the friction of the bullet speeding down the bore more uniformly. Uneven heating of a thinner barrel could cause temporary warpage, pulling it ever-so-slightly out of line.

Three days into sniper school, our shoulders were beaten black and blue from the vicious recoil of the rifle. We had little choice, since using extra padding was immediate grounds for dismissal. In less than a week, two men were dropped for putting foam rubber under their shooting jackets. It took about ten days for our shoulders to toughen up and the rifle kick to become a minor inconvenience.

During the second week, a man was sacked when he fell asleep on hole watch. Two more men were let go because they couldn't perfect breath control, a critical factor since snipers had to be able to fire between breaths. Getting one's breathing under control to prevent the body from moving the rifle was a formidable task, even at the rifle range. To do it in actual combat—breathing hard, with the heart pounding—would prove to be a much greater challenge. To qualify as a Sniper Expert, I would have to learn to fire between heartbeats.

Shooting and scouting took priority in our training, with classes on survival skills, map orientation, and directing air and artillery strikes filling almost every spare moment. We had to spend what would normally be free time attending to the vagaries necessary to pass an inspection at any moment.

One of the most difficult problems we faced was learning how to quickly and accurately judge distances, complicated by the fact that as scouts and forward observers we had to switch from meters to yards readily. Normally, the military uses the metric system when calling for air and artillery support. Therein lay a problem. We had all grown up with the American standard of measure: inches, feet, and yards. Since we were most accustomed to judging distances in yards, we used the standard measure when firing the bolt rifle.

A valley made the target appear closer than it was, while a rise in the ground gave the impression that the target was farther away. As forward observers, we had more latitude when directing air and artillery strikes, and a meter or two either way wasn't so critical. There were other factors to consider when calling for support, and they would quickly become apparent when we were in Vietnam.

An important fact of our scout training involved searching mock Vietnamese villages, with accurate reconstructions of huts, bunkers, and rice caches. Each time some small detail would be changed, and we were damn well expected to find it. It might be something as inconspicuous as an AK-47 shell casing discarded in the grass, but it could tell the right man a lot about the condition of the rifle that fired it.

We also meticulously combed through simulations of abandoned enemy camps. There was practically no limit to the information that could be gleaned from careful scouting. It became second nature for us to determine details such as the number of troops, types of weapons, rations, how long the camp had been abandoned, and even the enemy's morale by observing the manner in which the camp had been maintained. Constantly being made aware of our surroundings was all part of the scout discipline, which I found to be nearly as challenging as the shooting aspect of our education.

Sniper training was intricate and focused on precision and detail. We shot moving silhouettes at five hundred yards and stationary targets at one thousand yards. At the end of our second week, we were expected to and did hit 120 out of 120 rounds fired. Some allowance was given on windy days, but not much. Breath control, adjusting to the wind, and movement of the target were the most crucial aspects of hitting the target.

We had a loose rule of thumb formula for judging wind velocity. For example, one- to three-mile-per-hour winds tingled the hairs on a man's arm. Three- to five-mile-per-hour winds slightly diverted a pinch of dirt trickled from the hand. Five- to seven-mile-per-hour winds caused a piece of cloth to flap. Seven- to ten-mile-per-hour winds rustled the trees and grass. In winds above ten miles an hour, a sniper had only experience and practice to go by.

"Doping in" (sighting in the rifle) was done on dry, windless days in hundred yard increments by turning a knob on the top of the scope. Elevations which fell in between hundred yard increments were compensated for by moving the rifle to position the hairs (crosshairs) above or below the target. Windage settings were made by turning a knob on the side of the scope. Once it was dialed in, the setting normally was not readjusted, and allowance for wind was done by aiming the hairs left or right of the target.

The complexities of hitting a moving target, especially at long distances, were mind boggling. In addition to the normal requirements for sighting in a target, the distance, speed and angle at which the target was moving, its size, and position the sniper was firing from (prone, sitting, or standing) all had to be factored within seconds. In theory, if everything went perfectly the target would be in the crosshairs. In practice, however, it was uncommon to shoot a target set neatly in the hairs. Corrections up, down, left, and right were almost always necessary.

The hours on the firing line were some of the most grueling I spent in training. In a six-day training week, we had to fire 720 rounds and spot the same for our partner. We became "stoned to the scope." I eventually found it harder to hit a target at five hundred yards than at a thousand.

Snipers rarely made it off the firing line before the chow hall closed. Sometimes Force Reconnaissance, the other school at ACT, was already there. The men in recon were as gung ho as they got and often verbally abused us as we stood silently waiting our turn. Comments like, "What ya got in the box, snipees, your diapers for the day," would start most of the recon boys laughing. They might not have thought it so funny if they knew that our ticket to leave the firing line was a new box of live ammo for the next day. A fight between recon and snipers could have been a disaster. Trainers walked between the two groups to keep one from breaking out. Oron, Bolstead, and Hill were stern as they repeated what would become a very irritating message. "You are temporarily deaf people. You hear nothing, absolutely nothing."

In front of the mess hall were what I called the "gray badges of courage," and they lay everywhere on the pavement. The men who made it into Reconnaissance Batallion or Scout Snipers didn't get into those units by going to sick bay. Most of us had bronchitis or viral pneumonia, and we would cough up fluid from our lungs and spit it on the asphalt. I still had viral pneumonia, so I added a few spots to the pavement myself. It wasn't very appetizing, but it was a good sign. As long as a man kept coughing up the mucus he was okay, but if he couldn't, he probably had developed bronchial pneumonia and would spend at least a month in the hospital. It was doubtful that either school would pick a man up again.

I don't know what motivated the other men to push themselves so hard to succeed, but a great deal of my motivation went back to that talk the gunny gave us in boot camp. We were at war, and the better trained a man was the better were his chances of survival.

*

ACT Co 8/69 Snipers
MCB Camp Pendleton, Calif.
February 25, 1969

Dear Mom,

It's 10:00 A.M. and we just finished a breakfast of C rations. It rained so hard last night, the power is out and the chow hall can't cook without it.

Liberty went fine. I got back in plenty of time. There's still one guy gone, he's a squad leader and you'll never guess who they picked to take his place. Hope he gets back today.

Sure was glad Laura could come. It seemed like a very short three days. I gave her the engagement ring and she said she loved it, but I'm not sure if it was the right thing to do.

As it stands now, I'll be home before I ship out. Just for a weekend or so. I found out Dave didn't ship out yet. He's with

the 28th Marines here at Pendleton. O'Grady is still at Del Mar
and I don't know where Nick is.

Later—we had to go unplug the drainage ditches, what a
mess.

Well, Mom, better get this on its way. Tell Grams hi and
you take care.

Love, J.T.

As we entered our fourth week at school, we were getting
pretty cocky and did not pass up the chance to take a little
revenge on recon. A lieutenant from their unit came out to our
range and asked if he could fire a bolt rifle.

It just so happened that Corporal Hill had taken us to the
range that day. Hill didn't like the obnoxious remarks made by
recon while in the chow line any better than the rest of us, and
he saw the opportunity of the moment.

Hill replied, "Yes, sir, of course. We'd be honored. Someone get the lieutenant a rifle and load it." So we did. Hill
handed the rifle to him and led him to the center of an empty
firing line, as we stood back, curious to see what was going to
happen.

Hill gave the lieutenant a shooting jacket and some quick
instructions on the use of the rifle in the prone position. Hill
didn't say anything about the heavy recoil, or warn him to keep
his eye away from the scope. The lieutenant lay down, strapped
the rifle around his arm, aimed at a target five hundred yards
away, and pulled the trigger. He instantly went limp. We
thought it was pretty funny, for a few seconds anyway, but
when he didn't move and a pool of blood started to form on the
ground, we realized he was hurt.

He started to get up as we gathered around him, and we were
more than a little surprised at the amount of damage. The scope
had cut a circle around his eye down to the bone. Hill gave the
lieutenant his handkerchief, and by the time we got him up,
he'd nearly soaked it with blood. We all offered our own
handkerchiefs, but he refused and took out his own. He also
declined Hill's suggestion that a couple snipers take him to sick
bay.

We watched a very humbled recon lieutenant stumble toward his jeep. Before he got to it, Sergeants Oron and Bolstead
drove up. They figured out in no time what had happened. We
were all trying to buy that bloodied handkerchief from Hill, but
he wouldn't sell it. We had drawn first blood on recon.

Bolstead helped the lieutenant to his jeep and headed to sick bay while Oron called us together. The somber expression on his face reminded us we had obviously gone too far; after all, the guy was an officer.

"I see we had a mishap on the range today. Corporal Hill, you were in charge. What happened?" Hill was still holding the bloody handkerchief when he answered.

"Sure, Sarge. Let's see, uh, we were just setting up this morning when that Lieutenant Anderson, I think that's his name, came by. Well, anyway, he asked if he could take a few shots. I know he wasn't supposed to be here, but he had the brass so we cleared the line and got him a rifle."

"Corporal Hill, did you give Lieutenant Anderson instructions on the proper use of the bolt rifle?"

"Sure, Sarge, but he was in a hurry, and I may have missed a thing or two."

"By thing or two, you mean you didn't tell him to keep his eye well clear of the scope, right?"

"Well, yeah, Sarge, that may have been a point I missed. Like I said, he was in quite a hurry." Oron had to tell us to stop laughing.

"Corporal Hill, is there anything else I should know?"

"I can't think of anything right now, Sergeant Oron."

"Does anyone have anything they would like to add to what Corporal Hill has told me?"

"No, sir!"

"Is Corporal Hill accurate as to what happened?"

"Yes, sir!"

"Okay, that's how my report will read. The lieutenant was, in his haste, mainly responsible for his injuries. I'm sure he'll be too embarrassed to make anything of it, but you've made extra paperwork for me, Hill. Therefore, I want an accident report from you before chow tonight. Well, what the hell are you guys standing around for? Hill get these people on the line; they've got some caps to bust. I'm going to check on Lieutenant Anderson. As for that handkerchief, it belongs to the whole platoon, and the highest shooter each day will have the privilege of carrying it. Is that clear, everyone?"

"Yes, sir!"

I do believe Oron got as much satisfaction at recon's misfortune as did the rest of us.

We were becoming weary of the demanding training schedule and were primed to let off some steam. When, where, and how was the question. One thing was certain, if it happened against recon, it would be serious. More effort was put into keeping the two units apart.

We finally came uncorked on the night of February 24. I got off guard duty at 10:00 P.M., and there was already a party going on in the barracks. I don't know where all the hard liquor came from, but most everyone was drunk and getting drunker. Someone handed me a bottle of vodka, and the party claimed another victim. It took a giant leap toward disaster at about midnight when a pillow fight escalated into a water fight. Some pillows broke open and the combination of water and feathers made for an interesting mess. To make matters worse, two overhead light fixtures were broken and glass on the floor was cutting bare feet.

The noise brought Sergeant Oron to the barracks. He just stood there in disbelief, but not for long. A half a dozen men picked him up, carried him to the head, and put him under a cold shower. We saw it in his eyes right away. Anger, not your day-to-day anger, but the oh-shit-we-fucked-up-royally kind of anger.

I really have to hand it to Oron, the way he kept his cool. He didn't say a word; he didn't have to. If it's possible to sober up instantly, we did it. We followed him back into the barracks and he called everyone to attention. He said nothing while he picked his way through the rubble. He didn't look at anyone or turn around when he reached the other end of the barracks. He spoke in an ominously low tone.

"White-glove inspection at oh-six-hundred hours," and he was gone.

To fail a white-glove inspection would probably get us all kicked out of school. With one guy on hole watch, nineteen of us worked right up to the last minute to be ready.

One seemingly insurmountable problem we had to solve before passing inspection was how to replace the two broken light fixtures. A small raiding party was sent out to borrow, as it were, the fixtures from other barracks. Although nobody wanted this assignment, three guys actually volunteered. Private First Class Thomas headed this small clandestine operation. If they were caught in another unit's barracks, they would be considered thieves and might not make it out alive.

We all worried about them until they returned, soaking wet but safe, two hours later. They had procured three fixtures, two of which came from the recon barracks. The only way I can explain their ability to pull off such a seemingly impossible stunt is a type of invisibility we were becoming skilled at as scouts. The extra light fixture was a bonus. Thomas used his finger and shoe polish to write a dedication on it. "Presented to Sergeant Oron by Recon Battalion, Feb. 25, 1969." Oron had a twinkle in his eyes as he accepted the gift.

"Maybe there's hope for you guys yet. We're rained out of the range today, so take commander's time. You're free to do what you wish, short of destroying the barracks again. I do suggest a few of you, and you know who you are, study up on map orientation and procedures for calling air and artillery support. Good day, gentlemen."

"Good day, sir!"

He cradled that light fixture like a newborn baby when he left for his quarters.

It was like breaking a fever, we knew we were going to make it.

On February 28, 1969, we graduated with a short, low-key ceremony. The only people present were Lieutenant Colonel J. L. Day, commanding officer; First Lieutenant J.W. Bellow, officer in charge; Sergeants Oron and Bolstead; and Corporal Hill.

Of the twenty of us to receive our diplomas that day, three-fourths were actually assigned to Scout Sniper units in Vietnam. After thirty days or so in Vietnam, requalification at Da Nang would cut another quarter of my graduating class.

*

Stg. Btn.
BCN
Camp Pendleton
March 20, 1969

Dear Mom,

I know you thought my hand was broken. I'm sorry for being so poor to write.

So far things are going pretty good. We're getting in a lot of long hikes and short nights. We leave here Wednesday to go to Mainside until my port call comes up. I hope I make that first port call, I'm getting restless.

There isn't a whole lot of news since I talked to you on the phone. The chow here is the best I've gotten in the Corps.

Well, Mom, I know this isn't much of a letter but I promise

to do better when they let up on us a little. Tell Grams to take
care. You take care of yourself, too.

                                                        Love, Joe

With school behind me, I was about to enter the last and
most ominous portion of our training, staging. Staging Battalion was a backlog of thousands of men in final preparation to
be sent to war, and it had a vague feeling of unreality to it.

We were loosely grouped into military specialties. Immuni-
zation records were double checked, orders were cut, and
classes continued. These classes were different from anything
we'd experienced before. We watched training films on the
horrors of venereal disease. The myth of the dreaded "Black
Rose" started there (a strain of VD that we could only get from
Vietnamese prostitutes). It was rumored to be incurable, and if
a man got it, he'd be sent to an island for the rest of his life.
We were young and naive enough to buy the story. It took all
of twenty-four hours in Vietnam before we learned the truth.

One class was particularly memorable: what to do if you are
taken prisoner. Until that point I hadn't given the idea much
thought, but what the instructor was telling us started me thinking. Some of the things the captain relayed were tragically
humorous. Name, rank, and serial number of course, but most
of what I was hearing was a holdover from our experience with
the Japanese during World War II.

"Act crazy," he said. "The Oriental mind has respect for
someone they consider nuts, and for the most part they tend to
go easy on screwballs."

This tactic may have worked at times with the Japanese if a
man was a good actor. However, Charlie didn't fall for this
trick. As a matter of fact, such conduct would more likely than
not get someone killed on the spot. If the North Vietnamese
read the terms put down in the Geneva Convention, there was
little compliance on their part. Screw the rules, they'd been at
war for a long time. They were out to win.

Posey, Walters, and I were still together and would be
through our "out posts" (final destinations). We were tired of
training, and now the Corps was building us up for the real
thing, and we didn't know what the real thing was.

Men got edgy thinking about their impending destination.
Although orders were passed down that trips to Tijuana were
forbidden, we usually ignored them. Most of us went for what
might be our last lay and some tequila.

Time passed quickly enough, and we got the word of our unit destination and flight dates on March 28. I would be going to the 5th Marine Regiment, and after considerable inquiry, I found out it was at a place called An Hoa, Vietnam. I wondered about the name An Hoa. Where was it and what was it like? The answers to these questions would have to wait. With a four-day liberty before my April 3 flight date, I decided to fly home for a couple days, knowing I wouldn't see it again for over a year, if ever.

Posey and Walters decided to stay in California and party. I guess Walters didn't have much to go home for. He had a great story he recounted time and again. He came from a large, poor family, and he swore he was born in an abandoned train caboose. A few years later he showed me the caboose, still sitting in the same junkyard it was in when he was born.

Posey said his old man would just put him to work in their family-owned bar in Columbus, Ohio. The two of them would pal around in California, and although I doubted seriously that they could find much new in the way of mischief that we hadn't already tried, I told them to try and stay out of the brig, at least until I got back.

My family, except for my older brother who was in the navy, and Laura greeted me when I got home. Some of my old high-school buddies were still around, but they had changed. Or was it me? Most of them were trying to stay in college or getting married, hoping to avoid the draft. Whatever the consequences, my course was firmly set, and in that respect I suppose I had a slight advantage.

I had mainly gone home to see Laura. I think I was trying to convince myself that getting engaged just before being sent away was all right. Instead of minimizing my personal relations before leaving, I was intensifying them. It was as though perfumed letters from that special someone would assure my safe return. When I left to meet my port call, there were kisses, tears, and promises.

I finished last-minute preparations to go to Vietnam, and two days later I rode to El Toro Marine Air Station with Walters on a rented motorcycle. I told Bruce I'd be seeing him soon and boarded the 707. I sat by a window and watched the last-minute hugs and kisses from wives and girlfriends. I thought about Laura and felt very much alone.

We flew to Anchorage, Alaska, to refuel and take on more passengers. No one was allowed to deplane, but I was content to stare at the snow-capped mountains in the distance, so much like the ones back home. There were no empty seats when we left Anchorage for Hawaii.

We had a three-hour layover in Hololulu, and most of us eagerly filled that time in the airport bar downing Singapore slings as fast as possible. It was the shortest three hours of my life. Just when everyone started to get rowdy, we got the word to return to the plane ASAP. After a final head count, we flew straight to Okinawa. This stretch of our journey was the worst, nearly thirteen hours of being cramped in a jet that felt like it was still on the ground. No movement, only the noise from the engines to indicate we were flying at all. We landed in the middle of the night, jet-lagged and exhausted. After boxing and labeling our Stateside uniforms, everybody was issued jungle utilities and boots. We wrote home, killed time in the EM club, and tried to talk to the men returning from Vietnam on their way to the World (the States) about what the war was like. Most of them wouldn't talk about the war at all. I wondered if it was because we were too dumb to understand or if it was something else. I figured the best thing to do was to try to put the next thirteen months out of my mind.

Chapter II * Welcome to the War

*

1st Division
Okinawa
April 5, 1969

Dear Mom,

Well I'm almost there. I'm in Okinawa and should be leaving for Da Nang today. It doesn't seem like home is halfway around the world. We've been here a couple days. I was feeling pretty blue when I got here, so I went to the EM club and got drunk.

Right now it's raining hard. They've processed my papers again and gave me my last shot before leaving here.

Posey and Walters are already here, too. Posey and I got the same flight to Da Nang, but Walters doesn't know yet when he goes. We were hoping we wouldn't get separated, but we did.

I sent a telegram, but I don't know if you got it or not. I doubt it. Probably won't get this mailed until I get to Da Nang.

I'm sort of getting a case of the nerves. The B-52s take off from the Air Force base here around the clock to bomb targets in Vietnam. It's kind of good to know they're there.

Well, Mom, we have to finish processing our papers. It's twelve noon here and we leave at 8:00 tonight. Will write again as soon as I get an address. Tell Grandma hi.

Love, Joe

The tension of thousands of troops passing to and from Vietnam was in the air, and it made Camp Butler a dangerous place, especially after dark. Still, I liked Okinawa. When not processing, I was either at the EM club or watching the planes take off, mostly transports and B-52s. We

weren't allowed off-base liberty, but my last day there I paid a
cabby to get me out. He then went bar hopping with me until
2:00 in the morning. Somehow he managed to get a very drunk
Marine past the SPs (shore patrol) and back on base without a
pass.

Ten hours later I would board another civilian 707, identical
to the one we flew to Okinawa on, only the mood was different
this time. There wasn't the usual horseplay and banter. I was
lost in thoughts of things past and far away and of the unknown
ahead. It was obvious that I wasn't alone.

The reality of Vietnam and the war intruded on our thoughts
as soon as we arrived: a very spit-and-polished warrant officer
boarded the plane the instant the door opened. His only words
were "Welcome to the Republic of South Vietnam, gentlemen.
Due to conditions in the Da Nang area tonight, you are to move
quickly from the plane to the bunkers as directed by the signs
outside." My first thought was that this was probably a drill.

I spent my first night in Vietnam in a dark, overcrowded,
sandbag bunker with one flashlight and the occasional flame
from a cigarette lighter to break the gloom, listening to the
sounds of war. There were explosions all night, some seemed
near, others far away. I could only wonder what the hell I had
gotten myself into.

*

HQ Co, 5th Marines S/S
FPO/San Francisco, Calif.
An Hoa
April 10, 1969

Dear Mom,

I'm sure you think it's about time. I started to write last
night, but we had incoming mortars. By the time we could
leave the bunkers, it was past time for lights out.

I sent two Mars-O-Grams today, one to you and one to
Laura. It takes about twenty-four hours for them to get there.
I filled out a form like a telegram of no more than twenty-five
words. They send the message by ham radio to a ham receiver
in California and the person in California sends it on to you by
phone. It's free and they call till they get a hold of you.

I'm at a combat base called An Hoa which is about twenty-
five miles southwest of Da Nang. This is the 5th Marines base
of operations. It's a big camp, maybe two miles in diameter,
set in a large flat valley with mountains on three sides. It's sort
of a cork in a bottle neck and was put here to stop enemy

movement north and south. It was just about leveled two months ago during Tet when the VC blew up two ammo dumps, setting off 46,000 artillery shells. Since then it's quieted down and only receives a few mortar and rocket rounds each day.

As for my outfit, I'm with the sniper platoon. The platoon is part of Headquarters Company which is attached to the regiment. If you count the captain, gunny, two sergeants, and three central squad leaders, there's only 30 of us in the platoon. We have different duties, so they rotate two-man teams from place to place. One other guy I went through Sniper School with is here, too. We're the only new guys here. Most of the rest of them have been here four months or longer. They know their stuff real well. Within the next couple days I'll be assigned to one as his partner and spotter. I have to count on my partner to keep me in good health and teach me what I need to know.

This is the best sniper platoon in the division. It's so good the VC have put a bounty on our heads. Somehow they know the names of every man in the platoon and how many kills he has. They want some of these guys pretty bad. It doesn't bother me, since they have never collected it. We've lost one sniper in nearly a year and that was on a booby trap.

I had to go to sick bay this morning with many mosquito bites on my face and arms. I forgot to use repellent. I'll remember tonight.

Walters was sent to the 7th Marines and Posey is in a regular grunt company here. He's trying to get into the sniper platoon. I've seen him several times.

One thing you learn fast here is responsibility. You're responsible for other people's lives. Friends are different here from anyplace else. I don't know how to explain it, but there's a common bond between guys. We share everything. If someone swipes a case of beer or gets cookies from home, he puts it on the table and leaves it. No one will be a pig about it, but if he wants some, he gets it. If you've got it and he doesn't, let him use it.

As far as needing anything, I could use a pair of leather boot laces. I have lots of uses for those, also some white cotton socks. That's really all.

It takes mail about a week to get home and five or six days to get here. Don't worry! I'm in the best outfit here. My sergeant takes good care of me. He even makes me take my malaria pill every Sunday.

Well, Mom, let me know how you are doing and tell Grandma hi. I will write whenever I get a chance. Take care.

Love, Your Youngest

The helicopter was a symbol of Vietnam and for good reason. They were the trucks of the war. They brought our supplies, mail, and most importantly medevac (medical evacuation). Rarely was a medical facility more than fifteen or twenty minutes away.

My first ride on a chopper was from Da Nang to An Hoa. Orders stated that everyone had to have a helmet and flak jacket to be allowed to board a helicopter, which made sense. Thirteen of us, most of us new in-country, boarded a Chinook (twin rotor copter). We lined up along both sides facing each other and sat on the seats as trained, except for two salty-looking grunts. They did something I thought strange. They took off their flak jackets and sat on them. Surely that couldn't be comfortable. I finally leaned over and asked why they did that. Their reply was to the point. "To keep bullets from blowing your balls off when they come through the bottom of the bird." From that moment on I sat on my flak jacket a hell of a lot more than I wore it.

Stepping off the chopper at An Hoa was like having a hot, wet towel slapped on my face. I was stunned by the heat and humidity and the smell of burning shitters. Carrying a full seabag while walking the quarter mile from the main LZ (landing zone) to headquarters was an ordeal. I presented my orders to the office clerk, with so much sweat running into my eyes I could barely see.

Sandbag City was our name for An Hoa. Hundreds of thousands of sandbags were neatly formed into bunkers, trenches, and walls. The command bunker and field hospital were underground, covered with sandbags and dirt. The ceilings and walls of the tents had four-foot-high sandbag walls around them, except for ours. Our CO (commanding officer) felt the wall would only serve to concentrate the explosion of a direct hit. He was probably right, and I'm glad to say his theory wasn't tested while I was there.

An Hoa was at sea level and too far inland for the sea breeze to cool it off. Rarely did the temperature fall below seventy degrees at night. During the day it could reach up to 130 degrees, with 100 percent humidity.

It was a major fire base, and there was an almost constant rumble from mortars and big guns lending support to a Marine or army unit in trouble somewhere. When the big guns fired, dust seemed to magically rise from the ground and settle on everything.

Still, An Hoa was home. There was a small PX and an EM club that usually closed early on account of brawls. At times, the music of the Doors and Jimi Hendrix coming from radios and tapes all over the base nearly drowned out the sounds of outgoing artillery. We listened to Hanoi Hannah who usually played better rock music than our own station.

An Hoa was a busy place with a main road out that would eventually get you to Da Nang. There was a small LZ on the west side of the base for VIPs and a much larger LZ at the south end for troop movements and supplies. The east side had a metal airstrip big enough to land C-130 Hercules transports and Bird Dog spotter planes.

The main LZ and airstrip were favorite targets for enemy rockets and mortars. At night they would hit the airstrip, and before the sun was up, Seabees were busy filling holes and replacing damaged panels. The day after I arrived at An Hoa a C-130 landed, and Charlie promptly blew one of the wings off with what must have been a chance hit with a rocket, at least that's what everyone figured. The plane was towed to a repair area where it sat for a good two months before a Skycrane helicopter gingerly brought in another wing. The new wing was put on, and before the plane could get to the runway and off the ground, an enemy mortar blew the other wing off. It was again towed to the maintenance area where it sat for three months before another wing was brought in and that hapless C-130 was able to leave An Hoa. It had become a familiar sight as I choppered in and out and was like losing an old friend when it was gone. It surely cost the U.S. more to get that plane out than it would have been to push it off the runway and blow it to hell.

The main LZ caught more than its share of rockets and mortars. In this case, it was usually during the daylight when choppers continuously brought in cargo and mail and took troops out to any number of destinations. It was so dangerous that helicopters unloaded, loaded, and were on their way in no more than five minutes.

At the north end of the LZ was a large bunker with wooden benches neatly cemented into the ground, notorious for its ability to allow shrapnel to pass through the walls where it would ricochet around the inside of the bunker. During a rocket or mortar attack, men would invariably get low against the nearest wall. I couldn't see being crushed if a near miss blew the wall in. Since there really was no safe place, I would pick a bench near the center of the bunker, use my pack as a pillow, stretch out, and usually fall asleep. An old soldier's adage is "never run when you can walk, never walk when you can stand, never stand when you can sit, never sit when you can lie down, never stay awake when you can sleep." I slept through some pretty heavy rocket barrages, awakened occasionally by the sound of shrapnel hitting a support beam or bouncing off the metal walls, only to fall back asleep knowing any incoming would delay my chopper about half an hour. Every time someone would get wounded in the bunker, they were hugging the wall. Most were minor wounds, and those guys would be pissed. It could have been worse, like being buried under several tons of sandbags.

★

Scout Snipers
Delta Co. 1/5
April 20, 1969

Dear Mom,

Have some slack so will try to get a letter off. I'm at Delta Co. 1/5 base camp, which is about 15 miles from An Hoa. I'm teamed up with two other snipers here, Chuck Mawhinney and Dan Collier. Chuck is the best sniper we have and he's been here almost 11 months. I couldn't have asked for a better partner. Dan's been here about a month.

I went on my first patrol this morning and Chuck shot three NVA. We found one body; the gooks carried the other two away. We searched him and found some important maps and drawings of Marine installations. He also had a lot of money. We figured he was a courier and paymaster. This whole area around An Hoa is heavily booby-trapped. Snipers don't have to walk point, but we have to watch our step real close. They're everywhere.

I've learned a lot in the short time I've been here. For one thing, the papers and TV back home don't give an accurate representation of what's going on here, so if you read or hear something that happens in my area don't take it for full face value. Ask me and I'll tell you all I'm allowed to. Another thing is how much contact there is here. There's a lot more fighting during the day than I expected, and at night it gets five or six times as heavy. We can work any way we want to, mostly the hours around sunset and sunrise. Our skipper wants to hang on to us as long as possible, so he usually goes along with what we want.

One thing I can say for Vietnam, it has some pretty areas. On three sides of us we have the greenest mountains I've ever seen. I'd rather be looking at the ones at home. It's awful hot here and as it gets further into summer, the worse it is. A couple of days ago it got up to 125 degrees. When we're at base camp we wear shorts and no shirt during the day. At night we sleep with all our clothes and boots on. My bed partner is my M-14. It's not as pretty as Laura, but it will have to do. Where I go, it goes.

You ought to see some of the bugs they have here. There are ants an inch long and centipedes ten inches long. The mosquitoes are unbelievable, at night they come out in the millions. I'm glad I have a camera cuz it's really hard to describe some of the things I've seen.

I have a couple of ideas for a box you can send me. Paperback books are good. Also could use a few can openers. For some reason it's hard to get hold of a church key.

Love, Joe

P.S. Thought I had better make a list of some of the things I'll be writing about. This might help the confusion a little. NVA—North Vietnamese Army. They're trained in the north and are the best the Communists have. They've filtered down here so much lately, they outnumber the VC. VC—Viet Cong, farmers by day and fighters by night. They may be plowing a field and turn around and shoot you in the back. Gooks—the most common term we use for NVA and VC. Bolt rifle—our model 700 Sniper rifles. Grunts—regular rifle men. Short Timer—getting short, a Marine who has less than three months left over here. A short timer usually gets extra cautious, he figures he's made it this far and he doesn't want to louse it up at the last.

My first days at An Hoa were spent processing orders and making endless trips to the armory and to a clearing snipers used to sight in their new rifles to find an M-14 I was comfortable with. After spending so much time firing the bolt rifle with its telescopic sights, it was difficult to get used to working with iron sights again. The M-14 was preferred by snipers for several reasons. The most important was its accuracy at long ranges and proven reliability. A side benefit of using the M-14 and the bolt rifle in combination was that they both used the same basic round and in an emergency they could share ammunition. The M-16 round would fit neither rifle. I would soon be going out as a spotter to provide close-in support for the team leader, and I was desperately trying to get used to the heat and humidity. Most of the time, spotters took all shots up to five hundred yards and spent countless hours looking through binoculars and Starlite scopes. The bolt rifle had to be earned. Only team leaders carried the bolt rifle, mainly because they had already proven themselves in combat. Normally to be a team leader, a man had to be a spotter for two months, though there were exceptions.

A scout sniper platoon was run by a captain (usually called just "the skipper") followed by a gunnery sergeant, staff sergeant, and sergeant. Two or three central squad leaders ran the rest of us in two-man teams, a team leader and a spotter. The sniper team was the smallest combat unit in the military capable of functioning independently of others in the bush. We were self-contained units and had no set number of patrols. We had the prerogative, as I was to learn, of planning our own hunter-kills, and although we always tried to respect the skipper's plans, we had the option of foregoing a hunter-kill and going on patrol instead, or vice versa. Without these freedoms and prerogatives, we would not only have been singled out for attack, we would have attracted too much attention and lost our effectiveness.

I soon learned to tell the difference between the sound of incoming and outgoing ordnance and to always watch for the nearest bunker or low spot in the ground.

I was less than a week in-country when my squad leader, Dave Meeks, came into my tent and told me to saddle up, he was taking me to team up with a couple of snipers already in the bush. The team leader was getting short and had noticed a slight case of nerves in his partner. During the ten-to-twelve-mile truck ride from An Hoa to Delta Company (1st Battalion, 5th Marines), Dave told me to watch the kids.

"Sometimes they come running up to the trucks like they're begging and will throw a grenade in." I watched them as we rode along. They were all begging for something.

Delta Company was on a barren hill surrounded by rice paddies and fields about a quarter of a mile from the road. I first saw the company a mile away. What I didn't see until we jumped off the truck near a small village were the bodies, fourteen of them, lying together on grass mats alongside the road.

The truck drove on, leaving Dave and me standing in dusty silence. The smell of human blood cooking in the midday sun hit me as my mind raced to absorb what I was looking at. I was trying to match bodies to body parts and visualize that mess on the ground as ever having been living people. It dawned on me that they were mostly women and children. I looked at Dave who was closely watching to judge my reaction. He matter-of-factly told me, "The VC assassinated the village chief at a meeting this morning. They killed everyone in the hootch (hut)." Dave turned and started up the narrow path that led to Delta. As he walked, he warned me to stay on the trail and not step on anything that didn't look right, even a gum wrapper. "Welcome to the war, Ward," he added grimly.

I had heard enough about Chuck Mawhinney to form the mental picture of him as an eccentric man with an obsession for killing. I almost panicked at the idea of meeting him, let alone being his partner. When Dave introduced us, all my preconceived notions about him disappeared. He was slight of build and quiet, almost to the point of being shy, with a quick, if somewhat strained, smile. Chuck Mawhinney was a professional in every sense of the word. Dan Collier, on the other hand, did fit the image I'd formed of him. He had dark circles under his eyes, and his pale, drawn face betrayed more than a "slight case of nerves."

Before sunrise the next morning, Chuck and I left base camp with a squad and a first lieutenant on a routine patrol. Dan stayed behind. Chuck wanted to see how I handled myself. About an hour away from camp, the point man spotted some NVA moving through a large clearing nine hundred yards in the distance. The squad crouched low and the word was passed for "snipers up." Chuck was already running toward a small rise about seventy-five feet away on the other side of a rice paddy, with me right behind.

The lieutenant was yelling and swearing as loud as he dared for Chuck to slow down and watch out for booby traps. If Chuck heard him, he didn't give any indication, and in a few seconds he assumed a kneeling position. As trained, I took my spot two feet to his left rear. By the time I focused my field glasses and confirmed that they had weapons, Chuck had his breathing under control, and the first shot rang out.

A VC at the center of the column dropped. I heard myself say, "Hit," the same way I had said it so many times at the rifle range. It came out of my mouth calmly, well-rehearsed. All the VC, all but one, began running and dragging their fallen comrade toward the tree line they had come from. A second shot broke the early morning quiet and a man toward the front of the retreating column fell. "Hit," I said as I watched them pick up the second body and make the safety of the trees. The man that started for the opposite tree line had made two mistakes. His first was getting separated from the main unit. His last was trying to rejoin them with a sniper watching. Another shot rang out, and he fell behind a rice-paddy dike. For the third time in barely half a minute, the word "hit" came from my mouth. I felt nothing. The reality of the situation hadn't sunk in yet.

To get a confirmed kill, a scout sniper had to search the body for weapons and documents, then fill out a kill sheet. The front side had the name of the team leader and his spotter, rifle number, scope number, date and time, number of enemy, direction of movement, type of weapons, and map coordinates where the body or bodies were left. It also had a section for details which literally meant doing a cursory postmortem while looking for weapons and documents. A single bullet leaves the body relatively intact, which to the trained eye can yield valuable information about enemy troops in the area. The sex and approximate age were noted. The skin, fingernails, eyes, and teeth were checked for signs of malnutrition and disease. The condition of the uniform, equipment, and the food he or she was carrying were also logged. The back side of the sheet had spaces for the number of confirmed killed, probable killed, wounded, and more space for noting details. It then had to be signed by the highest ranking officer present. We rarely had time to fill out sheets on the spot, but the instructors at sniper school had done their jobs well. Our powers of observation were fine-tuned to the point where the data could be gathered mentally and transferred to kill sheets when we got back to a more secure area.

At that point Chuck was sitting on one hundred confirmed kills and getting short. For a reason known only to him he wanted to break that one hundred mark, but we would have to cross nine hundred yards of open terrain to get to the body. The lieutenant was concerned that we may have interrupted part of a larger enemy force that would ambush us when we got there. A brief, intense discussion between Chuck and the lieutenant resulted in a compromise. He wouldn't allow the two of us to go unless we could find volunteers to make up a fire team. Soon we were off on a very long nine hundred yard walk, my eyes glued to that tree line on the right.

We couldn't see the body until we got to the dike it had fallen behind, and there I saw something I couldn't believe. The man lay, spread-eagled on his back, and most of the rear and side of his skull was gone. Some of his brains were in his pith helmet, some on the ground, and the rest was slowly oozing from the hole in his head. Yet he was still breathing. I turned to Chuck to tell him the guy was still alive, but he hushed me with a wave of his hand and said, "Come on, let's get this done."

The fire team set up on each side of us, concentrating on the tree line that had us all worried. We began our search, Chuck took one side and I took the other, going through pockets and feeling the material for papers that might have been sewn into the fabric. The first thing I came upon was a three-inch-square color photo of a young Vietnamese woman. I found myself wondering if it was his wife, girlfriend, or sister. Chuck answered my question when he lifted the man's hand and I saw the wedding band. I put the picture back in the same pocket I'd found it and in a benumbed state continued my search, fighting the impulse to give the dying man a personality. Three hours or three minutes later—I couldn't tell, time and my mind were playing a soon-to-be-familiar trick on me—Chuck brought me out of my daze when he stood abruptly and placed a match-ammo round on the man's chest, an intimidation technique that served two purposes. It was a warning that a scout sniper had shot him, and the round Chuck had left had a different lot number than the ammo he was actually using, which helped confuse the enemy intelligence network.

Chuck had a wad of money in one hand and an AK-47 (the standard NVA issue rifle) in the other and said, "Let's get out of here." My thoughts snapped back to that tree line and the dangerous position we were in. I took one last glance and noticed the wedding band was still on his finger.

I told the fire team we were finished, stuffed the maps and documents into my pockets, and hustled to catch up with Chuck who was well on his way to rejoin the squad. Behind me, I heard someone say, "This bastard ain't dead yet," followed by the sound of M-16 fire. Later that day, the wedding ring turned up as stakes in a poker game at base camp.

That was Chuck's last patrol as team leader. When the lieutenant signed his kill sheet, Chuck turned to me and said, "The war's over." A few days later Chuck went to An Hoa and finished the rest of his tour as central squad leader, but for me the war had just begun.

Normally, a sniper had to serve at least two months as a spotter before he became eligible to be a team leader and carry the bolt rifle, but in less than two weeks after getting in-country, I would be carrying one. I inherited the rifle with the words, "Take care of my baby," and the man who turned it over to me was a local legend. Chuck had gotten the rifle as soon as it came into the armory, broke it in, and then carried it for a year. Although he logged 101 confirmed kills and over 150 probables, I could have put that rifle in any sporting goods store and sold it for new. I vowed to keep it that way, and with the weather and rigors of combat, I spent a tremendous amount of time doing just that.

In addition to the bolt rifle and the M-14, many of the snipers carried other specialized equipment. One such item that was passed along by the team leaders was the Australian bush pack that I carried. Not only was this pack better balanced, it was easier to open, which could save a life in an emergency. I also carried a Turkish battle axe, which was similar to a regular machete but with a hooked end.

*

HQ Co. 5th Marines
Scout Snipers
An Hoa
April 27, 1969

Dear Mom,

This is the best day I've had here yet. The company I was out with came into An Hoa, so we did, too. I got the cookies you sent and three letters.

We just got in from the bush. I haven't cleaned up yet and believe me I need it. I have three confirmed kills already. It's not like the movies when a GI kills his first enemy soldier. It wasn't as bad as I thought it would be, especially after I've seen what they can do to us. If people back in the States could see how dangerous Communism is and how fortunate they are to have what they do, there would be fewer riots and protests. The guys over here don't pay much attention to the protesters. I've also developed a real dislike for racists. Black men bleed just like white men. The color of a person's skin means nothing.

As to what I'm doing, this whole last week we mainly ran patrols, and except for a couple we did okay. The gooks have hit An Hoa every day, sometimes two and three times with rockets. This has gone on for about a week now, and so far they've hit two choppers and a tank. I don't know about any casualties yet.

You seem to be worried about my partner. Chuck is the best. He's got the highest number for kills of any sniper in the division and a general is coming here personally to promote him. You don't have to worry about my partner.

So, Nick's in the 4th Regiment. That would put him somewhere around Phu Bi, that's quite a ways north of here. Women here chew betel nut and it makes their teeth almost black. The men don't chew, but they do roll and smoke the worst smelling cigars. Be back. I'm going to the chow hall, it just opened and I haven't had a hot meal in three weeks.

I'm back. I ate so much I'm sick. It's Sunday here and they had steak and french fries, with ice cream even. Now all I need is a shower and I'll feel human. There's a water ration here, so I'll have to wait till 6:00 when they open the showers. Chuck just came in. He said two lieutenant generals personally pinned lance corporal stripes on him. Now do you believe me when I tell you he's got a lot on the ball? I'm getting paid the 1st and I'll be sending some money home. I'd better get this mailed.

> Love,
> Your much perked up son

The first week in the bush was a blur of patrols, hunter-kills, firefights, incoming mortars, C rations, and "snipers up." Chuck had me on the bolt rifle, and I was to be team leader. Dan would be my spotter, which was quite a disappointment for him. Dan's nerves were getting worse. I could only hope Chuck had crammed enough into my head in a week and a half to stay alive and keep my partner that way. I was racking up kills and started smoking marijuana to help detach myself from the constant death and destruction going on all around me. I was also introduced to the fetid smell of decomposing bodies left in the tropical heat and the depressing odor of napalm.

A two-man scout sniper team, well-trained in stealth and concealment, could move about the countryside with relative ease and safety, until the NVA put a bounty on us right after I arrived. Word spread that they would pay one thousand American dollars for a bolt rifle and three grand for a sniper they could skin alive. They didn't collect on the bounty, but it was a good tactical move on their part. Once while on a patrol on the outskirts of An Hoa, I came across a drawing of a sniper I knew from my home state, nailed to a fence post. The walls of the command bunker were literally covered with the photos, descriptions, and detailed sketches we had found of scout snipers.

As a safety measure, the brass decided that we should start taking out fire teams with us, then squads and occasionally platoons. At times, a quarter of our time was tied up with noisy patrols, constantly getting into booby traps, ambushes, and ironically taking enemy sniper fire. We decided to hell with the brass. They weren't out there getting shot at. We made a few modifications in our working routine, designed to confuse the enemy as to which snipers were working certain areas, and concentrated on direct-action operations.

Thick vegetation often caused patrols and company movements to bunch up, because the main rule for a movement was to keep the man in front of you in sight at all times. Bunching made it easy for the enemy to inflict serious damage when they sprang an ambush. The unit's CP (command post) with its key personnel, was usually located in the middle of a column for maximum protection, front and rear. A typical ambush would come from about forty-five degrees on either or both sides toward the front and was often initiated when the lead squad hit a booby trap. With the front of the column disabled, it was possible for the enemy to concentrate more of its fire at the center where key people were located.

Scout snipers were dangerously conspicuous. We were the only ones in the column without helmets and flak jackets, and a bolt rifle is pretty hard to disguise. We also didn't carry extra ammo. An exhausted sniper who couldn't get his breathing under control was as good as no sniper at all.

Chuck had warned me stay back in the column. It often meant a longer run to get to a firing point but was safer. His words were lost in my zeal to prove myself worthy of being made a team leader, but were abruptly reinforced on my third patrol. Dan and I were walking near the front of the command

post, behind the radioman. We were on a narrow rice-paddy
dike, approaching a thick tree line three hundred yards to the
right front. The radioman was holding a PRC-25 handset to the
side of his face, talking, when he violently spun halfway
around, facing me. His arm flew out to the side hard enough to
break the cord to the handset. I could hear firing as the man in
front of him fell dead, shot through the heart, and an engineer
in front of him was hit with shrapnel from an RPG (rocket-
propelled grenade). I dropped to the ground, hitting so hard
that it knocked the wind out of me. I looked up to see the
radioman down on one knee, looking at his arm, repeating,
"Jesus Christ, I've been shot." By the time I crawled the few
yards to reach him, the noise from AK-47s nearly drowned out
his voice. He was still kneeling, so I pulled him down by his
collar.

We were returning fire, and the deafening roar of a firefight was quickly building. The radioman kept wanting to raise
his head and look at his arm. With one hand I held his head
down and reached over him with my other hand to pull his right
arm to where I could look at it. The bullet had entered his
forearm just under the elbow, traveled most of the way through
his arm, made a ninety degree turn, and ended up just under the
skin in the middle of the back of his hand. We were in an
impossible situation, pinned flat on top of an exposed rice-
paddy dike, with the firefight becoming more intense. With my
right arm over his neck to keep him from getting up again, I
managed to get a battle dressing from my first-aid kit. Unable
to tie the dressing one handed, I put it over the hole and held
on. As abruptly as it started, the firefight was over. It probably
lasted fifteen minutes, but lying helpless on that dike it may as
well have been fifteen years. A medevac was on the way, and
a corpsman was taking care of the guy. I didn't know the
radioman's name and never saw him again, but I appreciated
the fact that he stopped a bullet that would have probably hit
me in the face.

Etched in my mind was Chuck's warning. Routine patrols
and company movements were two of the most dangerous
situations where snipers had the least amount of control and
were surrounded by too many men. After the incident with the
radioman, I rarely worked near the command post again. I
thought more and more about what obvious targets my partner
and I were. Salty grunts knew to give us extra room, but once
a new guy kept closing up behind me. I finally turned and

warned him, "If you don't want to get shot, you better double space behind me." From the look on his face, he must have thought I was going to shoot him, when what I meant was that if I drew fire, he'd probably get hit, too. Either way, he didn't get near me again.

★

Scout Snipers
An Hoa
May 1st, 1969

Dear Mom,

I'm at An Hoa and will be for another day or two, then Dan and I go to Da Nang to the Sniper School range there to requalify.

Last night Charlie (gooks) tried to break through the perimeter and we took at least 200 mortars. At first it looked like Charlie was going to push the issue and we thought we might see some action. They withdrew after a couple hours and it was fairly quiet the rest of the night.

We got paid yesterday, so we all put in some money and managed to talk the Seabees out of some beer. It's more valuable than gold around here.

I got a letter from you and Laura yesterday and they were much appreciated.

It's cloudy today and the temperature is only about 100 degrees. I never thought 100 degrees could be cool, but it is compared to what it's been.

In your letter you said Mike is at a base 11 miles southeast of Da Nang and as near as I can tell, it's probably Hill 37. Send me his full address and I may be able to look him up. It sure would be nice to see a face from home.

Well I better get over to the post office and get a money order to send with this letter. I'm doing okay. I did have a good case of diarrhea and I've already gone to sick bay to get something for it. Everyone gets it here. It comes from drinking the water in the rivers and villages. Do take care. I really appreciate your faithful writing.

Love, Joe

Every sniper had to go to the rifle range in Da Nang to requalify to stay in their units. If we didn't requalify we would be "sent down" (placed in a grunt outfit). Although requali-

fying was important, a few days out of the bush in the relative
safety of Da Nang was a real help to a man's nerves. The
diversions of Freedom Hill with it's USO, EM club, good
chow, and an air-conditioned movie theater could almost make
a guy forget he was in the middle of a war.

Sniper school was a serious but friendly competition between snipers from other Marine units. Six of the best long
shots in the world were after a small but rare prize. With first
place came a common Zippo lighter with some very uncommon engraving on it. One side had the insignia of the Scout
Snipers, the Grim Reaper. On the other side, the words "1ST
PLACE SCOUT SNIPER SCHOOL 1ST DIVISION USMC VIETNAM
1969" were followed by the name of the winner. When Dan
and I left Da Nang, my name was on it, and I constantly kept
reaching in my pocket to make sure it was still there. Later,
that three-dollar lighter was to become the object of an incident
that would come back to haunt me as much as any other memory of the war.

A few months later I would find myself sitting on a hilltop
twenty miles from Da Nang, watching huge fireballs punch
holes in the clouds as VC sappers (suicide teams) blew up the
main ammo dump by the sniper school and Freedom Hill. The
next day I learned that Freedom Hill and the school had been
leveled. Amazingly only a few men were killed. None were
snipers, but the blow to morale at losing Freedom Hill was
immediate and widespread.

★

HQ Co. 5th Marines
Scout Snipers
An Hoa
May 3, 1969

Dear Mom,

Hi from Satan's playground. I'm afraid a few of my letters
got lost or delayed a couple weeks ago when they shot down a
chopper with mail on it.

To answer your questions, here it goes. As for where An
Hoa is, I'll think of some way to show you how to locate it.

Do I think the VC are as good as you hear? Yes, most
definitely. Ho Chi Minh has sworn to wipe out the 5th Marines.
He'd vowed to eat Christmas dinner 1968 in An Hoa. It was
close, but he didn't quite make it. When the 5th first came
here, most of the fighting was against the Viet Cong. Then

"Uncle Ho" started sending full divisions of NVA through here. The NVA is well trained and will stand and fight. They're experts at getting us to fight on their terms. The NVA even has a rest center in this area at a place called Go Noi Island. Although there are sometimes two or three regiments of NVA there, every sweep we've made only turns up booby-traps. It's quite a trick to hide that many well-equipped troops.

The shellings are another story. There's something the papers don't tell. Charlie uses mostly mortars and 250-pound surface to surface rockets. The rockets don't leave much when they hit and they're so fast that by the time we hear them coming in, they've already hit. Another thing, they have tanks. They're using them to bring artillery down from the mountains.

I'm 29 miles southwest of Da Nang. I'm not far from Mike. I'm trying to figure a way to get over to see him.

How close are we censored? Actually we're not. We have to use a little common sense. Like I said, they shoot down mail choppers, too.

How do they get maps of our camps? Usually the kids draw them. Civilians aren't allowed inside the perimeter, but they can see all they need from the edge. You wouldn't believe how detailed these maps are. When I told you we have civilians on base, that's only at the larger camps like An Hoa. There's quite a few civilians who work here and they're watched pretty closely.

The food in the rear isn't bad and they offer three meals a day. I only eat supper cuz it's too hot to eat in the daytime. When we're in the bush we get nothing but C rations, so snacks come in real handy. As for candy and things like that, try to find stuff that doesn't melt at 130 degrees. The Kool-Aid is great. The water in the bush tastes bad and it smells bad. The water in the villages isn't very clean, so diarrhea is common. When you get it over here, you'll swear you've signed your butt away to the devil.

Hope I've answered your questions. Got a letter from Dave. He seems to be doing okay and says he's about the only one in his outfit that hasn't gotten a Purple Heart yet.

I was feeling homesick last night. Mail call sure picked me up. I'm doing fine. Oh, by the way, I've been here one whole month. Actually I feel like it's been more than six months. Time doesn't go fast over here. Take care.

Love, Joe

Snipers were billeted in five tents a short distance from the HQ command bunker and the field hospital. Under the worst-case scenario, a breach of the perimeter, the snipers in An Hoa at the time of a major attack would be part of the last line of defense for the command bunker, using M-14s with Starlite scopes. We also had the dubious honor of cleaning up after an attack, which meant ferreting out any sappers that may have gotten in. Cleanup was hairtrigger. If we did find a sapper, our chances of getting off a shot before he blew himself and us up with twenty to forty pounds of high explosives were poor at best. Sappers wore only a loincloth and had wire wrapped above each joint to tourniquet a missing arm or leg so they could keep going. Their usual targets were ammo dumps, hospitals, and command bunkers. Sappers were bad news. Dave Meeks and I managed to take one prisoner after a vicious assault by a large force of NVA on the night of the tenth.

*

HQ Co. 5th Marines
Scout Snipers
An Hoa—Arizona
May 18, 1969

Dear Mom,

I suppose you're frantic for a letter. Maybe you'll understand why I haven't written when I tell you what I've been doing.

First of all, Dan and I got back to An Hoa on the tenth. Later that night the enemy hit An Hoa with everything, even gas. It started at about 12:30 A.M. and didn't stop till 7:00 that same morning. They got some sappers inside the lines, but they didn't do much damage.

The next day we caught a chopper out to Delta Co. As soon as the chopper landed we got hit. By the next afternoon they hit us four more times.

We had eight medevacs in 24 hours and two of them died before they got there. One of the guys killed was the lieutenant for 2d Platoon. We called him Chip and he was a great guy. He was the first officer I made friends with. After everything calmed down I did something I swore I wouldn't do—I cried. All at once it all seemed so senseless. At first I thought we should be here and that there was a reason for us being here. Now I don't know. The whole thing has dampened my spirits.

Today's the 18th and we've been on the move every day and at night. Right now we're about halfway between An Hoa and Da Nang. This is the first place we've set in for more than one night, so I have a chance to write a couple letters.

We did get mail yesterday. It's the first since the tenth. As much as I was down in the dumps, that mail call was heaven sent. They probably won't send out my packages, so don't be worried if I don't say anything about getting one.

Since we've been moving we've had sixteen medevacs, twelve from wounds and the rest from heat and malaria. So far Dan and I are doing okay.

You may think I'm pulling your leg, but it's even hotter here now. It's been getting up to 130 degrees. You can see why we have heat casualties. The grunts are carrying 100 pounds of gear and ammo. It's not unusual to drink three to five gallons of water per day. I've started using Hallizone tablets in my water, so maybe I won't come down with diarrhea again.

The Kool-Aid is welcome. Matter of fact, I'm all out and was hoping for some in the mail today, but I didn't get any mail.

By the way, I've got boils. I would appreciate it if you would run down some medicine and send it, also a bottle of vitamins would come in handy. I better close, I have to write to Laura. Take care.

Love, Joe

A red flare meant the perimeter had been breached or that a sector was in imminent danger of being overrun. On the night of the tenth, red flares were going off in nearly every sector on the north, south, and west side of An Hoa. Early in the fight, two Marines manning a machine-gun bunker were killed, and three NVA with a plentiful supply of ammo turned the M-60 machine gun on us.

Several attempts to retake the bunker failed until a point-blank white phosphorus round from a 155mm gun quieted the bunker. Charlie could have flooded a huge number of troops through the hole in the perimeter. At that moment an angel of mercy appeared. A Spooky gunship (or Puff the Magic Dragon) darted in and out of the eerie glow cast by illumination flares. Spooky was a modified transport plane with three mini-guns mounted on each side. Mini-guns were something like Gatling guns with six rotating barrels, and they fired 6,000 rounds per minute. Every fourth round was a tracer, but the guns fired so fast that it looked like a solid red line whipping from the plane to the ground.

In amazement, I watched enemy tracers shoot from the ground toward the plane. I wondered what sort of man, and for what cause, would give away his position to such an awesome weapon. A slight change of course and a ten- or fifteen-second burst from Spooky's guns ended the enemy ground fire from that area. Often firing inside our perimeter, Spooky's ammo lasted for thirty minutes, allowing the grunts enough time to retake what was left of the bunker and seal the hole in our lines.

After Spooky cleared the area, our artillery and mortars began a massive barrage on enemy positions. The big guns (175mm cannons) were at times firing point blank over our heads, and we ended up getting shell shock from our artillery. We took heavy fire until daybreak of the eleventh when the enemy broke contact.

It was said that the night belonged to Charlie, and they knew with daylight would come air strikes. Besides, during the night thousands of artillery rounds had left the area so leveled they had few places to hide. The enemy suffered heavy losses. Over one hundred bodies, mostly sappers, were hung up in the barbed wire, and there was no telling how many others were carried away.

At sunrise we began our "cleanup." Meeks and I were searching the area near the mess hall, when we found a live sapper stumbling around in the open, so stoned on opium he'd lost his satchel charge and had no idea where he was. He became our prisoner and a survivor of a battle in which it was his duty to die.

After a sleepless night and a nerve-wracking search for sappers, Dan and I just had time to saddle up and catch a chopper to Delta Company. I should have clued in when my squad leader said, "I'm sorry, but I've got to send you out to Arizona Territory," the very words I would later say to teams when I became squad leader.

Arizona Territory, a place where the whole world seemed to come apart, was a flat seventy-square-mile area just northeast of An Hoa village. We choppered in to a recently defoliated area under fire, and for a week we were in constant contact with Charlie. Our surroundings were a mixture of dead and dying foliage covered with an oily film and the thick smell of the herbicide called Agent Orange.

We had just set in on the sixth day when we began taking fire and were pinned down. I was kneeling down and talking to Lieutenant Chip when an AK-47 round hit him in the throat, splattering my face with his blood. At that same instant, an RPG passed so close to my head I felt the rush of wind as it went by and exploded on the other side of a small rise thirty feet away.

The midday heat, fear, and rush of adrenaline caused me to sweat profusely. When I hit the ground, the dirt quickly changed to mud on my face and arms. I looked up to see Chip on his back, clutching his throat and making grotesque kicking motions with his legs.

I crawled to him and realized that there was little I could do but control some of the bleeding using a pressure point. The bullet entered near the Adam's apple and exited the left side of the back of his neck, hitting the jugular vein, missing his spine. The bleeding was serious, but manageable. The main problem was that the trauma had caused his throat to swell shut, and he was choking. It was a survivable wound if he could get some air. The RPG that had gone off just over the rise had blown the face off a staff sergeant in the command post. I sat with Chip's head in my lap, pushing hard on that pressure point, yelling louder and louder, "Corpsman up," unsuccessfully trying to drown out the sound of the firefight and the screams coming from the other side of the mound.

When the corpsman got there, he dug through his bag for the only thing that could save Chip, an airway to put down his throat so he could breathe. Of the three sizes of airways (small, medium and large), the medium was most often issued to the corpsmen who were limited in the amount of medical supplies they were able to carry. I held Chip's head while the corpsman repeatedly tried to insert the airway, his own anxiety growing.

"It's too big," he said.

"Keep trying," I shouted back at him over the roar of the firefight. Further attempts proved futile. He slammed the airway on the ground, grabbed a scalpel, and did a tracheotomy, but Chip's throat was too swollen, and it did no good.

A medevac chopper was landing, and before the ramp was down, the corpsman was on board, frantically trying to find a small airway. Again nothing, all they had were medium size. Six grunts grabbed Chip and ran to the chopper. It took off hard and fast.

It was beginning to quiet down except for our outgoing mortars. The staff sergeant died before the chopper got there.

I stood up, covered with muddy sweat and blood, and I took several steps before I realized one of my thigh pockets was bulging. Chip's blood had seeped through the material, half filling the pocket, and was dripping down the side of my leg.

I found Dan leaning against a tree, going on about how they should pull us out, we were all going to die. I sat down on my pack, too exhausted to think, and just stared at Dan as he rambled on. When I saw the corpsman who worked on Chip slowly walking toward me, I knew what he was going to say.

"The pilot radioed back to say he was sorry, they lost the lieutenant." As he walked away, I realized tears were making clean streaks down my face. I had to find the energy to change my uniform and wash up. Just the sight of me was making Dan worse.

The next day, with the company under half-strength and everyone showing signs of battle fatigue, we were emergency-evacuated from the hot LZ.

Our chopper was just gaining altitude when a bullet came through the bottom and hit a hydraulic line on the forward bulkhead, spraying everyone with fluid. Had we just survived a week in hell only to die in a helicopter crash? Yankee ingenuity would prevail when one of the door gunners calmly walked to the bulkhead and turned a valve, switching to one of two backup lines. He then removed his helmet—the visor was so covered with hydraulic fluid he couldn't see through it—returned to his gun, and resumed firing. If it wasn't for a coating of oil on everything and everyone, there would be no way to tell it had happened.

On nearly a dozen occasions, I was either attached to a company or on an assignment when we moved through areas that had been defoliated with Agent Orange. If a sector had been recently sprayed, a foul, oily film clung to everything. Trees, brush, and what would have been lush undergrowth were rapidly turning yellowish brown. At times dead and dying foliage, especially along river banks, stretched as far as the eye could see.

Nearly everyone who was in sprayed areas developed symptoms ranging from rashes, boils, numbness in the hands and arms to inflamed, infected joints. The corpsmen treated us the best they knew how by draining pustulous sores and using antibiotics and salves. Unfortunately, the real damage came upon contact when the active ingredient, dioxin, absorbed through the skin and moved throughout the body.

Of the approximately 3.5 million men and women who served in Vietnam, 53,000 would eventually be diagnosed as having moderate to severe Agent Orange contamination, with another 250,000 known to have been exposed. Over 18,000 have died as a direct result. Tragically, the immense, long-term effects on veterans and the people and land of Vietnam are just now coming to light.

We were aware of the reasoning behind the defoliation, but the hazards of even short periods of contact with the plants and ground were completely unknown to us. Sadly, the companies that manufactured Agent Orange knew of its dangers as early as 1957.

Chapter III ⋆ The Long Haul

⋆

HQ Co. 5th. Marines
Scout Snipers
Liberty Bridge
May 20th, 1969

Dear Mom,

Right now we're at Liberty Bridge which is about ten miles from An Hoa. We won't be here long. As it looks we're going to join an operation on Go Noi Island. Ten battalions of Marines and a bunch of army engineers are going in. We're supposed to level the place. If we don't go on this operation, we'll go to Arizona.

I got some mail yesterday. It's been awhile since I heard from home, so that mail call was most welcome. You must have been reading my mind when you asked if I needed vitamins, as I wrote a couple of days ago and asked you to send me some. We don't eat very often here and when we do it really isn't too healthy.

I feel bad about Mother's Day. I didn't even know what day it was. The school was okay. Actually I didn't learn anything new, but it did get me out of the bush for a few days. Am I anywhere near Arizona Territory? As a matter of fact, I'm looking at it right now. It starts about two miles from the bridge here and runs southeast along the foot of the mountains. It's about the worst spot around here. Companies go in there and get tore up pretty bad. There is a big operation going on there. It started yesterday. I hate to say it, but we probably will be going back to Arizona within the next three weeks. The 7th Marines have a lot of men there, so maybe Dave is there.

An Hoa is pretty large. The whole 5th Marine Regiment is

there plus about a battalion of army. At any one time there's probably 2,000 to 3,000 men there.

No, the monsoons haven't started yet and shouldn't for a couple more months. It showers about every two or three days. I would rather have it hot and dry, we have to do enough wading as it is.

Well, Mom, by now you should have gotten a letter. I know you are concerned when you don't get one for a while. There are a lot of reasons. Please don't worry when it happens.

Love, Joseph

If beans and bullets make the wheels of war turn, then letters from home are the lubricant that keeps a foot soldier from being ground up in those wheels. So many guys didn't get mail. We shared news from home just like we shared everything else.

To get from An Hoa to Da Nang by land meant a long, dusty, teeth-jarring ride in a truck or a smoother, more risky ride on top of a tank. Mine sweeps traveled the road early each morning and usually found nothing. Charlie would often wait until the sweep had passed before planting a two-hundred-pound box mine in the road.

Few GIs who tangled with a box mine lived to tell about it. Strangely, riding on top of a tank that hit one was almost certainly fatal. The crew might survive, but the force of the explosion would wrap around the sides of the tank, concentrating where men sat, tearing and burning the flesh off their bones. I never hitched a ride on a tank. It was harder, but safer to ride in a truck or walk. When a truck hit a mine that didn't have a delay fuse, the front of the truck literally disappeared, while the back stayed intact.

Liberty Bridge was a large wooden span across the Song Thu Bon (the Thu Bon River), about midway between An Hoa and Da Nang. Charlie often floated contact explosives, camouflaged with foliage, downstream to blow up the bridge. Guards stationed along the bridge would shoot to pieces anything coming toward it.

At night, floodlights lit up the river, and guards strolled back and forth, throwing concussion grenades into the murky water to keep sappers away. It was said that the only damage done to the bridge was a couple years earlier when some drunk Marines set it on fire. The Seabees rebuilt the bridge, and it was jealously guarded, with a checkpoint on one side and a small fire base on the other. The fire base had a twenty-foot tower where snipers often pulled tower watch.

Every large fire base had a tower, and when not in the bush, sniper teams manned them. They were usually equipped with "Big Eyes" (large 50,000 dollar Starlite scopes) for night observation that turned the terrain into a detailed green panorama. During the day, we constantly surveyed the area through high-powered binoculars and rifle scopes. It was like watching the war through a microscope.

In late May I got the chance every boot Marine dreams of, the opportunity to get even with his DI. I was on a truck about to leave Liberty Bridge, and against all odds, one of the men on guard at the check point was Sergeant Graves.

He recognized me right away, and we chatted briefly. My admiration for Graves couldn't have been higher. What a seemingly impossible task he had in boot camp, to prepare boys for war, knowing that his own rotation to Vietnam was inevitable. At that time there were only three kinds of Marines, "Those in Vietnam, those going, and those coming back." As we talked on equal terms, I saw that thousand-yard stare in his eyes only men in war have. Graves made it home alive.

*

Scout Snipers
Liberty Bridge
May 24, 1969

Dear Mom,

I got your letters yesterday and you seem worried. I'm doing fine. We're still at Liberty Bridge, but that operation should be starting soon. This new offensive by Charlie is bad, but I don't think they can keep it up much longer. Every time a convoy comes through I look for Dave. Posey is on the other side of the bridge. I think I'll hitch a ride over to see him.

Love, Joe

The month of May 1969 handed the United States the sixth highest casualty rate in our ten years of the war. More significantly, we were inflicting fewer casualties on the NVA. The enemy had changed tactics. They realized they couldn't pull off another Dien Bien Phu. Under the worst conditions such as Khe Sanh, the Americans could call on unlimited firepower, and a head-to-head prolonged battle with the US was unwinnable. Charlie's answer was to split into small units, usually regiment-size or smaller, and employ hit-and-run tactics, making it extremely difficult to bring our firepower to bear. It was often like fighting ghosts, and the frustration of rarely seeing the enemy was having a greater effect on men than the high casualty rate.

Barely forty-five days in-country, and my respect for the tenacity and dedication of the NVA and Vietcong had grown immensely. Time and time again, like moths to a candle flame, they hurled themselves at a fire only the American military could ignite. Always losing, but knowing the candle was burning lower all the time.

The few prisoners we took were usually too wounded or sick from malaria to go on. A few *Chieu-Hoi*ed (surrendered) and for the most part were treated well. A small, select group of *Chieu-Hoi*s were reprogrammed and sent to us as Kit Carson scouts, so-called because they wore bright red western-style bandannas around their necks. It was my privilege to serve with these men on several occasions, traitors in their own country maybe, but among the few Vietnamese I trusted. I gained invaluable insight into the enemy's mind and tactics. Who could find a better teacher than the man who may have led an attack on our outfit scant weeks earlier? We did have to watch them, not for any direct danger, but their own bickering and infighting could quickly turn into a dangerous situation for everyone.

While at Liberty Bridge, my partner and I were billeted with two Kit Carson scouts, engineers, and a dog handler whose dog had just been killed the day before. The scouts began arguing over a crummy ten-dollar transistor radio, and one of them pulled the pin on a grenade and threw the pin outside. There he stood, holding the hammer down on that grenade so tightly his knuckles were turning white. He was shaking, either from rage or fear of what he was about to do. It became deathly quiet in that tent, as the seven of us stared at the grenade. The dog handler slowly reached down and clicked the safety off his M-16 and abruptly took aim. His voice broke the silence. "You'll die before it hits the floor," he said. The scout came out of whatever state he was in and reached up with his other hand to hold the hammer down. We made the other scout go outside and find the pin. He returned with it, and the two of them had to work together to put it back in the grenade. Obviously it wasn't safe to put even two of them together, so we separated them into different tents. The incident caused me to wonder about the North Vietnamese. If a man was willing to die and take seven other people with him for a transistor radio, what would he do for a real cause? That was the first time I considered that the US was in big trouble in Vietnam.

The South Vietnamese on the other hand were a more gentle people. It was hard to distinguish Vietcong from civilians. The women and children could be as deadly as any soldier. Still, the vast majority were decent and hardworking. The ARVN (Army of the Republic of Vietnam) was bad, either through their own incompetence or VC infiltration, and we tried not to work with them.

The local militia was different. Some of the most pleasant and rewarding times I spent during my tour were with them. These men for some reason, be it age or health, were considered unfit to serve in the regular army and provided immediate defense of villages and hamlets. They were poorly trained, if at all, and had a chronic shortage of decent weapons, but they would fight to the death to protect homes and families. I begged, borrowed, and stole weapons and medical supplies from our own overabundance so they would have a little more to work with.

An Hoa village was about two miles from the base. The town was a mixture of masonry buildings with tin roofs that served as shops and thatch hootches that were houses. It had a population of between three and five thousand people. Several times I was invited to eat with the village or hamlet chief and invariably was treated like an honored guest. Like most Americans, at first I knew little about the Vietnamese culture and customs. Before my first such invitation, I was only aware that the Vietnamese considered it an insult to point the soles of one's feet toward a person. I spent most of my time worrying over what to do with my big feet and nearly missed out on a delicious meal.

A village chieftain lived in a large bamboo-and-thatch hut, with a hard dirt floor, an earthen hearth with a continuous fire burning under a large black cast iron pot, and the ever-present opening to an underground bunker. The only obvious difference between a chieftain's hootch and that of any other villager was that it was bigger, and he also seemed to have a very large family. There were reasons for both differences. Many of those selfless old men took in orphans and displaced people who had no one and nowhere else to go. Somehow they could always make room for one more. It became my routine to snatch a couple cases of C rations, gratefully accepted by the chieftain as he mentally calculated how many mouths he could feed with them.

On my second assignment to the militia, I was teamed up with a very special man. Lee Oot was a civilian interpreter and liaison officer, assigned to me to help bridge the language and cultural barrier between myself, the militia, and the villagers. He quickly became one of my best friends. Whenever Lee and I worked together, we would spend many hours talking about the ways of his people, the war, and sometimes America. I was first introduced to Lee by Chuck Mawhinney when he took me to An Hoa village for the first time. Lee was the one who made the village safe for me. As a lone American in a Vietnamese village, it was likely that the VC would target me for assassination, but Lee had his own intelligence network that gathered information from the militia and from the villagers, who also got information from friends and relatives in other hamlets. We found Lee's intelligence reliable and timely. While VC retaliation was always a risk, Lee's network and my good relations with the villagers minimized that risk.

Lee and I became good friends and I was concerned about what would happen to him and his family. Service personnel could sponsor Vietnamese civilians for emigration to the US, and with my security clearance and being part of headquarters, the paperwork would have been easier for me than for most other American soldiers.

I once offered to pull some strings to get Lee and his family to the US, and the instant I said it, I knew I'd made a mistake. His polite, but immediate refusal told me what I should have already known. Vietnam was his homeland, and he wouldn't leave. We were both aware that the war was not going well, and an American pullout would certainly lead to a Communist takeover. Lee was too closely associated with the Americans and would, without a doubt, be among the first executed.

CAP (Civilian Assistance Program) was a very important and successful aspect of my tour. The acronym ''CAP'' was used at various times by the Marines for a variety of programs, such as the Combined Action Platoon, which was a squad of Marines that would be based in a village to organize and fight alongside a platoon of local militia. As it pertained to snipers, the Civilian Assistance Program was an open-ended project and participation was voluntary. Most of the snipers were involved to some degree. Most of us knew little and asked few questions about the activities of other snipers. My security clearance as a sniper made it possible to provide Lee and the militia with weapons, medical supplies, and field rations; I usually just signed for the supplies as no one challenged a sniper carrying the bolt rifle. CAP was more to me than the slogan "winning the hearts and minds of the people." I was committed to the idea that our presence in Vietnam didn't give us a right to tread on the people or on their way of life.

Civilian assistance in the bush was frustrating and often heartbreaking. The rural population was torn apart by the war and had little reason to trust anyone. The NVA and VC came in the night to kill, kidnap, rape, and steal. The Americans came during the day to search and destroy.

I made a personal commitment to keep my CAP door open. Lee Oot and An Hoa were the keys to that door. If I failed to persuade a frightened mother to let her dying baby be treated by a corpsman, I made a greater effort to get medical supplies to the village. If I failed to get an orphaned kid out of the bush to the safety of an orphanage, I worked harder to help the militia save An Hoa from attack. The gains far outweighed the losses. As my tour progressed, I spent more and more of my spare time working with Lee, the militia, and the villagers.

On a particularly hot day, Lee and I were sitting under a tent made from ponchos, with all four sides open to allow any breeze at all to pass through. There were kids milling around, and we would have normally shooed them away, but Lee was giving me a crash course on the Vietnamese language, and we paid them little note. I took out that treasured lighter I'd won at sniper school, lit a cigarette, and laid it on the ground beside me. When I next reached for the lighter, it was gone. I looked everywhere for it, when it dawned on me that one of the kids had managed to steal the lighter. I flew into a rage, shouted, *"Lai dai,"* (Vietnamese for "come here") and tried to get my hands on one of them. They disappeared like a puff of smoke. I stomped back into the tent swearing as only a Marine can, and there was Lee, head in hands, sobbing softly. As my anger turned to puzzlement, I said, "Lee, that lighter was important, but not that important."

He slowly looked up and half-heartedly mumbled, "I no cry for your lighter, I cry for the children, that they must steal to live."

I sat down, put my arm around his shoulders, and quietly added some American tears.

My best efforts over the years to locate Lee have been fruitless, but at times I assure myself that Lee did leave the country before the purge and is content somewhere. Lee taught me so much, but the most important thing I learned from him was that compassion is the only thing that can balance the forever-lopsided scales of war.

★

Scout Snipers
Go Noi Island
May 28, 1969

Dear Mom,

I got your letters yesterday. You should have gotten a letter by now. I had so much on my mind and was kept so busy that I couldn't write.

We're farther into Go Noi Island now. We've been joined by three more companies and by the first of next month the rest of the battalions should be here.

We've had a lot of casualties from booby-traps and have made contact with the enemy five times. The worst thing about this operation is the walking. I can't tell you its name right now.

It's been cloudy, but not much cooler. It rained last night, just enough to keep the mosquitos down. As we were walking up to where we're set in now, the point man found a 1,000 pound bomb. Well, we called for engineers to blow it up after we passed. We didn't get 200 meters away when we saw the engineers come running up yelling for everyone to make tracks cuz they had lit the fuse, and it was going to blow. They thought we were further away than we were. A bomb that big will throw shrapnel 1,000 meters in all directions. We looked pretty ridiculous with everyone trying to run and watch for booby-traps, too. Dan and I took advantage of the first hole we came to and jumped in. When that thing went off, big trees disintegrated. No one was hurt, but the engineers are taking a lot of ribbing.

I'm sure there are some packages waiting for me in the rear, so I'm anxious to get back to An Hoa. I'm in need of a shave and shower, too.

The supply choppers just brought in hot chow. I can't believe it. It's the first time I've seen hot chow in the bush.

You said you thought about sending canned fruit. That would be great. It's the best thing for this hot weather. You might try putting a couple cans of beer in, too.

Well, Mom, guess I'll close. Take care and quit that worrying so much.

                                                    Love, your youngest
P.S. I'm the youngest in age only.

Operation Pipestone Canyon on Go Noi Island was an exercise in insanity. Huge Rome plows (similar to large personnel carriers with rotating blades that can devour a twelve-inch-thick tree instantly) and a few tanks and armored personnel carriers moved on-line, shredding and mashing everything in their path, as we plodded through the rubble behind them. Villages were burned, rice scattered, and bunkers blown up. We saw little of the enemy, as though they had set the stage and left. What remained was an endless maze of booby traps of every description, from punji stakes to our own dud bombs. Medevac choppers were coming and going constantly.

A natural impulse during a firefight was to drop behind a rice-paddy dike and hope that it would provide some protection from incoming fire. Charlie defied that logic on Go Noi by hiding punji stakes in the water along the trail on the opposite side of an ambush. After seeing a grunt with a two-foot-long punji stake that entered his groin and exited his buttock, I knew Dan and I would have to force ourselves to dive toward enemy fire, and it would have to be a reflex action. We would be left in the open with a long, low crawl to the next dike, but I swore that if Charlie was going to get us, he'd have to shoot us, not watch as we impaled ourselves on bamboo spikes.

It seemed like everything was booby-trapped. Charlie knew our habits, and one was that when an American patrol entered a village, most guys would drop their packs and sit down against the nearest palm tree to rest. The very last time I did it, I heard a loud pop and was immediately engulfed in a thick cloud of white smoke. I rolled furiously away from the tree, wondering why I was still alive. After the smoke cleared, the engineers probed the base of the tree and discovered I had managed to flop my ass squarely on an 81mm mortar round.

"You were lucky," they said. "The detonator was wet and didn't burn fast enough to set the mortar off." Stupid was more like it, I thought.

The constant attrition from booby traps and our inability to pin the enemy down was straining the troops to the point of despair. Although Dan and I tried to stay with Delta Company as much as possible, we serviced other companies when requested. One such request drew us into a nightmare.

A certain company had planned a silent night movement of seven clicks (while a "click" usually meant a kilometer, in the snipers we understood it as 1000 yards) to reach a village suspected of being sympathetic to the VC. We moved out in total darkness, holding onto the web belt of the man ahead to keep from getting lost. Barely one click out, an explosion at the front of the column sent shrapnel whistling over our heads. We all sat where we were in the middle of the trail to await a medevac chopper. I had a friend from ITR named Leptman in the lead fire team and before word was whispered back through the column I knew he was hurt. I resisted the temptation to work my way to the front to check on him. He had tripped a booby-trapped mortar and was so mangled that he lay there, dying, with one of his own legs under the back of his head. The men in front and behind him were killed, and nearly all of the lead squad had to be medevaced.

My mind went blank as I watched the strobe light rhythmically flash our location to the chopper and listened to the strained voices of corpsmen trying to save what was left of the lead squad. I was more numb than bitter at Leptman's death and starting thinking of my own mortality. The chopper came and went, and silence and darkness returned as we moved on.

After hours of stumbling through the blackness, we finally reached our objective. The company set up seven hundred yards from the village and waited for daybreak. I leaned against my pack and fell asleep, forgetting to roll my pant legs down and tie the straps. Minutes later I was rudely awakened by a painful sting just above my boot top, followed by another higher up my leg, then another. I bit the palm of my hand to keep from breaking silence as a five-inch centipede wiggled its way up the inside of my leg, biting each time I tried to grab it. As it headed for my groin, I started to panic. I finally smashed it near my thigh pocket. My leg was throbbing from seven fiery welts as I unfastened my pants and felt around for the pieces of the little monster. There was a corpsman two or three men back from Dan, and although Dan was only three feet away, it was so dark I had to find him by feel. I grabbed his sleeve and pulled him close.

"Tell the doc I just got bit to hell by a centipede," I whispered.

In similar fashion he passed my message on to the next man, as I lay back, wiping sweat from my face. In a few minutes Dan turned back and whispered for me to hold my hands out palms up. In one hand he dropped some pain pills, saying, "Take these now." In my other hand he put an antitoxin pill. "Take this if you're getting sick." I swallowed them all and in about twenty minutes was feeling better. The sun would be coming up soon, and I had to be functioning when it did.

Early light revealed a small village of eight huts on the far side of a large, dry, rice paddy and a thick fogbank a hundred yards farther on. As I scanned the village through my rifle scope, it seemed deserted except for a couple water buffalo in a pen at one end. Water buffalo can't pen themselves in, so I knew there must be someone around. Without warning, three young Vietnamese men broke from a hut toward the fogbank, running with all they had in them. Someone shouted, "Sniper, can you see them?" Sure I could see them, that was my job, and what I saw weren't VC.

"Weapons?" I asked Dan who was watching through binoculars.

"Negative," he replied.

"Confirmed, no shot," I said, figuring they may have been draft dodgers or ARVN deserters. Seconds later they disappeared into the fog. At that all hell broke loose. Except for the command post, the whole company began running toward the village, yelling and shooting. The skipper and gunny tried in vain to call the men back, but their voices were drowned out by the din of over one hundred automatic weapons. Two lieutenants took off after their platoons, stooping down to pick up rocks or whatever they could find to throw at their men. One even threw his .45, but it was useless. Someone was going to pay for the booby trap of the night before. Over a hundred men swarmed over the village, tossing two and three grenades at a time into each bunker and hut. It was over in five minutes and the command post slowly moved into the village, with Dan and me bringing up the rear. I had given him the bolt rifle and was using his M-14 as a cane to take some of the pressure off my leg. I was totally unprepared for what I saw as we entered one end of the village. Sixteen women and children lay dead on the ground the full length of the village. One grunt had propped the body of a nine- or ten-year-old girl against a post, put a cigarette in the kid's mouth, and was taking pictures of her. My impulse was to shoot the guy.

Everyone and everything in that village was dead. Shit, I thought, they even killed the chickens. As I limped on, I was amazed that these clean-cut, all-American boys were capable of such an act. When I got to the far end of the village, the water buffalo were dead. One was lying on its side riddled with bullet holes, the other, its legs locked, was standing motion-less, leaning against one side of the pen. I approached the gunnery sergeant and asked him what he thought. He shook his head and walked away to be alone. I did the same. The skipper was in a frenzy, making the men scour the area for any signs of misplaced artillery on which to lay the blame. Amazingly, some grunts found a half dozen old mortar craters a short distance from the village. The captain had his out, and I heard no more about the incident, but my belief that we were morally superior to the enemy was gone.

★

Scout Snipers
Operation Pipestone Canyon
May 30, 1969

Dear Mom,

I'll just fill you in on the last 24 hours. We've moved again. Other than one of our own helicopter gun ships firing on us, yesterday was without incident. We stayed up last night watching B-52s fly missions in the area. They were dropping what we figured to be 500, 750, and 1,000 pound bombs and didn't get closer than two miles away, which was close enough.

It's been raining off and on for the last couple days. I went down to the river and took my first bath and shave in a week and a half. I was definitely in need of one.

I better close if I'm going to get this on the next bird out. Tell all hi and you take care. I'm doing okay.

Love, Joe

P.S. The name of the operation we're on is Pipestone Canyon.

Twilight, May 29. Dan and I were back with Delta Company as it entered a small clearing with three huts, suspiciously abandoned. The absence of any animals or cooking fires was a sign to be careful. First Squad moved in and in proper order yelled, *"Lai dai,"* a couple times at the entrance to each bunker before tossing a frag (M-30 fragmentation grenade) inside. They would then step to the side and watch to see if the grenade came flying back out. The command post entered the clearing. Smoke was still rolling out of the bunkers, but I had my eye on something else. There was an isolated hootch two hundred yards away on the tip of a small peninsula that protruded into a large open area, which would afford Dan and me a good view for at least three thousand yards in three directions. I rounded up a fire team to go with us. The skipper's last words were, "Be careful."

We set out, not knowing that in the meantime a wounded VC was pulled from one of the bunkers. It didn't matter that there was only one, we had made contact with the enemy, and a Cobra helicopter gunship quickly showed up to provide protection for the medevac chopper requested for the wounded man.

The five of us were isolated from the main company but in radio contact. We searched the hut and only found two mama-sans (old women) and a pig. We were making our way to the vantage point I'd picked out, when the Cobra gunship flew over about 150 feet up, did a 180 degree turn 200 yards out, where it hung motionless. We waved as it went over, and I told the radioman to contact them so they would know we were friendlies. It had assumed an attack mode, one we had seen used against enemy positions often, only this time we were the target.

The radioman didn't have time to contact the chopper before the nose of the gunship lowered and we knew we had a serious problem on our hands. The crew opened fire with the mini-gun and automatic grenade launcher.

We were cut off from the bunker in the hootch, and the only cover we had was a small crater five feet across at most and three feet deep. The mama-sans ran into their bunker as the five of us crammed into that little hole. It was poor protection, especially when bullets were coming from above at 6,000 rounds per minute. The ground vibrated with the impact of bullets, some hitting within inches of our position. The pig, standing a few feet away, fell over, riddled by bullets. The first two bloopers (grenades) hit the roof of the hootch and blew huge holes in it, while the rest landed randomly. Each of us knew we were about to die. Every second that passed seemed an eternity.

The radioman couldn't be heard over the noise, and it was only a matter of time before the mini-gun made a pass directly through our position. The seconds ground by, ever slower as we were covered by dirt kicked up by bullets. After sixty seconds the chopper broke contact thanks to the radioman in the command post.

Stunned and in complete silence we stood up, looking at each other in amazement. The ground all around us was churned up as though someone had prepared it to plant a garden.

Our moment of contemplation was interrupted when the pilot came over the radio and matter-of-factly said, "Sorry about that. Was anyone hurt?"

Our radioman tersely replied, "Not a fucking scratch, man. You're damn poor shots," and with that he switched the radio off.

The mama-sans were having a fit about their pig, so we strung it up from a beam in their hootch. They cut the pig's throat and caught the blood in a large earthen bowl to make into candy, which was considered a delicacy. None of the animal would be wasted. I declined an offer to stay for candy, but did accept a handful of cookies made from thin slices of baked corncobs and found them to be quite tasty, as we walked back to the company.

The medevac chopper appeared on the horizon at the same time we rejoined the command post. I saw the VC sitting on the ground, with shrapnel wounds in his foot and calf. His eyes were bloodshot from the concussion, and he was talking so fast I couldn't understand a word he was saying.

Suddenly, that sixty seconds of sheer terror turned into anger. I raised the bolt rifle, clicked the safety off, and put the end of the barrel to the tip of his nose. I was asking myself, had we nearly died because of this piece of shit? If he was talking before, he was suddenly giving me his whole life history. A lieutenant saw what was happening and strolled up next to me and said, "No one here gives a damn, but he's mighty gabby, and intelligence would like him alive."

We were all walking a tightrope, with sanity on one side and insanity on the other. I'd come very close to falling off the wrong side. I had at least two pounds of pressure on a 2.8-pound trigger pull.

The company set up a night position in the village, and Dan

and I sat on top of a bunker, taking vicarious revenge as we watched B-52s lay waste to the countryside in front of us.

The early morning haze hadn't completely cleared when we entered the area bombed the night before. It didn't take much effort to imagine we had just stepped onto the surface of another planet. For several hundred yards on both sides and for at least two miles in front of us, no structure or plant of any kind was left standing. The area was covered with craters forty to seventy feet wide and at least thirty feet deep. Everything was leveled by the force of the explosions and covered by dirt and mud thrown out of the craters. Smoke drifted eerily from something still burning at the bottom of some of them. As we threaded our way between one hole after another for more than an hour, a grunt joked, "What if the gooks had B-52s?" No one really laughed. What if they did?

*

Scout Snipers
Operation Pipestone Canyon
June 1, 1969

Dear Mom,

You'll have to excuse the paper, it got wet. It's been raining pretty steady for the last three days. It's miserable trying to sleep in three inches of mud. I haven't had any mail for four days. Every day I hope they'll send it out with the supply bird, but it doesn't come.

Dan and I got the word yesterday that one of us will be going to the rear. We have a new first sergeant and he has changed things. They ruled that private first classes can't carry bolt rifles anymore, so it looks like I'll have to give mine up. I guess I'll find out soon. Right now we're set in along the river and are acting as a blocking force for sweeps coming our way.

Well, Mom, I shall close. The chopper is coming in about an hour and I want to write to Laura yet. Take care. Tell Grams hi.

Love, Joe

The first sweep to reach us was a battalion of ARVNs and true to form, upon sighting us they opened fire. We were taking small-arms fire and mortars, and the skipper didn't waste any time getting their commander on the radio. He got right to the point, "If you don't cease fire immediately, a bunch of pissed-off Marines are going to unload on you!" They broke contact in a big hurry and set in on the opposite side of the river, which was as close as the skipper would allow.

We had carried the brunt of the war so long, the South Vietnamese had either forgotten how or lost the will to fight. There were a few disciplined and courageous ARVN units, but they were by far the exception, not the rule.

★

Scout Snipers
An Hoa
June 2, 1969

Dear Mom,

Dan and I got into An Hoa yesterday and there were packages and a bunch of mail waiting for me. It was like Christmas with all those goodies. I sure appreciate everything you sent.

As far as news goes, here's what's up. I told in a letter I wrote before I came in that PFCs couldn't carry bolt rifles anymore. Well my squad leader said that I was doing a good job and that I would keep mine, so I'm still team leader. I'll be going out tomorrow and will be out until the first of next month.

To answer your questions, here it is. Delta Company is D Co. We use the phonetic alphabet for clarity, C Co. is Charlie Co., B Co. is Bravo, and so on. Delta Company is part of 1st Battalion 5th Marine Regiment. It's abbreviated like this, D1/5. We try to stay with Delta as much as possible, but there's a lot of companies in the regiment and we work with most of them. I like Delta Company. It's smaller than most, but it's one of the best around. Delta is usually out front where the action is.

Yes, the boils on my face and neck are clearing up. We usually have plenty of salt tablets. The corpsmen carry them and I have some of my own.

Being team leader means I'm responsible for my partner, when we go out on hunter-kills or on patrol, I have control of the squad, fire team, or platoon that goes with us.

The foot powder will come in handy and the white cotton socks help a lot. It's a constant battle to keep our feet in good shape.

Sorry to hear about Nick. There's no telling what he's got, they've got diseases here they don't even have names for.

I had better close. I'm enclosing a money order and some film to be developed. I'm working on my third month here. Two down and 11 to go.

Like I said I'm going back to the bush tomorrow, so don't get too worried if the mail service slows down a little.

Love, Joseph

Delta Company was somewhat unusual in that it had about 150 men, or 95 men less than most companies, but it was a disciplined, kick-ass outfit. The skipper treated his men well and had their respect. After a particularly grueling forced march of several clicks, we set up in an abandoned village. We were out of rations and water. A resupply chopper was supposed to meet us at the village, but a screwup delayed it nearly four hours. When it did arrive, a grunt took a case of C rations to the hootch where the skipper was. I heard him bellow, "Get 'em out of here, I'll eat after the men are fed." That was the only time I heard him yell at any of his men.

Every day I would submit plans for a hunter-kill or patrol to the skipper, and he would either adjust the company situation a little to accommodate me or guide my thinking in a different direction. We always ended up with a practical and effective action.

The gunnery sergeant with Delta Company was much like the skipper. A gunny in the Marine Corps has a complicated job to perform. He's a buffer between the men and the skipper and is responsible for everything, from always having fresh batteries for the radios to settling disputes.

Delta was like a large family, and I always felt more comfortable with them than most other companies. I guess it was partly the fact that Delta was small, and although the snipers usually tried to not get close to the men in any company, it was especially hard with Delta. To lose a man was to lose a family member. Whether I knew him or not, it went down hard.

*

Scout Snipers
Go Noi Island
June 9, 1969

Dear Mom,

Will try to get this finished before the chopper comes. We're still on Go Noi Island. This operation is going full blast now. There's part of the 7th Marines, the 26th Marines, the 5th Marines, 101st Airborne, "ROKs" (Republic of South Korea Marines) and some ARVNs are here.

We got hit last night and when we searched the area this

morning, we found some dead NVA. No one in our unit was hurt. Tomorrow we start sweeping.

Dave's outfit isn't on this operation, but I got a letter from him and he said he was going on an operation into "Dodge City," which is close to An Hoa. I guess he's doing okay. Like me, he's already had enough of Vietnam.

Did I see Posey? I wrote Laura about what happened to him. He stepped on a booby-trap and broke both legs and an arm and caught a lot of shrapnel. I guess he's back in the States now. I'm enclosing more film. Most of the pictures on this roll I took from the chopper.

Well, Mom, I'll close and get this ready to mail.

Love, Joseph

During a major sweep, a large force of at least a company or battalion size would move in a long horizontal front to push any enemy into a blocking force, thus catching them in a deadly cross fire. On Go Noi Island, sweeps rarely turned up anything of consequence, except once. On the morning of June 16, we were blocking for a company of ROKs when the Koreans made contact with a couple hundred NVA.

Dense jungle kept us from seeing the battle, but we could hear it. It was vicious, and we tried to keep track of it over the radio. An hour after their first contact, with no sign of the enemy retreating our way, the skipper radioed the ROK commander to offer help, we were only a few minutes away.

"No, thank you," was his reply.

"I guess he knows what he's doing," the skipper said as he hung up the handset. Another two hours passed, as we listened to the fierce firefight just out of our sight. The enemy had only one logical route of retreat, and that was toward us. But where were they? The battle was winding down and still no sign of enemy troops. A few minutes later the mystery was cleared up when the ROK skipper, speaking in broken English, radioed, "Enemy been eliminated."

That was no understatement. They had caught a company of NVA by surprise, and in a relentless frontal assault that would make any Marine unit proud, wiped out an equal number of NVA. Not a single enemy soldier made it to our blocking force. The Koreans took no prisoners, and when he said the enemy was eliminated, he meant exactly that. The last body count I heard over the radio was two hundred, with eleven Koreans dead.

A grunt once told me, "Don't fuck with the ROKs." At the time I didn't know what he meant. I had heard they didn't even bother to put barbed wire around their base in Da Nang. If anyone was caught stealing from their compound, he was hung from a post at the entrance for several days. Although ruthless in combat, the Koreans were quite capable of compassion and had a sense of human dignity as intense as their ability to wage war. I held them in awe, and no doubt Charlie did, too.

An operation the size of Pipestone Canyon drew on so many different units, the logistics were immense. The ingrained pride of the Marines had to give way at times. When medevacing from an LZ, the Marine Corps had a tendency to circle high overhead until enemy fire was suppressed. The army did it differently. They came in at treetop level, hard and fast, often having to reduce their speed so quickly that the rear rotor nearly hit the ground. They would be in and out before the Charlie really had time to target them. We used army medevacs whenever possible.

After a firefight in which we had several wounded, a Marine medevac took up its position and circled high overhead. We were still receiving light small-arms fire, and the major piloting the chopper wouldn't land. Precious time was wasting, and the radioman kept telling him that we had some people in bad shape. The radioman finally had enough. He called the medevac and told the pilot, "If you don't come in and get these guys out, you can forget about the gooks 'cuz we'll shoot your ass down." The pilot promptly landed and picked up the wounded. Strange war. I had just heard a lance corporal give a major an order and seen it carried out.

The air force provided close-in jet-fighter support, at times dropping their ordnance less than two hundred yards from our own position and often braving withering enemy fire to do it. Countless times they helped us out of touchy situations. I was once out with a squad on patrol when we were ambushed by what must have been a company of NVA. We were pinned down in two feet of mud behind a rice-paddy dike and needed quick, heavy support. I called in an air strike, and within minutes an air force Phantom appeared, loaded with napalm and going lower and faster than any fighter I'd seen on a bombing run. A quick exchange with the pilot confirmed that he was on the right trajectory and had exact coordinates, extremely important since we were, at best, 150 yards from the enemy position. He opened up with rockets, and then dropped a full load of napalm dead on target. Fifteen seconds later he was out of sight.

The whole sequence didn't last a minute, but in that short time he had completely quelled all hostile fire. I called for artillery strikes to cover our rear, as we headed back to the company. I was about to call the pilot to thank him, but he was already talking to Da Nang air control. I listened as he calmly described a "small" problem he had. He'd come in so low, he had sucked the tops of some trees into one of his air intakes. He made it to Da Nang and landed safely. I asked air control to relay our appreciation.

Only two months into my tour, and I was getting word nearly every day of friends from the States and men I'd met there, being killed or wounded.

★

Scout Snipers
Go Noi Island
June 13, 1969

Dear Mom,

Well, another day. It's quit raining every day, so now it's extra hot. Just sitting writing this I'm sweating like someone poured a bucket of water on me.

I got some mail yesterday. Don't worry about me getting mail. It comes through eventually.

We're still on Go Noi Island. I don't know how much longer we'll be here. I heard they were going to pull us back to An Hoa for a day or two and then send us to Arizona Territory. Now don't get worried if I do go to Arizona. There's more use for a sniper there anyway. We just got the word to move out soon, so I'll get my gear ready and write more if I have time.

June 16, 1969

As you can see, it's taken me three days to finish this letter. I think they plan for us to cover every square inch of Go Noi by foot. We've just about done it.

I sent more rolls of film and some other things a few days ago. Let me know if you get them all right.

Well, this filthy country is finally catching up to me. I have a bad rash on my left ankle. I got some salve from the corpsman. It better clear up soon cuz it itches like mad. We haven't been near any water that we could bathe in for over four days. Needless to say, we're all getting pretty ripe. I feel miserable when I get this filthy. They have to fly our drinking water to us.

Mom, could you put a tube of zinc oxide in the next box? My nose gets so sunburned, it bleeds every time I rub it or bump it.

Better close and try to get a couple more letters written. You take it easy.

Love, Joseph

P.S. Excuse the dirty paper, a chopper just landed and blew everything away.

One of the first things I did when the company set in was to put up a small shelter made from two ponchos and take off my boots and socks to dry. Sweat and constant wading through streams and rice paddies made it impossible to keep my feet dry for any length of time. I was religious about taking care of my feet, but to no avail.

While on Go Noi Island, I came down with a bad case of ringworm and jungle rot that started on my ankles. The corpsman tried to bring it under control in the bush, but it was getting worse and spreading. I didn't want to go to the rear, but I was losing my small personal battle with bacteria.

It didn't take long before my legs, torso, and arms were covered with bright red circles from the size of a dime to three inches in diameter. By June 16, I itched so badly, I wasn't getting any rest. The following day, when I looked in my shaving mirror, it was all over my face and scalp. The way I carried on motivated Dan to saddle us both up in record time while I went to talk to the skipper. I looked like I'd been mauled by a big octopus, and when he saw me all the captain could say was, "Shit, Ward, how did you manage that?"

Dan and I were on the morning supply chopper back to An Hoa.

*

Scout Snipers
An Hoa
June 20, 1969

Dear Mom,

A quick note to go along with a roll of film. I'll be in An Hoa until I get this mess on my feet and ankles cleared up. The Doc says it's ringworm and jungle rot. It would make you itch just to look at me.

I hope you can read my writing, it's pretty sloppy. I had to stand lines last night and I haven't had any sleep cuz we were on 100 percent alert. I'll try to catch a few winks after I have written a few letters. They made us get haircuts today. I'd rather be in the bush, things are too petty here.

You wanted to know more about Posey. I asked the corpsman who took care of him if any shrapnel hit him in the crotch or face and he said it hadn't. At least that much is in his favor.

Well, Mom, I better cut it off here. I'm putting some film in with this. Most of the pictures are of Go Noi Island, some air strikes, and whatever. Take care.

Love, Joseph

Undoubtedly, the most common response when a guy heard about a friend being wounded, especially if it was from a booby trap, was, "Did he get it in the crotch?"

Corpsmen had what I considered to be the toughest job in the world. They saved men, knowing their lives were shattered forever. It's true that soldiers about to die ask for their mothers, if they can talk. Corpsmen became their surrogate mothers and would sit with these dying men, softly talking to them as they slipped away.

★

Scout Snipers
Da Nang Hospital
June 28, 1969

Dear Mom,

I sure have gotten behind in my writing. I just came back from four days in Da Nang at the Naval Hospital. When I came into An Hoa with that fungus, I got a secondary infection in my feet and ankles. It got so bad I could hardly walk. They decided to send me to the hospital where it's clean and I could stay off my feet. They wanted to medevac me, but I said I'd take a scheduled bird, which I was sorry for. By the time I got to the hospital, I could wring the blood out of my socks.

When the doctor saw me he said, "My God, what did you do, walk on the tops of your feet?" My feet started to improve overnight and three days later I was out again.

Well, anyway, I'm on light duty and medication. You keep asking what I want in the packages. What you've been sending is fine. Dried soups and a few canned things, like fruit and sardines. Well I guess Laura started school by now. If she needs any money, let me know. I have about 500 dollars on the books, and if I can help her out, I sure want to.

I'm up for lance corporal. I don't really care about the rank, but the extra 20 bucks a month will come in handy.

You asked if we drink the river water. Yes, we do. It's dirty and no telling what's in it, but it's wet.

Well, Mom, I must write to Laura before I go to sick bay. Don't worry, cuz I'm healing fine.

Love, Joseph

After several days in An Hoa, spending most of my time on my cot with my legs elevated, it was obvious the jungle rot was getting worse. The pain in my feet was murderous and my ankles were so infected that I couldn't bear the feeling of blood rushing down to them. I would hold my urine as long as possible, calculating different ways of making it to the pisser. When I could hold it no longer, I eventually scooted there on my ass. I spent two days trying to urinate, switching from one leg to the other, lifting each in turn up to my buttocks in an attempt to keep the blood from rushing downward. A black grunt who was using the urinal next to me and watching my crazy antics said, "Good rhythm, brother."

The doctor at the field hospital decided my condition was too serious to handle there and arranged for a medevac chopper to take me straight to the hospital in Da Nang, but I elected to take a regularly scheduled bird on June 24.

The naval hospital was kept cold to minimize the spread of infection. After an intense routine of soaks, shots, and being smeared all over with an ugly and uncomfortable yellow cream, I began to improve. I quit wearing the green military issue completely and had Mom send what must have been at least a hundred pair of white cotton socks. After having two brothers in the South Pacific during World War II, she knew what to send in her invaluable packages. White socks, hard candy, dried-soup packets, and Kool-Aid to help kill the taste of local water.

In such a wet country, it was surprisingly difficult to find drinkable water. The villagers relieved themselves in the rice paddies, and the rivers were perpetually dark brown from silt washing downstream and usually had leeches. Even if a river was nearly black with silt, a man would jump in to fill canteens and wash off the grime of war. Helicopters brought fresh water in five-gallon plastic containers when they could get through, but it was rarely enough.

At one point during operation Pipestone Canyon, the com-

pany had been moving along a river, and after days without a
bath, I couldn't resist the temptation to strip and jump in. As
I drank water like an animal and filled canteens, Dan strolled
upstream for security. Before long he came back and said, "I
think you better come see this." I climbed up the bank and
followed him upstream about thirty yards to a point where the
river made a small bend. There, floating face up in the water,
was a dead VC. He was naked and bloated twice his size. His
genital area had been shot to pieces, and he must have died a
terrible death. Suddenly my whole world became two naked
men, one standing on the bank, alive, and the other floating in
the water, dead. I thought, you bastard! You came back from
the dead to get even, didn't you? I promptly threw up. Personal
hygiene was as difficult as fighting the war.

If cleanliness was next to godliness, then He and I were
rubbing elbows one day when we moved past a friendly village. Three enterprising young women were hastily setting up
business near a local well. A box of C rations would buy a guy
a bath with clean well water. It was too good to be true. I
couldn't have dropped my pack faster if we were in a firefight.
I snatched two boxes of C rations and was off!

The gunny, ever watchful of the men, wanted to know what
the hell I was doing.

"Winning the hearts and minds, Sarge," I shouted as I
sprinted toward the well. What fortune; I had gotten there first.
I handed one of the girls the C rats. She bowed and gave them
to a kid who ran with them to the village. In seconds, she had
all my clothes off and was hand-washing me from head to toe.
The youngest woman carried water in wooden buckets and
poured it over my head, giggling when the cold water took my
breath away. The cobblestones, worn smooth by countless
baths taken there by the villagers, were soothing to my tired
feet.

It was an extremely sensual experience, just the sheer pleasure of being really clean. I had stepped out of the war for a
few brief minutes, only to be brought back when someone
shouted, "Hey, sniper, hurry up!" I looked up to see a line of
thirty or so men, each holding boxes of C rations.

I watched the line grow longer as I sat on a rock and changed
into clean fatigues. The company had come to a halt and the
skipper knew things were just going to have to run their course.
It didn't take bullets to stop a company of Marines dead in its
tracks, just three classy ladies.

Before day's end we would be filthy again, but not then, not right then. Thanks to Lee Oot's guidance, I was often able to at least gain a glimpse and sometimes entrance into a culture, with customs and pleasures centuries old, that was often dumbfounding to our western way of thought. It was hard to cut through the fog of death and destruction to find the beauty of the land and people, but it could be done. As my tour progressed, I not only adopted many of the ways of the Vietnamese, but often found myself identifying more with them than I did my own people.

★

Scout Snipers
An Hoa
July 5, 1969

Dear Mom,

This is late. Happy Birthday! All I can say is, chalk up one more occasion that I have to make up when I get back. I sure hope you had a nice day, I just wish I could do more.

I got your letters with the pictures. Talk about me being thin, it looks like you could use a little extra meat on those bones. Are you sure you feel okay?

I don't like the idea of you staying home and worrying. I would feel better knowing you were taking advantage of every chance you have to be doing the things you want. Life's just too precious to waste. I'm sending you some money. Call it a late birthday present.

Another thing while I'm thinking of it. If for any reason you're notified that I've been wounded, PLEASE be calm. Most likely a Marine will come to you in person. A friend of mine in snipers was hit about two weeks ago. His mother had a heart attack when she saw two recruiters walk up to their house. She has since gotten better, but you must keep a cool head. Besides, I'm not planning on getting hit.

You say I don't smile much anymore in my pictures. Well, maybe that's true, but don't think it's always like that. We have some good times, too, it's just that they aren't very often. When we come in from the bush for payday, someone usually comes up with a couple cases of beer and then we resort to just plain ole hell raising.

We had incoming rockets about an hour ago and one caught an ammo truck on fire down by the air strip. I haven't heard any earth-shaking explosions, so I guess they got it put out.

I don't know who my new partner is. I won't know till I'm ready for the bush again. Oh, yeah, as of yesterday, they've put a security wrap on our platoon. I'll have to wait till I get home to tell you the reason.

I haven't had a letter from Laura for five days now. I guess she's caught up in the swirl of school. I am anxious to hear from her.

Well, Mom, this has been a gabby letter. Take care.

Love, Joe

Except for sniper school, Stateside and in Da Nang, we never saw or heard about snipers from other units. We were all silent, neither to be seen nor heard. By necessity, we were also an elusive group, every aspect of being a sniper was geared toward evasiveness. At times we seemed to be everywhere, and at other times we were nowhere. Confusing to say the least, but that's the way we liked it.

Standing orders stated that snipers were not to talk to reporters, and when word got around that they were in the area, snipers simply disappeared. With a security wrap on our platoon, we became extremely closed-mouthed. The reason for this cloak and daggery was of course the cloak-and-dagger-department, CID (Counterintelligence Department, a branch of the CIA, not to be confused with the Criminal Investigation Division). Our outfit's reputation had caught the attention of CID, who had planned some operations in which I would reluctantly become involved.

*

Scout Snipers
An Hoa
July 8, 1969

Dear Mom,

Will put some film in with this. Most of the pictures are of Da Nang. I'm in An Hoa. Two more days and I should be back beating the bush. I'm kind of anxious to get back in the swing of things.

We didn't get our usual incoming rockets this morning. It was almost a disappointment, Charlie's slipping. This isn't much of a letter, but I wanted you to know I'm getting along fine.

Love, Joseph

Charlie knew An Hoa couldn't be taken, but he still waged a war of nerves with rockets and artillery from a mountain range four miles away called Nun's Ridge. They fired a few volleys and I'm sure were long gone when our big guns opened on the ridge. Along with the casualties, the rockets had a greater impact on routine and morale.

A hit on the chow hall not only killed several men, but it meant C rations for everyone until the mess hall was put back together. A freak hit on the water line that supplied the base shut off the showers and almost started a riot among the men wanting to wash up, especially after coming in from the bush.

The simultaneous *whoosh* and explosion of incoming rockets and artillery was so common, we often didn't bother to go to the bunkers. They usually came in salvos of six to ten, but it wasn't unusual to take several rounds a minute for an hour or longer.

★

Scout Snipers
Liberty Bridge
July 15, 1969

Dear Mom,

A quick note to let you know what's up. I'm back at Liberty Bridge. A team leader named Dave Meeks needed a partner for a job. I'll be with him for a while, then go back, get my gear and bolt rifle, and new partner. Dave and I will be going out with Echo Co. between the 17th and 20th. We'll be choppered to a place in the mountains. That's all I'm allowed to say right now.

I got a letter today just before I got on the chopper. About an hour ago a grunt cleaning his rifle had an accidental discharge and shot a guy through the stomach. They didn't think he would live till he got to Da Nang.

I don't hear from Laura very often. Don't say anything to her. I think she could do a little better. Oh, well.

It's hot tonight. They said on the radio that it was 85 degrees in Da Nang, so it's probably 95 or 100 here. That's pretty gruesome for 10:00 at night. I've never seen the mosquitoes so bad. If I see one single mosquito or fly when I get home, I'll go stark raving mad.

Got to go now. As usual, tell Grandma hi. Take care.

Love, Joseph

With so many men carrying lethal weapons, accidents often occurred. When near large groups of GIs, my partner and I had to watch ourselves and others closely.

At Hill 55, I watched in disbelief as two bored grunts played quick draw with .45s, and one accidentally shot the other dead. While with Zulu Company, 2d Battalion, 5th Marines, someone inadvertently threw a live LAW into the company fire. It blew up, killing two men and injuring four others.

Drugs played their part. I awoke to a commotion in our tent one morning at Hill 65. A man had died in his bunk during the night of a heroin overdose. We threw a poncho over him and moved to another tent. We'd spent the night in that tent with a corpse, and in an inexplicable way we all felt tainted. I had to wonder if it was an omen.

★

Scout Snipers
Liberty Bridge
Operation Durham Peak
July 21, 1969

Dear Mom,

I just got back from getting mail. I can always count on you to write. If it weren't for you, I would hardly get any.

You can probably tell I'm not in a very good mood. I guess I'm just tired, the last few days have been pretty full. I'm with Echo Co. 2/5 and for three days we've been practicing rappeling, sliding out of a chopper on a 150 foot cable. At first it was okay, but after awhile it gets very tiring. The reason for it is that tomorrow we're going to the mountains on a new operation.

We'll be the first unit inserted and the whole area is covered with a double canopy so choppers can't land. The operation is named Durham Peak. The only reason I told you about all this is that by the time the mail leaves we will already be there.

I haven't heard from Nick or Dave. I guess they don't have any more time to write than I do.

It's raining again. Like it does every day and will for the next two months.

Things have quieted some here. I think the US is making a terrible mistake by pulling troops out. All they are doing is giving the enemy time to build up strength, and then after we've pulled out enough troops, they'll just come down here and take over. Of course, certain politicians couldn't lose face by sending troops back over here if things go bad. There's no way in the world these ARVNs can fill in cuz they're just not good enough. I can't help getting the feeling that the US is selling South Vietnam short and by the time they realize it, it'll be too late. Maybe I'm wrong, I hope so.

We've been listening to Apollo 11 on the radio. They have just finished walking around on the moon and are back on the ship. I sure would like to be one of those guys.

Well, Mom, I better get this in the mail. Tell Grams hi. You take care.

                                                    Love, Joseph

Dave Meeks and I were partners again, with Dave as team leader. Dave was the same squad leader who first introduced me to the bush. He and I had just been given a rotten assignment, inserting with Echo Company, 2d Battalion, 5th Marines, into an area of the Central Highlands that was heavily vegetated. Due to the dense jungle, visibility would be severely limited. We were carrying M-14s with Starlite scopes as the bolt rifle would be of little or no use under these conditions. I had a sense of foreboding about this mission from the start.

It was still dark at 0530 hours on the 22d when Dave and I boarded one of five Huey gunships, with five men in each chopper: a squad of grunts for fire support, the captain, the gunny, the first lieutenant, four engineers, one radioman, one corpsman and one Kit Carson scout. All of us together didn't make half a light platoon. We were to surprise the enemy, if any, secure the area, and blow an LZ so the rest of the company could insert.

After an all-too-brief chopper ride we reached our objective, a canopy of treetops about one hundred feet high, with another layer thirty feet lower. The sun was just breaking the horizon as we hooked up to the cables and swung over the sides. There was only one thing on my mind and that was to get to the ground alive.

If there was an element of surprise it was on us. As we came out from under the top layer of trees, it was immediately apparent we were in trouble. We'd just dropped in on a company of NVA, and RPGs were going off in the tree branches above and below us. Our gunships returned fire with rockets, and most of them were exploding in the treetops. Shrapnel was flying everywhere, and we were already taking casualties.

I sped my descent, hoping the second barrier of trees would afford some protection, but coming out from under the bottom canopy was even worse. The crack of AK-47s sounded like a million crazed crickets. I was barely in a controlled fall and probably would have broken my legs when I hit were it not for the cushion of thick jungle.

Meeks and I had to reestablish contact quickly, which proved very difficult. The foliage was so dense, and it was so dark under the trees, I couldn't see a single man who'd made it safely to the ground. Dave and I were close enough to hear each other's voice over the firefight, but we couldn't see each other.

By persistently calling one another's name, we eventually got together. It didn't take much discussion, we knew it wasn't good. We were pretty sure we were near the middle of our unit, but had no way of knowing if anyone had survived on either side of us. We decided to treat it as an overrun situation and stay put until things calmed down. We sat quietly back-to-back, each of us scanning side to side, ready to shoot the first leaf that rustled without an American voice behind it. I was becoming aware of a steadily increasing pain in my back, as though someone had given me a hard kidney punch. I wondered if I had hit it when I landed.

The firefight, if you could call it that with people shooting through leaves and vines, was beginning to wind down. I untied the bandolier of M-14 clips while Dave pulled up my shirt. "You've got a great-looking bruise the exact size and shape of an M-14 magazine," he said. I picked up the bandolier and looked at it. There it was, a piece of shrapnel one inch long and a quarter inch thick. It had penetrated the clip and two bullets and was just sticking out of the inside of the magazine. It had hit with considerable force, but I hadn't felt it during my frantic slide to the ground.

It was quiet, except for the cries of the wounded and the voices of the remainder of our unit struggling to regroup. Dave and I tried to make sense out of our predicament. I knew Charlie should have rolled over us and that the only thing stopping them was their ignorance of our numbers. Had they known, we would all be dead. Nearly a third of us were killed or wounded during the rappel in. The captain, corpsman, one engineer, and a grunt were dead. Another engineer and the radioman were badly wounded and would have to be carried. The lieutenant and another grunt were walking wounded.

Dave and I took up rear guard, pushing ourselves up the steep hill on our asses, with our guns pointed down the small trail we were making. Two grunts took up the task of cutting a trail with machetes, and when they weren't able to lift their arms any longer, two more men took their places. The trail was barely wide enough for two men to crawl past each other. Using ponchos to carry our dead and wounded, we struggled to reach the top of a hill seventy-five yards away where, with the help of the two remaining engineers, we could get our casualties out. Our progress was agonizingly slow, four or five yards a minute at best.

Dave and I soon had our turn at the front, and the machetes were dull. We passed them back and called for sharp ones. In the meantime, we used our Turkish battle-axes, and our pace picked back up. By the time sharp machetes were passed to the front, we were too exhausted to keep swinging, and two more men took our places.

We tended to the wounded as we carried them up the steep hillside, but the jungle was about to win our battle against time, when it began to thin slightly. We were nearing the hilltop, and the engineers were working their way to the front while the rest of us held up.

An engineer returned after a few minutes and passed the word to collect all the claymore mines. We were able to come up with seven. When they reached my position, curiosity had gotten the better of me, and I took the mines to the hilltop myself. I had to know what they were going to do with claymores.

The engineer who took them from me satisfied my curiosity when he sat down and pried the backs off to dig out the C-4. They had strung detonation cord (high explosive wire, the thickness of a pencil) in a weblike fashion between trees, passing through a block or lump of explosive at the base of each one. Even with the C-4 from the mines, they weren't sure they had enough to do the job. I pulled back to a safe distance, and they let it blow.

When the smoke cleared, I saw their strange work of art. We

had lost a lot of C-4 in the rough rappel in, but with very limited resources, the engineers had blown a nearly perfect LZ. It was small, but big enough to land the medevac chopper that was circling in the distance.

Charlie must have been having the same problem of getting their wounded out because we had no contact while the medevac came and went.

We had a break to rest, ponder the events of the last forty-five minutes, and wait for a chopper to bring supplies and more C-4 to enlarge the LZ. When it arrived, it took heavy enemy ground fire, coming and going.

We were surrounded by NVA and would be our whole time in the mountains. The rest of the company came in under heavy fire, and there wasn't much we could do to stop it. It was next to impossible to find the enemy in the heavy jungle that surrounded us.

At the cost of four dead and four wounded, we had taken a hill, merely a number on a map and a place not worth giving a shit about. I asked the Kit Carson scout what he thought. He said, "This bad, very bad." That was all I needed to hear. Dave and I picked a spot just within the perimeter, away from the rest of the unit, where we stayed on guard the whole time.

A company of men in the bush required a steady source of ammo and supplies, a lot of both. The first scheduled supply chopper got shot up so badly, it had to turn back, trailing smoke, a day's rations gone. An early morning attempt the next day met the same fate. Repeated attempts to resupply us over the next two days proved useless. We were stranded on a hill, surrounded by a large enemy force that had moved in after our initial insertion, and were unable to get supplies in. We ran out of food and water about the same time.

Another day went by, and the skipper called for three volunteers to go down the hillside in hopes of finding a stream. He got his volunteers, and I watched as they disappeared into the wall of green below the LZ, each with three five-gallon, plastic water cans tied to his back. Three hours passed, as the skipper paced nervously back and forth, before they reappeared from the jungle, water cans empty. We were well into our fourth day without any resupply at all. It had become a serious situation.

Although we were only receiving occasional incoming mortars, when a chopper tried to get in, Charlie raised so much hell it couldn't land. They'd cut our supply line and were content to just let us dehydrate, certain death in the intense heat. Mid-morning of the fifth day, everyone was desperately hoping the supply bird that appeared on the horizon would get through. He was carrying a full sling under the chopper, most of it water cans. A quarter mile away he started drawing fire that grew in intensity.

We watched and wondered how far they would get before turning back. There was something different about the pilot—he wasn't slowing down or turning away. With the binoculars I could see that it was an army chopper. It was taking such heavy enemy fire, water was streaming from bullet holes through some of the cans in its cargo sling.

I thought, he's going to make it or die trying. He got to a point just outside of our perimeter where he made a hard climbing turn and released the sling. I tried to watch the sling full of supplies as it fell to the ground and keep an eye on the helicopter at the same time. The supplies hit at the edge of a steep incline that led to a ravine far below. The chopper climbed and was soon out of sight. It had to be full of bullet holes.

Almost all the food went down the ravine, gone for good, but ten cans of water got hung up on the incline. Two grunts were lowered by ropes to retrieve them. It didn't amount to a canteen and a half for each man. That pilot risked it all to get us the equivalent of fifty gallons of water.

Fortunately, I had a partial answer to our limited food situation in my pack. I always carried the dried-soup packets Mom sent. I had four left. I got them out as Dave carefully poured both of us a cup of water and began heating them. We could quench our thirst some and get a little nourishment, too. It had been nearly three days since we had eaten, and we slowly savored that cup of soup sent halfway around the world. The temptation to use the other two packets was almost too much, but we resisted, and they would be our breakfast in the morning.

Early the next day a supply chopper showed up with four Cobra gunships, and their fire power, combined with the company throwing out everything it had, enabled the supply chopper to barely get in and out. The first chopper brought water, a 106mm recoilless rifle, and all the shells the bird could lift off with. They weren't ordinary rounds, they were beehive shells. When a 106mm recoilless rifle fired this kind of round, about halfway in its trajectory the round split open, unleashing eight thousand flechettes (inch-long steel darts). Finally, Charlie had a problem.

A dozen supply choppers were circling a couple miles away while the recoilless was assembled. When the rifle was ready, the first bird headed our way. As expected, green tracers started streaming toward it. With the first *boom* and *zing,* the flechettes tore through the jungle. The tracers stopped and started from another area. Again, *boom, zing,* and the tracers stopped. The guys were firing that rifle faster and faster, and the choppers were finally able to make it in.

Before long, the supplies that had been building up in the rear got through. Pretty soon Dave and I were staring at a pile of food we couldn't eat in two weeks, from canned bacon to bottled catsup.

The very next morning, we got the word to move out, and couldn't carry a tenth of those supplies with us. We'd just gone four days with practically no food and water and found ourselves pouring water on the ground and carrying armloads of food to throw into the company fire.

I stood there and watched as tons of supplies went up in smoke and wondered what we had accomplished.

*

Scout Snipers
10 miles south An Hoa
July 18, 1969

Dear Mom,

It's starting to storm, so I'll write as much as I can. The wind is blowing like mad, and it'll be raining soon.

You wanted to know where I am. I'm in the mountains. Yesterday a company next to us got hit, and when they tried to medevac the wounded, the gooks shot down two choppers. Our company sent a platoon to help get the crews out, and Dave and I went along. We were just about up to the closest bird when we got pinned down. We called in air strikes and they were pretty close. Well, I raised my head up at the wrong time, and got hit by a piece of wood blown off a tree. It raised a good size lump on my forehead and it is sore today. Except for Dave calling me ''Block Head'' it's okay now.

Well, they got the astronauts back safe and sound. You know something, last night I was lying there looking up at the moon and I got to thinking, there's an American flag up there. It's something to be proud of.

We just got the word that we may go back to the bridge.

After the last few days, I can say I don't mind if we do. I'll write and let you know.

We're not with E Company anymore. They wanted us over at G Company. They call it "Goofy Golf" and to tell the truth, I don't have much confidence in the company.

I've decided to go to Sydney, Australia, for R and R. I think I'll try to take it in October or November.

Well, Mom, the rain has cut me some slack and let me finish this. This is my last piece of paper. I'll figure something out. I'm getting along fine, so don't worry. Take care. Bye for now.

Love, Joseph

We began moving every day, often having to cut a path through dense jungle, and set in at night on a progression of hilltops. Since we were constantly changing locations, the enemy had more trouble interrupting our supply line and turned their attention to us. They were lobbing at least a hundred mortars in on us each night. I was developing a special hate for the sound of incoming mortars.

There was a battalion (four companies) from the 5th Regiment involved in operation Durham Peak. Charlie was keeping up the same pressure on all four companies. We figured there had to be at least a regiment of NVA with a good supply line. Finding them in the rugged jungle terrain, however, was incredibly difficult. Climbing one hill and small mountain after another was bad enough, but when we encountered heavy resistance from one particular hill, the skipper got pissed and ordered a blockbuster (fifteen-thousand-pound aerial bomb). We pulled back and covered our ears.

The air force dropped it right on target, and a seemingly endless explosion rolled over us. Afterward we walked to the top of the hill without firing a shot, and we were amazed at the destruction and dead NVA. A bunker complex was smashed flat, as though a giant hand had pushed it down.

Less than six months later, I was with a company barely five miles from the same spot that took the blockbuster, when Charlie hit us with rocket fire from a hill a mile away. The skipper called for artillery strikes and was surprised when he was switched to fire command on the USS *New Jersey*. We were eleven miles inland, and the *New Jersey* was seven miles off shore. The skipper had barely given the coordinates when a single 2,200-pound, high explosive round roared overhead like an invisible freight train and hit the hill with a tremendous explosion. That first round stopped all enemy fire. They were either dead or in shock from the concussion. The skipper said, "You're right on target, *New Jersey,* have at it." We listened as the first full salvo thundered overhead and smashed into the hill. Our stomachs were pushed in and out from the shock waves of the explosion. In no time at all the second salvo was on its way, soon to be followed by a third. In scant minutes, the *New Jersey* had placed sixty thousand pounds of high explosives exactly on target. The company broke into cheers as the hill literally disappeared.

When the ship called back to see if we needed more help, all the skipper could say was, "No, thanks, *New Jersey,* there's nothing left to fire at."

Although the Marine Corps is part of the navy, there exists a friendly, and sometimes not-so-friendly, rivalry between the two services. The fierce pride of at least one company of Marines had to give way to admiration that day at what one navy ship eighteen miles away had done.

★

Scout Snipers
Mountains
August 2, 1969

Dear Mom,

A note to go with these rolls of film. We haven't had mail for a week now.

I just wrote to Laura, so I guess this will be pretty much a repeat. We're still in the mountains and we're still with Golf Company. Yesterday a patrol found an NVA hospital cut into the side of a mountain. They decided we better stick around and see what else we could find.

Later—They just called "Snipers up." There was 120 NVA about three clicks away carrying wounded up a ravine. They were too far away for us to shoot, so we called in air strikes.

The corpsman told me yesterday I had dysentery. He's giving me medicine, which should keep it from getting any worse. Dave had it a couple weeks ago and he was real sick. I'm not as bad as he was. A guy has to run to keep up with all the crud that can be caught here.

I'll close now and get this ready to go on the next bird.

Love, Joseph

I stood up on the morning of August 1, and the ground quickly came up to meet me. I was so dizzy I had to crawl on my hands and knees to get to a corpsman I knew. I told him I was weak, seeing double, and had the shits. He knew right away what was wrong; I had dysentery. He gave me a big shot of antibiotics and started me on tablets. At one point I couldn't move, my body felt like it weighed a ton, but in twenty-four hours the corpsman had me recovering from a disease that usually lasted about a week.

A rule of thumb was get to know the corpsmen right away for medicine and the engineers for C-4 to heat chow with. C-4 burned with an intense heat and was much faster at heating water or chow than the alcohol heat tabs in each box of C rations. Likewise, the corpsmen and engineers tried to stay near the snipers, since we knew the safest spots in the perimeter to sit in.

During our travel in the mountains, I spent a considerable amount of time with the Kit Carson scout. He showed me the subtle aspects of scouting, easily overlooked, that no amount of training Stateside could teach a man. If the berry bushes and banana trees were stripped of their fruit, it meant an enemy force had passed through that area in the last forty-eight hours. It may have been something as inconspicuous as the twigs of a particular type of bush broken in a certain way, which was a directional signal for following troops to go by. Once, he stopped me from walking into a booby trap. He saw the trip wire; I didn't.

*

Scout Snipers
An Hoa
August 26, 1969

Dear Mom,

I know you've been frantic for a letter and I'm sure sorry. I may be able to get caught up on my writing some.

I'm in An Hoa right now. I've been through a lot in the last three weeks. Dave and I got switched to another company and we went to Arizona Territory. The 7th Marines pulled out of Arizona and we went in. I knew we were in for a rough time.

The reason I'm in An Hoa is that Dave Suttles was wounded this morning and we medevaced him, so I had to get his rifle and gear back to the rear. He's not the same Dave I went out

with. I'll be here till I get a new partner and there's no one
available right now. I don't think Dave is too bad, I should hear
about him tomorrow. He caught shrapnel in the back of the neck
and butt. I'm okay, so don't worry about me. The only thing
wrong with me is my nerves. I'm trying to get R and R in
October cuz I really need it.

Today was the first mail I've had since we went into Arizona. They kept sending it out, but the choppers couldn't land
to get it to us, so they finally quit sending it. I got a couple
packages from you and the pictures. Thanks so much for sending them. I'm going to answer your questions tomorrow or the
next day after I've had a chance to rest and regroup my thoughts.

Mom, this is a poor letter, but I'm going to close. I need to
write to Dave's parents, I think they would appreciate it. I
haven't even cleaned up yet. The important thing is that you
know I'm fine. Take care, and I'll write soon.

Love, Joseph

I picked up another partner, Dave Suttles, and we were attached to a company in Arizona Territory.

To send a company into Arizona Territory was like rubbing an
eraser over coarse sandpaper. Casualties were high and steady.
In time, a company would wear down to a demoralized, under-
manned unit, no longer capable of conducting effective operations. I went into Arizona often and never failed to see this
happen.

Arizona Territory was a flat plain consisting of rice paddies,
fields, and scattered trees and undergrowth. It was about twenty
miles long and varied from five to twelve miles wide, bordered
on the Da Nang side by a quarter-mile-wide, waist-deep river
and a mountain range on the other. It was a persistent thorn in
the sides of the 5th and 7th Marine Regiments, and just the
thought of going into Arizona could get a man down.

To begin with, there was no safe way to get there. We either
had to ford the river, holding onto a nylon rope to keep the
current from washing us away, and hope we didn't get hit while
helpless in the water, or chopper in under fire. Either way, Charlie would hit us coming and going and constantly peck away at
us while there.

As we choppered toward Charlie Company, my mind drifted
back to my last time in Arizona.

Dave Meeks and I had been attached to Hotel Company when

we crossed the Dien Ban River. The last man wasn't out of the
water, and we were already pinned down by AK-47 rounds
coming at us three feet off the ground.

The front of the column was returning fire with M-60 machine guns and everything else they had, but before long the
word was passed back for "ammo up!" The machine guns
were running out of ammunition. Ron and I were crouched
behind a burial mound, in a cemetery dotted by grass-covered
earth mounds, three feet high and six feet long, which afforded
good protection. I was quite content to stay where we were, but
again the word came back for more ammo.

A strange thought crossed my mind as I pictured the barrels
of those machine guns glowing red with heat. A gun crew
carried a spare barrel which could be changed in a few seconds.
They traded between the two, allowing each barrel time to cool
off, but they sure weren't bothing with it at that point. The next
cry for ammo was more urgent.

There was a saying drummed into us in training: "When
you're pinned down, you move or you die." I leaned over and
peeked around the grave to the next mound ten yards ahead and
saw a grunt curled in a fetal position, locked tight with fear. He
was a FNG (fucking new guy), and this was probably his first
firefight.

He had the handle of a can of gun ammo clutched tight in
one hand. I kept thinking, come on snap out of it, go. I handed
the bolt rifle to Ron and did one of those things a guy regrets
as soon as he does it. I crawled up to the grunt, and when our
eyes met, I could see he was looking through me, not at me. He
had a death grip on the can. When I managed to jerk it away
from him, I saw a change come over his face.

I started crawling toward the guns, dragging the ammo box
along. Pretty soon I was in a low crawl, pushing the box ahead
of me. By the time I reached a point where I could see the
smoke from one of our machine guns, bullets were hitting the
ground and trees all around me. I suddenly realized that I'd
gotten myself into a situation I probably wasn't going to live
through. I rolled over, and with both hands flung the box as
hard as I could toward the gun. I lay flat and watched the
gunner's assistant scramble out, snatch the ammo, and return.

That was good enough for me, and I started crawling like
mad back to the safety of the graveyard. I hadn't gone far,
when I saw that grunt who'd froze making his way toward the
guns. He was doing the craziest low crawl I'd ever seen, mov-

ing along like an inchworm with a can of ammo in each hand.

I got behind the first mound I came to and watched him make two more trips in like fashion. On his third trip he looked at me, sweat dripping from his face, and smiled. I just nodded, and he was off. We both knew what he had done: he'd overcome the paralyzing fear that grips a man in combat to do his job.

When the firefight was over, I went to look at the machine guns. They were really burned up, the insides of the barrels scored beyond hope and so warped I doubted if they could have hit a target twenty yards away. We were fighting hardcore NVA in Arizona, many with experience combating the French.

My thoughts snapped back to the present as the door gunner opened fire, signaling our descent and that we were being shot at from somewhere.

By the time Dave Suttles and I joined Charlie Company, even with replacements, they were down in strength by 20 percent. The skipper was desperate to cut losses, and when we got off the chopper, he hustled us away for a conference. He was a newly commissioned captain and hadn't been in-country very long, and sure as hell had never seen anything like Arizona.

He was a good skipper, but after a week of watching his men fall dead and wounded all around him, he was looking for a solution. All the air and artillery strikes seemed to have little effect. I stopped myself short of telling him that it would be that way his whole time in Arizona, and we could only help him out so much. It was the most dangerous place around, but paradoxically it was a sniper's paradise. Long fields of view gave us the chance to use the bolt rifle the way it was intended to be used. This same advantage also applied to the enemy, and sniper duels were not uncommon. A year and a half before I arrived, a duel killed both a sniper from the 5th and an NVA sniper when they fired at exactly the same time.

The skipper agreed to let me cover Arizona my way. We would forgo some of the daytime patrols, and Dave and I would move out before sunrise or just before sunset in hopes of catching enemy movements. With limited light or on a moonlit night, the bolt rifle was good up to one thousand yards. Dave would carry a radio, so if we got into a jam we could call air or artillery strikes to cover our withdrawal.

We did get some good results over the next two weeks, but it was only a finger in the dike. I logged eight confirmed kills and many probables. The intensity of enemy activity prevented us from conducting body searches, therefore making the majority of my shots only probable kills. On two occasions, we spotted enemy troop movements so large, I didn't even consider using the bolt rifle. Instead, I called in heavy-artillery strikes, and after seeing that they were on target, we pulled back to the company.

Snipers weren't required to stand lines in the bush, but in Arizona we did when asked. It meant the company had worn down to a point where it could no longer maintain an effective perimeter. We relieved weary radiomen in contact with a night ambush or listening post somewhere out in the darkness. We went on night ambushes. On one August ambush, while getting to our assigned position we passed so close to the enemy, the smell of fish, which was a major part of their diet, nearly overpowered us. For the same reason, they surely knew we were there because Americans smelled like soap. We must have passed scant yards apart in the night in total silence, as though both groups of men were too weary to go at it.

A night ambush is a monster, unique to itself, and required a ritual beforehand. Camouflage grease paint was applied to faces, necks, and arms; shotguns were loaded; a final weapons' check was made; and noisy gear was taped down. The shotguns would deliver the majority of firepower for the first three to five seconds, with M-16s filling in. Although a properly sprung ambush could be over within seconds, it usually meant sitting in the night for hours, absolutely quiet. We communicated with the company via an occasional silent press or two on the radio button to inform them of our status.

The day before Dave Suttles was wounded, we caught a squad of NVA in a predawn ambush. After sitting motionless all night, I was exhausted and getting a bad feeling about it.

An hour before first light, the trap was sprung when enemy troops began moving into the kill zone. The night lit up from the muzzle flashes of pump shotguns and M-16s. In two blinks it was quiet again. A flare was thrown onto the path. The result was three dead NVA. The first two were shot to pieces by the shotguns, and the third man caught most of a magazine from an M-16. We took three prisoners, two regulars and a nurse. Two to four enemy had escaped into the thick growth on a hillside which ran for a hundred yards along the ambush site.

Counterintelligence was in on the ambush and interrogated

the enemy. In frustration when one prisoner wouldn't answer, an agent took him by the hair and rubbed his face in the brains of one of his dead comrades. He still refused to talk. The other prisoners were bound and sitting back-to-back in a small clearing. I didn't need to see more of the "interrogation," and I relieved the grunt guarding them.

A whimper was coming from the nurse, which grew in intensity as the sun began to rise. Something was wrong. As soon as it was light enough, I saw a pleading look in her eyes that I couldn't ignore. I turned her around and saw the reason. One of the counterintelligence agents had tied her hands so tight, they looked like rubber gloves full of air and were turning black.

Prisoners became the "property" of the counterintelligence division but when I saw her hands, I stormed up to the agent I'd come to dislike by then anyway. "I'm going to loosen the bonds on the woman," I told him in a tone that was hard to mistake. Counterintelligence agents carried a lot of weight. The guy could have had me arrested, but didn't for two reasons. First, I was part of regimental headquarters which presented a problem, even for the brass, and second, he knew it wasn't overly smart to piss off the snipers. To piss off one sniper was to piss off all the snipers. Our free-fire ability and our reputation for elusiveness gave rise to some fear and uncertainty where the snipers were concerned, even among fellow Marines. He just gave me a dirty look and didn't say a word.

I returned to the prisoners and pulled the nurse to the side. I spent quite some time looking for a place where the swelling hadn't completely covered the rope before I forced my battle-ax down hard between her wrists. She slowly crossed her arms against her chest, as a torrent of tears ran down her face. This is bullshit, I thought as I went to get the corpsman to check her out.

"Her left hand might come out of it, but she'll probably lose the right one," he said.

My dislike for that agent was growing rapidly. When a sweep of the hillside netted two more prisoners, one an NVA captain, I was quick to remind the agent of the Geneva Convention rules for the treatment of captured enemy officers. Through clenched teeth he said, "Okay, sniper, you be responsible for him."

I led the captain to a spot a short distance from the rest of the prisoners and leaned him against a rock. He showed signs of malaria and was too sick to make a run for it anyway. I laid my rifle out of his reach and squatted down to get a close look at our adversary. What I saw changed my attitude about the war for good.

I hadn't had a chance to really study a live NVA officer, and our eyes locked in an icy stare. I offered him water—no response. I offered him a cigarette—no response. I was mesmerized by this look into the enemy's soul and found myself thinking, give me a thousand men like this, and I could conquer the world. There we were fighting a whole nation of them on their terms. I knew then we would pay dearly for being in Vietnam. I abruptly stood, feeling as though I'd just seen my own death. I called the corpsman to check him, and he offered him quinine tablets for the malaria. There was no response, just what I expected.

A chopper landed, and the prisoners, along with the counterintelligence agents, were not long out of sight when the pilot radioed us to say, "Hate to tell you this, but one of your prisoners just jumped out." Jumped out my ass, I thought. He or she was thrown out to make the others talk. I was sure it wasn't the captain, he was too valuable alive, but which of the others it was, I didn't know and didn't want to know.

The next afternoon, against my better judgment and still fatigued from the ambush the night before, I agreed to take a squad out on a short, routine patrol. But in my weariness, I forgot an important fact—nothing was ever routine in Arizona.

Two clicks away from the company, we were caught by a quick hit-and-run ambush. The first mortar round hit a few yards to my right rear, wounding Dave and two grunts behind him.

I called in an air strike, which I'm sure dropped a load of napalm on an empty tree line. My next priority was a medevac, and once that was done, we returned to the company, my anger at myself growing with every step.

A sniper team is exactly that, a team. If your partner went off to take a piss, you knew where he was going and when to expect him back. A tight bond quickly formed, and to lose your partner was no light matter. I caught the afternoon supply chopper to An Hoa.

When a sniper returned with his partner's gear, an informal ritual took place. The snipers in the rear at the time followed me to Dave's tent. If I put his gear on top of his cot along with his rifle, he was still alive. If I put his gear under his cot and headed to the armory with his rifle, it meant he was dead. I put his pack on his cot with his rifle, and as I sat down, the chatter began: "How bad is he?" "Where did he get hit?" "What did he get hit by?"

The questions seemed to run together, as emotional and physical exhaustion overwhelmed me. Someone handed me a can of soda, and I slowly sipped it as I tried to answer everyone. I was bitter. I hadn't lost a partner in action until then, and I felt I should have been able to prevent it. I finished the soda and reluctantly headed toward Gunny Fergie's (Ferguson) tent to report in. Fergie was a great guy, and he knew how I felt. In the past, he'd had to make the very same report. His job was tough. He had to report to the skipper who would take it hard, too. I guess if shit ever flows uphill, that was one of those times.

He finished his report and told me to get some hot chow and clean up. He would try to get some beer for the guys later. As I pushed the screen door to his tent open, he asked, "By the way, Ward, do you know anything about the pot smoking going on in the platoon?"

"Yes, why?"

"Well, the skipper found some marijuana cigarettes on the ground between the tents this morning, and he wanted me to check it out. Do you smoke it?"

"Yes."

"I've never tried it," he said. "What's it like?"

"Oh, it's okay, Gunny. It's not like drinking. Do you want me to get you some?"

"No, no, I was just curious," he said in a distant tone of voice.

"Anything else, Gunny?"

"No, that's all."

I stopped by each tent and told the guys there between assignments to be more careful with their pot. Nothing more was said about it.

The chow hall and showers weren't open yet, so I went to my tent to write Mom and Dave's parents. I wanted them to get the story first-hand. After a shower and hot chow, I felt better, but was having trouble patching the cracks in my normally steady nerves. True to his word, Fergie later came by my tent. "This is from the skipper," he said as he put a case of beer on the table and walked out.

★

Scout Snipers
An Hoa
August 30, 1969

Dear Mom,

Just got back from chow. I had lines last night just like every night, so I'm not getting a whole lot of rest. At least I'm getting some good chow. Yesterday was the first time since I got in-country that I've had any salad. It's just about all I ate and it sure was good. There's a new guy in charge of the mess hall and the meals have really improved.

There was a letter here from you dated the 25th, so I'm caught up on my mail. This letter had the flicks you took and I sure enjoyed them.

Mom, I'm having a hard time getting what I think written, so please bear with me. I'm sure you're still worried because of not getting any mail for so long. When I wrote you that letter on the 26th, I think I was about to have a nervous breakdown. My hands were shaking. Actually, my nerves have calmed down, but I'm pretty depressed. Just when I thought I could take about anything, we went back to Arizona and it really got to me.

It may sound like I'm crying in my beer, but I'm sort of confused. I know you'll probably be unhappy with me when I tell you that I haven't told you everything when I write and there's still a lot of things I won't tell you cuz I don't think I should.

I had best get on to other things. The weather has been hotter than it has been so far. The monsoons are due to start next month, so I guess the summer is really pouring it on in a last effort.

No, Dave Young and I weren't in the same unit. He's in Golf 2/7 and I was with Golf 2/5. The 2 stands for 2d Battalion and the 7 and 5 stand for the regiment. When we were at Hill 65 just before going into Arizona, I found out that Dave's unit was at Hill 22 which was about 8 miles away, and I didn't have time to get over to see him. He didn't say anything about being wounded in his letter.

As for Dave Suttles, the last word I got was that he was in Japan and that he wasn't hurt as bad as I thought. I wrote his parents and explained what happened.

I've got a lot of stuff to send as soon as I get some money. I have five rolls of film and some coins and documents. I only have one roll of film left and they don't have any more at the

PX, so I could use more, if you would send it. Don't worry
about getting me anything for my birthday, it's a lost occasion
for me this year.

Do me a favor, will you? I've forgotten Laura's birthday.
This place just pushes a lot of things out of a guy's mind. Don't
tell her I forgot. Well, Mom, I've rambled on long enough and
I want to write to Laura, so I better get cracking.

I know this is useless to say, but please try not to worry too
much. Take good care, and I'll write again when I send that
stuff.

Love, Joseph

There were too few snipers and too many people requesting
us. From tower watch and lines to clean up after an attack,
being in the rear—whether it was in An Hoa, Liberty Bridge,
Hill 65, Hill 55 or any number of fire bases—meant little rest,
only a short break from the bush. In An Hoa, the fact that we
could fire without clearance prompted the grunts to bribe us to
a bunker in their sector with pot and booze. Such offers bought
me duty at the most dangerous bunker on the perimeter several
times. It was in an area called no-man's-land, and was somewhat separated from the other bunkers. Charlie often probed
and hit An Hoa from that area.

At midnight on the twenty-ninth, I was standing watch with
the Starlite, fighting the urge to sleep. A new guy I'd brought
out as my partner and two grunts were sleeping. In another
hour my partner would relieve me.

While scanning the area in front of the bunker, I thought I
saw something about 450 yards out. Maybe I'm just tired, I
thought. I looked away from the scope and rubbed my eyes.
When I looked again, I saw two sappers making their way
toward our position through the maze of barbed wire and trip
flares.

I could drop one of them for sure, but I would blind the
scope from the muzzle flash long enough to allow the other to
get away. I knew where our claymore mines were located and
decided to let them keep coming. I woke up the rest of the guys
and got headquarters on the field phone to tell them there would
be fire from our sector and keep the rest of the bunkers from
opening up. I returned to the scope to watch the sappers'
progress.

They moved like cats, but were heading toward a line of
claymores fifty yards out, each capable of blasting seven hun-

dred steel balls outward in a fan-shape pattern. One of the grunts had his hand on the detonator, waiting for me to give the word. When they were fifty feet from the mines I told him, "Now," and ducked. He turned the switch, and four clay-mores went off simultaneously. The backblast sent rocks and dirt flying through the opening in the bunker, and illumination flares started popping over our sector before the smoke and dust had cleared.

I handed the scope rifle to the new guy and told him to check it out. After a time he said, "I don't see anything."

"Of course not," I said, as I sat on a case of grenades and leaned against the sandbags. "They're dead."

I was weary, and my last thought before I fell asleep was that I needed to see Lee Oot. It had been awhile since I'd been into the village with supplies, and I also wanted to see if Lee had any information on the increase in enemy activity.

My partner called my name at first light. "The grunts want to know if you wanna check out the bodies."

"You go ahead; I'm heading in."

Sappers didn't carry documents; besides, I knew what the bodies would look like. If I hurried, I could get to the show-ers before they closed for the day. After a shave and shower, I went to my cot to get some sleep. I woke when the new guy came in and listened to him describe the bodies to a cou-ple of team leaders. He'd counted 127 holes in one of the sappers.

I looked at my watch. It was nearly 10:00. Remembering Lee, I emptied my pack on the cot, grabbed my rifle, and headed for the field hospital.

It was a two-mile walk to An Hoa village, and I was too tired to carry ammo or weapons. Medical supplies would be lighter, and one of the corpsmen I knew at the hospital accommodated me quite well. He dumped handfuls of battle dressings, anti-septic, quinine, and miscellaneous items into my pack. The hospital bunker was so cool and quiet; I wanted to lie down on one of the cutting tables (operating tables) and sleep, but if I was to see Lee before I went back to the bush, I had to get moving.

We weren't supposed to go into the village alone or without a pass, but I often did. I had discovered early on in my tour I was carrying a ticket to go wherever I wanted—the bolt rifle. It could get me on a chopper to Da Nang for twenty-four hours without orders or through the checkpoint at An Hoa without a pass. I was never questioned about my movements when I carried it.

I'd missed the morning convoy, and it was a hot, dusty walk to the first militia outpost. I asked the men there where Lee was. Between my poor Vietnamese and their poorer English, it took a stick drawing in the dirt to tell me he was at a bunker on the other side of the village. I left them some things from my pack and slowly walked through the village.

I always enjoyed the sights, sounds, and smells of the Vietnamese people going about their daily lives. In the village, a guy could buy anything from banana beer (made from the local small, sweet bananas) and popsicles to opium or some kid's nine-year-old sister. I knew which shops were safe for a GI to buy at and took pleasure at the outdoor marketplace. Although Lee had made it as safe as possible, I was always vulnerable to VC assassination. Still, I felt at ease there.

Word that I was in the village spread quickly, and I soon found myself surrounded by a small mob of kids. I didn't have any gum or candy to give them that day. They were very persistent, and I was becoming more aggravated at the thought of them picking me clean in no time, when a clap of hands and a shout sent them scurrying.

I looked up to see one of the most beautiful women I'd ever encountered. Taller than the average Vietnamese woman, she had the fine features unique to a French Vietnamese. Before I could thank her, she disappeared behind her parasol and was walking away. I was awed by this brief encounter. I'd been to the village so many times and couldn't understand why I hadn't seen her before.

I hurried on to find Lee before the kids had a chance to regroup. He was already coming to greet me with his usual gesture, arms outstretched saying, "Ah, Joe, Joe, Joe." We always hugged, glad for each other that we were both still alive. I was in time for the noon meal with the militia and always ate with the people when I could. Not only was the food good, it was a welcome break from mess hall chow and C rations.

I told Lee to get a poncho and spread it on the ground. When he returned, I dumped the contents of my pack in the center. Lee just nodded; that was all the thanks necessary.

It had taken weeks of painful readjustment for my knees before I mastered the Vietnamese way of sitting, a low squat with the butt just off the ground and both knees against the chest.

Lee and I squatted and began talking, when a militiaman brought me a shallow bowl of rice wine. I reflected on my first meal with the militia and my introduction to the 190 proof wine. I had been given a bowl like the one I was holding, with what looked to be water in it. Great, I thought, I was parched. I took a big swallow and was immediately gasping for air. Everyone laughed, and Lee put his hand on my arm and said, "Slowly." He had that right. A warm, comforting feeling washed over me as I sipped the wine. Next came a bowl of rice containing vegetables and meat. It was delicious, but I couldn't identify the meat, it was unlike anything I'd tasted before. I held a piece of it up with my chopsticks and turned to a militiaman next to me. *"Bruck, bruck?"* I inquired, imitating the sound of a chicken. *"Ruff, ruff,"* he replied. Dog meat or not, it was good, and I was relieved it wasn't cat or monkey.

That same familiar, warm feeling was again easing my tired mind and body. While we ate, I asked Lee about the woman I'd seen earlier in the village. He told me her name was Ann Bae, and since she wasn't pure Vietnamese, she was somewhat of an outcast. She had married an ARVN lieutenant, who had been killed a year ago, and lived fairly well on her government pension. "Such beauty," I said, "is highly prized in my country. Would you take me to meet her?" He did.

She lived in an average hootch at the rear of the village. I took no gifts of any kind. To do so would mean by Vietnamese custom that the host or hostess would have to offer anything they owned in return, and I didn't want her to feel that way. She welcomed us inside, rushed into the bunker, and returned with a small folding chair for me to sit on. When I refused the chair and squatted down, the ice was broken.

She somehow came up with a cold can of American beer and squatted down facing me. I was barely aware of the beer I was holding, as I stared at her flawless face, wondering how such a flower could survive amid the insanity that was Vietnam. Lee quietly slipped out of the hootch, and we were alone.

Suddenly I was tongue-tied. I thanked her for the beer, and the only thing I knew to talk about was her dead husband. I was surprised at how good her English was when she answered. "He killed in VC ambush, ten months ago."

A war is a damn poor place to fall in love, but that's what I found myself doing as we talked. Impossible as the situation was, passions surfaced quickly as in any war. I would be going home at some point, and there was always the possibility that one of us could be killed at any time.

Ann's hootch would often be my first stop when I went to the village to see Lee, and she always greeted me with a can of beer. I usually took her candy and cigarettes and some little something from the PX. Whether we had time to make love or not, it was always an intense exchange between a man and a woman, worlds apart, but totally together.

★

Scout Snipers
An Hoa
August 31, 1969

Dear Mom,

Just got back from church and I'm glad I went. I had to share my song book with some major, but other than that it was okay.

Wanted to put a note in with all this stuff. The coins, paper money, and some of the papers written in Chinese were in a bunker I checked out when we were in Arizona. There was also a badly wounded VC, but I won't go into that.

The one roll of film was taken in the mountains. The other is mostly of Arizona. I really don't need any pictures to remind me of Arizona. I hope all this stuff gets there okay.

Love, Joseph

A "tunnel rat" (a small guy that checked out tunnels and underground bunker complexes) asked me if I wanted to check out a bunker that had just been fragged.

Checking out enemy bunkers wasn't the safest thing to do, especially in Arizona. I wasn't sure my six-foot, three-inch frame would fit through the tunnel, but I hadn't done it before and I wanted to know what it was like. I borrowed a .45 and followed him on my hands and knees into what, from the outside, looked to be an ordinary bunker. The acrid fumes from the grenade were thick in the musty air of the tunnel as we slowly made our way along, the "rat" constantly probing the floor and walls with a bayonet for booby traps. A faint sound was coming from inside the bunker itself, and we stopped to listen. We knew what it was; it was the unmistakable sound of someone choking on their own blood. I cocked my .45 as we moved toward the dark opening ahead.

Tunnel rats were highly respected, but I was thinking, a guy had to be crazy to do this.

When we reached the bunker, he quickly moved his flashlight all round, briefly stopping at one spot, then he began moving the light around again. "Holy shit," he said as he moved into the open space of the main bunker. "Come look at this."

While I crawled next to him, he was training his light on a figure lying by the wall to the right. There was the source of the noise, a Vietcong female, about twenty-five years old, with an AK-47 rifle still strapped to her back. She must have been pretty close to the grenade when it went off—I couldn't see an area on her that didn't have a shrapnel hole in it. She was only seconds away from being dead, but the rat handed me the flashlight while he checked to see if she had armed a grenade and was lying on it. He carefully reached under her and felt around.

"Not a chance," he said, reaching out with a hand sticky with blood and took the flashlight from me. "Look," he added as he shined the light around the bunker. It was only then that I realized we were in a large chamber, with tunnels leading off in several directions. The place was full of supplies. This was an old tunnel complex that had escaped detection for years. As he played the light from tunnel to tunnel, I felt like we had just entered the untouched tomb of a pharoah. There were weapons, ammo, rice in large wicker baskets, stacks of documents, paper money, coins, and crates of medical supplies. Many bore a shipping stamp that read, DONATED TO THE PEOPLE'S REPUBLIC BY YOUR FRIENDS AT BERKELEY COLLEGE. It wasn't the first time I'd seen such markings from various universities and organizations in the United States. What really caught my eye was the silk. At least three hundred rolls of black Chinese silk to be made into uniforms, more than enough to make a man rich in the States. The rat was wiping the blood off of his hands with what must have been a hundred dollars worth of it.

We stuffed our pockets full of money and documents and didn't put a dent in the pile. It was so cramped in the tunnel that we had a hard time pulling the woman outside where we laid her on the ground. She was barely breathing, and her eyelids would occasionally blink slowly. She had only two or three minutes to live. As we walked away, a weirded-out grunt pulled her pants down and forced a pop-up flare into her vagina and gave it a kick. Her abdomen instantly swelled, and her whole stomach burst open like a volcano with fire and smoke gushing out. God, was there no limit?

The grunts moved in and brought out the weapons, ammo, and documents; then the whole bunker complex was blown with massive charges of C-4. All that beautiful silk gone. The whole thing made me feel strangely sad inside.

*

Scout Snipers
Arizona–Da Nang
September 13, 1969

Dear Mom,

Well, they did it to me again. They sent me back to Arizona on the first. We were out there till yesterday and they pulled Ron and I into Da Nang to go to school again. I told my squad leader before they sent us out this last time that he'd be sorry if he didn't get me into school so I could get a few days rest. Well, he finally did. Ron and I are going to be here for six days.

Ron is my new partner and I like him better than any of the partners I've had so far. I hope nothing happens to mess us up.

I haven't had any mail since we left An Hoa twelve days ago, so I don't have any idea what's been going on at home. There's really not a whole lot to say. Arizona was the same except we had the monsoons, too. They finally came, and believe me it rains like nothing you ever saw.

During the cease fire for Ho Chi Minh's death, the gooks let up a little, but we didn't, which I was glad to see. Like I said, things were pretty much the same the last couple weeks as before. I'm hoping for a better assignment next time out.

These guys in Da Nang have got it made. There's recreation centers and PXs all over the place. I plan on using the EM clubs, too.

Oh, yeah, remember Walters who hung around with Posey and I back in the World? He's here at school, too. I was sure glad to see him. He had already heard about Posey. Walters is a sniper for the 7th Marines and he ran into Dave Young a few days ago. I wish I could be as fortunate. From what I hear, O'Grady's unit is about fifteen miles from here.

Mom, I'm going to close for now. I'll write soon. Take care.

Love, Joseph

On September 1st I picked up a new partner, Ron Feekes, and choppered to Hotel Company in Arizona. The monsoons were starting, and we spent most of our spare time cleaning our rifles to keep them from rusting. It was a struggle to keep personal gear dry.

Arizona was starting to affect me, and my nerves were getting thin. I started having nightmares, when I was able to sleep at all. Fortunately Ron was a rather naive, jolly guy, and I was able to draw strength from him.

The second night out we took at least three hundred incoming mortars. There were times when it was better to dig in and times when it was better not to. I had misread that night completely. In the pitch black, Ron and I dove into the nearest hole and found no bottom. As we slid downward, the first flares began to light up the area, and we realized we were in a very big bomb crater. I shouted at Ron that we had to get out of it, but we had trouble getting up the muddy sides of the hole. We clawed frantically to the top, and as we rolled over the edge, a mortar landed in the crater and went off, followed by a second one. When a mortar goes off in a crater, it peppers every bit of the walls. We had cleared that crater by a split second. We lay flat until the incoming let up. I had cheated death so many times, I felt like an old tomcat who had lost track of which of his nine lives he was on. Ron had handled the whole thing well. He would make a good team leader.

The following day we left base camp with a light platoon (twenty to thirty men) for a routine patrol. The monsoons had hampered our night and early morning visibility, so we were •mainly restricted to daylight patrols.

It had rained the day before, and it was particularly hot and humid. We had a long, uneventful patrol and were about three clicks from the company on our return when the lieutenant called a ten-minute rest break on a small knoll, thirty yards in diameter. I hadn't even found a spot to sit, when a grunt tripped a booby-trapped mortar round. His right leg was gone below the knee and his left leg was attached only by some skin and tendons. He took shrapnel in the groin, arms, and chin. I'd seen men with less severe wounds die, but he was fighting to stay alive. There was no shade, and the best thing we could come up with was my bush hat a grunt used to keep the sun out of the wounded man's eyes.

The lieutenant rushed up to me with a tired, pained look on his face. A medevac was coming, but enemy movement had been spotted a thousand yards away, heading in a direction that would cut us off from the company.

"Can you pin them down long enough to get the chopper in and out?" he asked.

"Hell, yes," I replied, knowing full well there wasn't a decent firing point and I would have to shoot standing up. To hit a moving target at one thousand yards is tough enough in the prone position, but standing?

Ron was watching through the binoculars and estimated about a platoon size unit moving in and out of a broken tree line at least one thousand yards away.

"Where are you going to shoot from?" he asked.

"You," I said. I had him cover his ears and stand as still as he could while I rested the bolt rifle on his right shoulder. I had the scope set for one thousand yards, corrected up and missed. I corrected up more and hit one. I had their range and pegged a machine gunner before they all took cover. When they tried to move again, I hit a man carrying a mortar tube. I had succeeded in splitting their unit, and they were trying to re-group.

Four more tried to move, and I dropped them. A few green tracers came our way and fell short. They were desperate to get out of the position they were in, but I swore they weren't going anywhere. After firing fifteen rounds with the bolt rifle, heat waves coming from the barrel made looking through the scope like looking through a glass of water. I don't know how Ron stood it, the muzzle was inches from his head. He must have felt every shot like a hammer blow.

Then someone yelled, "The chopper's coming!"

While the medevac came in, I fired the last few rounds, looking over the top of the scope completely because heat waves had made it useless. As soon as the medevac cleared, our own mortars and heavy artillery started, and I flopped down, wiped the sweat from my eyes and picked up shell casings. Ron was walking in a small circle, shaking his head, trying to throw off the shock of what I'd just put him through.

The lieutenant came up, handed me my bush hat, and said, "Thanks."

"For what?" I asked. He told me the chopper didn't take a single round of enemy fire.

"Is he still alive?" I asked.

"Yes. Give me your kill sheets, I'll sign them now. Third

Platoon is on its way to join us, and we'll check out that tree line.''

When we did check out the tree line, out of seventeen bodies, I found six that I knew I'd hit. The rest were blown apart by artillery. Charlie had just lost half of a platoon, yet as I filled out kill sheets, I couldn't push the sight of the mangled Marine out of my mind. It struck me that I had walked through that same spot and so had Ron and several other guys. Yet that particular man tripped the booby trap. Why?

On the night of the sixth, after a three-day slowdown by the enemy for Ho Chi Minh's death, we were hit hard. Within minutes of the first contact red flares were going off everywhere; we'd been overrun. I can't think of a more frightening situation than having enemy troops running free inside the perimeter, especially at night. Wherever a guy was at the time, he had better stay put. Standard procedure was to shoot anything that moved, whether it turned out to be a gook or a panicked Marine.

Ron and I sat in our foxhole, back-to-back, scanning in our side-to-side pattern, trying to make sense out of the total confusion around us. M-16s and mortars were going off everywhere inside the perimeter. Two massive explosions rocked us. One was so close that the ground around us seemed to twist and slammed us against the sides of the foxhole. A sapper had managed to throw his satchel charge less than ten feet from us. We were stunned. I had the sling on the bolt rifle wrapped around my arm. Instead of popping out of the hole, the rifle flew backward and its barrel hit me in the face. I didn't know my nose was bleeding. My head was spinning, and the next few minutes were a haze. Ron was in the same shape. He and I couldn't actually hear each other, but talked nonsensically in an attempt to prove we were still alive.

We didn't start to come out of it until incoming illumination rounds lit up the area like daylight. The company had barely held together. The noise of artillery strikes around the perimeter and the light from flares didn't keep Ron and I from falling into a deep sleep. We needed it to throw off the effects of the shell shock. Early morning of the seventh, I awoke to find us and our gear covered with dirt. It was a struggle to get up, every bone in my body hurt. I awakened Ron and asked him if he was okay.

"What?" he asked.

I spoke louder. "Are you okay?"

"Yeah, except for my ears." I knew what he meant; my ears were ringing something terrible.

"I'll go tell the skipper we're in no shape for a patrol today." I knocked some of the dust off with my bush hat and set out to find the company commander.

I hadn't gone far, when I came upon the body of a Marine. He had tried to move during the attack, and it looked like he had been crawling on all fours when a grenade went off between his chest and the ground. No one had even bothered to cover him. The rest of his fire team was sitting nearby, each man silently staring at nothing. They had just lost a brother and the anguish was clearly visible on their faces. I am not sure why, but the thought flashed through my mind that it was probably one of their own grenades that had killed him.

"Where's his gear?" I asked in an unintentionally loud voice. One of the men pointed to a pack nearby. I opened it, took out the poncho, and covered his body. I walked on, not wanting to see those tormented faces again.

I found the skipper bent over a map talking to the gunny and a lieutenant. When he looked up at me, it was obvious how tired he was. Before I could say anything, he seemed to mumble something to me, but he wasn't mumbling. I just couldn't hear him. I shook my head and pointed at my ears. He spoke louder.

"No patrols today!" I nodded and turned to leave, when I realized my face was covered with dry blood from the rifle hitting me in the nose. I walked around the inside of the perimeter and found everyone to be depressed. I came upon the remains of a sapper whose charge had gone off while still strapped to him. Only half a foot and what looked to be a piece of leg were left. That accounted for the first big explosion. I continued on and found one other sapper inside the perimeter. He had been shot before he could use his charge. There were seven dead NVA just outside the perimeter. Except for the five-foot-deep crater by our foxhole, that was it.

Suddenly the implications were clear to me. The sapper that had come so close to Ron and me had passed all the way through the company perimeter, into the command post, and back out. Since we only had one dead Marine, and the rest of the enemy bodies were outside the perimeter, it could only mean one thing: A fire team had failed to man its position. I thought back to that dead grunt and the rest of his fire team, the look on their faces was carved in my mind forever.

Ron and I rested the day of the seventh while our hearing slowly returned. It wasn't hard to see that the company was demoralized, and if for no other reason than to prevent a repeat of the night before, we would help man lines, our way. I would relieve the command post radioman, and Ron would move from foxhole to foxhole with the Starlite scope on the M-14. It would mean a long night, with Ron cautiously moving between each fire team, careful to identify himself at each one so as not to be mistaken for a sapper. Whether he saw an enemy or not was secondary. The presence of a night scope at each hole, even for a short time, would be reassuring to the men, and we would know they were staying awake. Ron would survey the area and report to me. I would always know where he was if something happened.

We needed a series of code words to pass to everyone on lines, I didn't want Ron getting shot by a jumpy grunt. We decided on "Sniper," the proper response being, "Sniper what?" Ron would then say, "Sniper up." He would have to go through this procedure at the thirty or so foxholes that ringed the company. I took the idea to the skipper, and before I had finished talking, he sent for the lieutenants to be sure there would be no confusion as to what we would be doing. The grunts were nervous, and a minor mistake could get Ron killed.

The night air was suffocating. The mosquitoes were so thick, repellent did no good. If I took a deep breath, I would suck several down my throat. I had my collar up and my sleeves rolled all the way down to afford some protection from the little pests. I sat monitoring the coded clicks for listening posts and the muffled chatter of a company set in for the night. Ron was working his way around the perimeter as planned. The eighth was my twentieth birthday and it looked like it was going to arrive uneventfully. Shortly after 1:00 A.M. I got my birthday present—the sound of incoming artillery followed by a brilliant explosion behind me. One of our own 155mm white-phosphorous rounds had hit dead center of the command post. Someone had made an improper "on call" (a set of numbers instead of full coordinates) and given the gun crew the company coordinates instead of a location outside the perimeter. The gun crew hadn't made a mistake, they were right on target for the information they were given. I ripped off my shirt as burning phosphorous landed on my collar and sleeve. Several men were rolling out of foxholes, tearing off different parts of their clothing. Amazingly, only one man was burned badly enough to be medevaced, and with a chopper coming, I didn't want Ron on the lines. I called him in.

I had blisters on the back of my neck and right forearm, and if I could keep them from getting infected, the corpsman could treat me in the bush. As the doc applied burn salve and bandages, the last bit of confidence I had in the company disappeared. It had too many unseasoned people, and I had doubts about the command.

Not all companies were tight like Alpha, Delta, or Charlie. When assigned to a questionable company, it was the team leader's decision whether to stay with it or not. It meant a lance corporal or corporal bucking heads with a captain and was no small matter. The situation had to warrant the action, and it had to be done properly.

Ron and I talked it over and figured they hadn't managed to get us killed up to then, so we'd hook it out a little longer. We would have to watch out for our fellow Marines as much as the enemy, maybe more so.

On the morning of the eleventh, we were out with a platoon and had just entered a perfect area for an ambush. When it came, it was from a tree line to our right front. I was ten paces behind the lieutenant, as I dove toward the direction of fire. I landed wrong, and it felt like I had broken a rib, as I started to crawl to the next rice-paddy dike. Three RPGs passed overhead. One hit and exploded twenty feet away. I had to get to that dike. I looked back to see Ron and a corpsman taking cover behind a small pagoda. My attention snapped forward again when the lieutenant yelled, "Firing the LAW!" Like a bazooka, the LAW had a backblast that could be fatal at forty feet. He was "boot louie" (new to rank with little combat experience) and had skipped a step in the procedure for firing the LAW—he hadn't looked behind him to be sure a man wasn't in the danger zone. I was that man behind him.

He already had the tube extended and the clear plastic sight flipped up, which exposes the trigger and arms the LAW. I was only fifteen feet away when I shouted, "Wait!" I made a crawling turn to the right, but I knew I wasn't going to make it. He pushed the trigger, and the backblast caught me from my knees down. My pant legs were shredded, my boot tops melted, and the force of the blast turned me back toward the dike I had been heading to in the first place. Except for a slight flash burn on my left calf, I wasn't hurt, but I was damned mad.

When I reached the dike, the firefight was nearly over, and I discovered the source of my original pain. I had landed on the bolt rifle hard enough to knock the scope out of line and bruise some ribs. I was about to have a serious confrontation with an officer. We were still taking some light small-arms fire when I stormed up to him shouting, "You asshole, what were you trying to do, blow my fucking head off?" He said something about insubordination, and I was ready to hit him with a rifle butt, when Ron intervened. He pulled me a step to the side and in a loud, clear voice said, "I had him in my sights, and if that back blast had hit you wrong, I would have shot him." I looked back at the lieutenant, and after overhearing Ron, a pale, sick look had come over his face. He wasn't a boot louie anymore.

Ron and I walked away discussing what we would have to do to get away from the company alive. We sat down a short distance away as the platoon regrouped. I cut what was left of my trousers off at the knees with a knife and repaired a melted boot lace while we talked. I had a plan. I had knocked the scope out of line, something Ron and I could correct when we got back to the company, but a bolt rifle is a delicate instrument, and if the mount was the slightest bit damaged, the scope itself wouldn't hold a setting. We would have no choice but to take it to the armory at An Hoa, and once there I could get us a different assignment. We could avoid a confrontation altogether. I hadn't ditched a company before, and I wanted to be careful.

When we returned to the company, I told the captain I would be firing from a certain sector to redope my rifle. After three rounds, we had the rifle resighted, but I fired a few more shots to make it look good. I went back to the skipper and told him I had a little trouble redoping and couldn't be sure if the mount was damaged until I used it again. I didn't know at the time that I wouldn't need such an elaborate scheme.

Early the next morning the company moved. About an hour out we halted on a plateau overlooking a small village seven hundred yards below. Ron and I had looked it over pretty well with the scope and binoculars and figured it to be a friendly village. To my knowledge no one else saw anything to indicate otherwise, which made the following events all the more sinister.

The captain had decided to call in air strikes, and before long, two Phantoms dropped full loads of napalm, which en-

gulfed the village in one huge ball of fire. Then came a call for
"Snipers up." The captain was pointing at a figure running
straight toward the company.

"Shoot," he said. I didn't need to look through the scope to
see it was a young woman carrying a small child. I wondered
if I was missing something. I looked through the rifle scope and
confirmed that it was a woman about twenty years old with an
infant clutched tight in both arms, running from the inferno that
moments before was her home. I was amazed that she had
survived the air strike.

"It's a woman and a kid," I told him.

"Shoot," he said, more insistently.

I looked into his eyes and saw he meant it. My frustration
with the company and him was just too much. I stuck the rifle
in front of his face. "If you want 'em dead, you shoot 'em."

"That's a direct order, Marine!" Without comment, I turned
to Ron and told him to get ready to catch the next bird out. We
walked to a spot which would separate us from the company
while the captain swore and carried on about a court martial,
the brig and such.

Officially, Ron and I were no longer attached to the company, and as we sat waiting for a supply chopper, we were
quite prepared to shoot anyone who tried to stop us. An hour
later the chopper landed, and we were running to board it,
when we met our squad leader getting off. He asked where we
were going at the same time we were asking him what he was
doing there.

We talked as we hurried to board the chopper. Helicopters
didn't stay long in Arizona. Dave Meeks had come out to tell
Ron and me that we were going to sniper school in Da Nang.
As we took off, I told him what had happened. He just nodded.

As soon as we landed, I went to the skipper, and he listened
quietly to my story. When I'd finished, he leaned forward, and
a sly grin creased his lips. "Fuck em; they'll never get another
sniper team." And they didn't.

That night I had the first in a series of frequent nightmares
that dogged me the rest of my tour. I dreamed that a sapper had
slipped into the perimeter during the dead of night and was
choking me with a garrote. Each time the dream was the same,
and each time I awoke in a cold sweat, my heart beating
wildly.

When Ron and I went to Da Nang to requalify, winning the
first-place lighter wasn't on my mind. I had to get out of the

bush for a while, and Ron was already showing signs of battle fatigue.

I'd come to know Da Nang pretty well, and between sessions at the range, we were going to raise some hell. I knew the only place on the lines where a guy could slip out to the local whorehouse and get back in without being shot. We could go to the air base and get the best chow in the US military.

There was also Freedom Hill with its huge PX. Only staff sergeants and above were allowed to buy hard liquor there, but if a bush-weary lance corporal stood by the main doors, a "staffer," a gunny, or someone else of sufficient rank would eventually stop and ask what he wanted. I was pulling this routine our second day at school when a major came up to me and asked what I wanted. Big brass just didn't do that. I was concerned it might be a trick.

"Uh, vodka, sir?" I stammered as I reached in my pocket for some money.

"Ah, keep your money," he said and pushed the door open. The major returned shortly and handed me a sack with two quarts of one hundred proof vodka. "Stay out of trouble, Marine," he said and walked away. He had given me enough booze to get all six snipers in the school drunk that night.

By a one in a million chance, Walters was in for school at the same time. Dear Walters. Oh, the stunts he, Posey, and I pulled back in the World. We were as tight as any three people could be. Only six months in-country, and already one of us had been badly wounded. When we spoke of Posey it was always about the crazy things we did together in the States. Neither of us dared to say it, but we knew with each passing day the chances increased that one or both of us would be killed or wounded before our tour was over.

If anyone had a worse temper than I, it was Walters. A couple nights before school was over we got drunked up at the EM club. On the way back to our tents, for some unknown reason he walked through a tent full of grunts. Something was said and a fight broke out. The next morning Walters went up for office hours (a preliminary hearing before High Mast which could lead to a court martial). Each sniper was called into the range commander's office and questioned about the incident.

Since one of the grunts was black, there was concern that it was racially motivated. I knew Bruce better than anyone and was called in first. The major in charge of the range knew snipers were hard to control, but the grunts were pissed, and he had to at least go through the motions. He asked me what I knew about it.

"Well, sir, I wasn't actually in the tent so I can't really say for sure."

"Was it because one of them is a Negro?" he asked.

"I have no idea, sir." The major knew he was getting nowhere, but he had one last question to ask as he leaned back in his chair.

"Tell me, Lance Corporal Ward, what do you think happened?"

"Major, I've known Walters a long time, and if he hits someone, then the guy probably deserves it." With that I was dismissed, and the next sniper was called in. He got the same story from all of us. "Stay tight and survive" was our motto. The whole thing was eventually dropped.

We finished requalifying, and when it was time for each of us to go back to our units, Walters and I cried and hugged good-bye. Ten years would pass before we would see each other again.

*

Scout Snipers
An Hoa, Charlie Company
September 21, 1969

Dear Mom,

Got quite a bit to catch up on so, here goes. Finally saw Mike O'Grady. It took a lot of walking and thumbing from Da Nang, but I got there. Mike is closer to An Hoa than he is to Da Nang. When we got there we spent the night and sure had a good time. He's doing fine, so you can pass that on to his mom and dad. I hated to leave the next day, but we had to get on back.

Ron and I got to An Hoa on the afternoon of the 19th, and I was glad to see those packages. I can't believe my birthday cake came through in perfect shape. We kind of had a late birthday party with cake and gifts. Everyone was anxious for me to open my packages, and it didn't take long for the guys to eat most of the goodies. I kept all the socks, foot powder, film, and as much stuff to eat as I could get in my pack. Since the monsoons are here, the foot powder and socks are precious items. Thanks for everything, it was great!

I sure must have been messed up the last time I wrote from

An Hoa after leaving Arizona. I thought I had already told you that Dave Meeks caught malaria and the next partner I got was Dave Suttles and he's the one that got wounded. Dave Meeks is back here and is my acting squad leader from time to time. Dave Suttles is doing okay and may come back to An Hoa on medical profile.

Right now I'm back in the bush and I'm with C Company 1/5, and we're about ten miles from An Hoa, not too far from Liberty Bridge. I've got my bolt rifle and two new partners, both of them got in-country about three weeks ago, but they're fast learners.

So Dave Young got his second Purple Heart, huh? If he gets another one, they'll send him home no matter how slight it is. I hear they may pull out the 3d Marine Division and Nick will probably be going with them. I'm almost through my sixth month and after the middle of next month it'll be downhill. Seems like a long time.

I've got another roll of film ready. It's got some flicks of Mike and my birthday cake on it.

Well, Mom, if I hurry, I can get this on the next bird. Take care and tell all hi. Thanks again for everything.

Love, Joseph

When Ron and I left Da Nang, instead of taking the first available chopper as our orders stated, I dragged Ron off on one of my excursions. I found out that Mike O'Grady was working supply at a fire base called Hill 37, several miles off the road to An Hoa. The next scheduled chopper to Hill 37 wasn't until late in the afternoon. I knew I wouldn't have much time with him, but if we hitched, we could be there well before noon. We would be a day late getting back to An Hoa, and I knew what the gunny would say. "Late again, huh, Ward?"

"Gee, gunny, I had trouble catching a bird."

Then his reply would be, "Yeah, sure. Go check in with your squad leader, I'm sure he has an assignment for you."

The first ride we caught was with two Korean Marines in a jeep. We hesitated a moment as I thought back to what that grunt had told me, "Don't fuck with the ROKs." The passenger was a captain, so I figured it was probably safe. When he curtly nodded toward the rear of the jeep we hopped in. Ron leaned over and with a big grin said, "Maybe they haven't had breakfast yet and we're it." As we rode the few miles to our turn off, I watched them in fascination. They seemed starched in place, heads erect and eyes forward. Their uniforms were immaculate. Class act, I thought as we got out at our stop. We thanked them, and the captain bowed briskly, then it was eyes forward again, and they were off. I was beginning to like and respect the ROKs. We walked a couple miles before a sky pilot (chaplain) picked us up and took us the rest of the way.

It wasn't hard to find Mike; Hill 37 wasn't all that big. He couldn't believe I was there. It was great to see a face from home and to know for sure that two of the four of us were still alive. Working in supply meant Mike was able to come up with a bottle of Scotch, and we sat down and proceeded to put the war out of our minds for at least one night. Our conversation went back to before the war, high school, and the truly bizarre things we did. The time passed much too quickly.

The next morning, Ron and I had to catch the first chopper to An Hoa. While we made ready to board, Mike disappeared and came running back with two bottles of Scotch. "Here, take these with you." I looked back as we walked to the LZ. He just stood there; his smile betrayed a hint of sadness. I waved, and we ran to our chopper.

We landed at An Hoa, and I went to report in to the gunny. I handed him our orders and he said, "Late again, huh, Ward?"

"Gee, Gunny, I had trouble catching a bird."

"Yeah, sure. Go check in with your squad leader, I'm sure he has an assignment for you."

When I got to my tent, my cot was piled high with packages. My birthday! I'd forgotten. It had been thirteen days since my surprise gift in Arizona. It didn't take long for the word to spread, and pretty soon every sniper in the rear was in my tent. Some of the guys were looking at me funny. I think they had been eyeing those packages for several days, waiting for me to get back. Hmm, this is serious, I thought as I separated out the packages I wanted to open myself.

Chaos reigned as I put the rest on the table. I had to shout over the noise of people tearing open boxes, "The socks, foot powder, and film come to me." While I opened the packages and read cards, I was pelted with socks, film, and an occasional can of foot powder. The gunny stopped by for a piece of cake, and I gave him one to take to the skipper. It wasn't *my* birthday celebration, it was everybody's.

The day Dave Meeks came down with malaria, I had never seen anyone get sick so fast. We were at Hill 65 in late Sep-

tember, manning one of two towers. This one was on a high
point, in a somewhat isolated part of the base. It was different
from the regular tower in that it had a .50 caliber machine gun
with a scope mounted on top, accurate to 3,000 yards. Snipers
sometimes manned this tower during the day and the main
tower at night with an M-14 and the Big Eye. We mainly
used the .50 caliber to keep people and boats as far away
from that sector as possible. It fired high explosive rounds,
and I'd just sunk an empty sampan on the river two thousand
yards out, when the gun jammed. A round slammed against
the side of the chamber, and as I unjammed it, thankful the
round hadn't gone off, I forgot about Dave sitting behind me.
I fired a few rounds to make sure the gun was working okay
and turned to say something to Dave, when he slumped into
my arms. He was fine when we came out, but in just a few
minutes he'd turned yellow and was so weak I had to help
him down from the tower. We'd both seen enough cases of
malaria to know he needed immediate medical attention. I
asked him if he could make the hundred-yard walk to sick
bay. He said he could, and I watched skeptically as he staggered away.

I used the field phone in the tower to call for a replacement ASAP. The only other sniper at the hill came to relieve me fifteen minutes later, and I rushed to sick bay. It
couldn't have been more than twenty-five minutes from the
time the gun jammed until I reached sick bay, where I found
Dave in a staging area for emergency medevac to the Da Nang
hospital.

His temperature was already 106 degrees and I couldn't
believe what they were doing to him. He was stark naked and
lying on a rubber sheet that circulated ice water through tubes.
He had been packed with ice, especially his groin and arm pits.
There was an IV in each arm, and to top it all off, a big fan was
blowing full blast across him. Every fiber of his being was
shaking from the cold. I knew he was burning up inside, and
if not brought under control, his temperature would keep going
up until he had brain damage or died. His teeth were chattering
so hard he couldn't talk. The only thing I understood him to say
was, "My gear." I was afraid he would break a tooth or bite
off his tongue. I grabbed a wet washcloth and stuck it in his
mouth. He bit down like a vise and shook his head, grateful for
even that little bit of relief. The chopper landed, and he was
whisked away. I gathered up his gear and walked back to our

tent, thinking every step of the way, Sweet Jesus don't let me get malaria.

By the time I heard Dave Young had been wounded for the second time, I had very serious doubts that all four of us would make it back alive.

★

Scout Snipers
Hill near Arizona
September 25, 1969

Dear Mom,

Got four letters from you yesterday. Sure did welcome them. It's been days since we had mail.

Yes, it does get chilly with the monsoons. Actually it doesn't get that cold, maybe 40 or 50 degrees, but that's cold when you're used to 120 plus. It hasn't rained the last couple days. I don't think it will stay that way long. We're expecting seventeen more inches of rain by the end of the month.

We're set up on a hill just across from Arizona, and we should be here a few more days. So far we've only made contact a few times since we came out to this company. This is a pretty good outfit, we've just been mostly going out on two-man scout-and-wait jobs like I like to do.

I heard on the radio the temperature at home was 50 degrees. Guess winter is almost there. We've got a joke around here about whether it's going to snow or not. The gooks would really be in trouble if it snowed about three feet.

I don't think anything Nixon does is going to stop this war. The only thing they're accomplishing by pulling troops out is making it harder on the ones that have to stay, prolonging the war. There's no way to win this war the way they're trying to do it now. To tell the truth, I don't see how morale stays as high as it does. I've sure grown to respect the guys I'm in the bush with.

Yes, they're short on snipers. We can't keep a team out with everyone, so we switch around a lot. It's nice to be wanted, huh?

Did we go to the EM club while in Da Nang? You know me better than to ask that. The chance doesn't come very often here.

As of today, I've got 220 days. Before long I'll have to start thinking about getting short. Tell Laura to hang on, I'll be there before she knows it. As for you, Mom, take it easy. Don't worry too much cuz I'm getting along much better than I was. Take care.

Love, Joseph

Ron and I pulled an assignment just before leaving An Hoa to hook up with Charlie Company. It was a hunter-kill with a twist. It wasn't one we planned and carried out on our own. It didn't come down from HQ, either, but from information Lee Oot had gathered. He'd heard about an NVA captain who had developed a bad habit of repeatedly going into the village of Giang Hoa, about 13 clicks north of An Hoa, to visit a lady friend.

Preassigned hunter-kills were the most dangerous and taxing jobs snipers had to deal with, and during my tour, I participated in approximately twenty-five of these operations, none of which were ever more than seventy-two hours long. Taking a radio only slowed us down and made moving silently more difficult. Once out, we knew we were on our own. Preparations for a hunter-kill such as this one, my twelfth, were extremely intricate. We went over the tactical maps repeatedly and saw two obstacles. The most dangerous was making a thirteen click movement without detection. The other was crossing the Thu Bon River without knowing how deep it was.

At 3:00 A.M. of the 22d, Ron and I were making ready to move out at first light. As usual, we donned camouflage, triple checked our equipment, and went through a last-minute rundown of procedures, but something about this particular hunter-kill had us both on edge. We finally attributed it to the long daylight movement and river crossing.

At 0500 we moved out and were half a click past An Hoa village when the sun peeked over the horizon. During the day, we had to continuously reroute our path to avoid contact with the farmers and civilians we encountered. To be spotted by anyone meant scrubbing the mission.

Less than an hour before sunset we reached the river. Ron crossed ahead of me, constantly probing the bottom to keep both of us from stepping into a hole. It was crucial that I not fall and get the scope wet.

It was almost dark when we reached the opposite bank, where we set in for the night. We removed our fatigues, laid them out to dry, wrapped up in ponchos, and took turns sleeping and keeping watch. We were cold and tired.

Before dawn we were on our way again, moving at a snail's

pace in the darkness to avoid booby traps. The sun was up as we neared the area of our planned firing point. We had to crawl the last five hundred yards and camouflage into our firing point eight hundred yards from the trail. We soon discovered the trail supposedly used by the captain was a heavily traveled path. We were going to be kept very busy separating our target from the villagers. It was not an ideal situation.

The trail, which led from a bushy knoll where the captain normally came from to the village, was over a mile long. The surrounding area was flat and exposed. Giang Hoa was a village of about 100 to 300 people. The buildings were all thatched huts, surrounded by patches of thick trees and knee-high grass.

My job was to watch the knoll and wait for him to appear, if he did. Hell, as far as I knew he may have changed his routine and wouldn't show up that day at all. Ron's task was to cover the area from the target point to the village.

Soon villagers began to use the trail. Old men pulled carts of fresh vegetables, women carried baskets of rice balanced by poles on their shoulders, and several people rode bicycles. Ron looked at me and in frustration said, "Damn, Ward, it looks like a freeway down there!"

"Yeah, and it's almost ten o'clock already. We can't give the guy much longer before calling it off. You know, I think he's waiting until he can blend in with the villagers," I replied. Ron nodded in agreement.

With the morning sun came the heat and humidity. Soon a swarm of gnats descended on us like a shimmering cloud. Our situation was deteriorating rapidly. We both had to roll over and piss lying down. The smell of urine was as irritating as the gnats. It wasn't unheard of for a sniper with diarrhea to crap while in position. We had to tolerate the smells and insects. Moving would give away our position. As we wiped the sweat from our necks and faces, a solid black mass of smashed gnats covered our palms. We just looked at each other and shook our heads.

"Noon, Ron, we give him till noon. If he hasn't shown up by then, we book."

"Good fucking idea, man."

At 10:40 a man cautiously emerged from the knoll, paused briefly to look around, and began walking toward the village. He was dressed in civilian clothes, but his actions were strained. Even at 1,200 yards away, I sensed he was nervous. The field glasses were more powerful than the scope, and when

Ron looked at him, all he said was, "Fuckin' A. It's gotta be him. He matches the description, and I can see part of a holster sticking out from under the bottom of his shirt."

That familiar feeling of nervous anticipation came and went. I wiped the sweat from my eyes and watched as he shuffled closer to the kill zone. Questions raced through my mind. Why would a man of his rank persistently maintain such a dangerous routine as going to the same village time and time again? Why did he go during the day? Was he more afraid of a night ambush or more at ease in his attempt to blend in with the peasants? Then a frightening thought interrupted my speculation. What if the guy wasn't an officer at all, just a "snufflie," an expendable man rumored to be a captain? Charlie would certainly trade the life of one low rank to flush out a couple snipers. I quickly dismissed the idea as too gruesome to contemplate and focused on the job at hand.

At nine hundred yards I slowly began to put pressure on the trigger. At eight hundred yards I squeezed off my shot. The bullet hit him in the chest with enough force to lift him up and backward several feet. The people on the trail scattered like chaff in a breeze. We waited for twenty minutes. I watched the body lying on the trail, while Ron surveyed the area for a hint of anything out of the ordinary. Then we made our move. Stiff and sore from lying in position so long, we wiggled out from under the leaves and twigs that were our cover. If it was a trap, we would soon find out as we worked our way toward the motionless figure on the trail. When we reached the body, I did the search while Ron kept watch. It was obvious the man was well fed and groomed. Before I had put the bullet through his heart, he was very healthy. I checked the clothing for documents and found nothing. I paused briefly, wondering about the woman in Giang Hoa, waiting for a man who would never arrive.

"Captain Lovelorn," I mumbled.

"What?"

"Nothing, Ron. Just talking to myself." When I removed the pistol from his belt and saw the red star carved into the handle, my sentimentality faded away. I put one of my own match rounds on his chest and stuck the pistol in a thigh pocket.

"I'm finished. Let's get!"

We moved at a slow, steady jog for over a click, before stopping to rest. I filled out a kill sheet with few details. Re-crossing the Thu Bon River in the daylight helped make the

trek back much easier. We sauntered into An Hoa completely
exhausted and more than a little filthy. I went straight to Fergie's tent and laid the kill sheet on his desk. He just nodded.
Neither of us said a word. I went to my tent and fell asleep
while cleaning my rifle.

If nature ever played a trick on the Earth, it was giving it the
monsoon rains. Rain doesn't exactly describe it; deluge is more
fitting. We would often grab a bar of soap, strip to the buff, and
take a shower during a downpour. It was late September and
already everyone complained about not being able to stay dry.
Monsoon season had just begun.

Late September also found Ron Feekes and me attached to
Echo Company 1/5. Everyone was intently watching the middle of Arizona Territory. An ambush had been sprung, only it
was no ordinary ambush. We watched and listened in helpless
rage as a battalion of Marines was mauled by a regiment of
NVA. Because of the intense air and artillery strikes the Marines had called in, it would have been suicide for us or any
other unit to get to the trapped Marines. Any pause long enough
to allow us to reach them would have also allowed the NVA
time to overrun them. The Marines had to get out of the trap
themselves and were outnumbered five to one. We witnessed a
desperate struggle between 3,000 men go on all day long.

The trapped battalion was getting artillery support from every fire base within range. Hundreds of artillery rounds hit
enemy positions. Then there was a brief lull in the shelling.
Almost immediately, several jets went in and dropped napalm
and one-thousand-pound bombs. As soon as the planes cleared
the area, the artillery barrage began again. By noon, the smoke
and dust from thousands of artillery rounds and bombs hung
ominously over most of Arizona, as though the thin haze could
hide the killing ground beneath.

We listened intently over the radio, hour after hour, to the
largest sustained battle we had seen. Late in the afternoon, the
enemy began to buckle under the pressure of artillery and air
attacks that took a backseat to no other war.

Our accepted formula for casualties was three or four men
wounded for each death. Although we couldn't keep track of
the number wounded, the final death toll gave us a pretty good
idea. Fifty-three Marines were dead, including the battalion
commander, which equated to an entire company of casualties
total. Estimates of enemy dead and wounded ranged from sev-

eral hundred to over two thousand. When the difference in the size of the two units was considered, neither side really won the battle. There were more well-trained, well-equipped and experienced NVA arriving in Arizona all the time.

Snipers were an elite unit. We had gone that extra mile in training, from boot camp to sniper school, but there were so few of us. Besides the captain, gunny, sergeant, staff sergeant, and two or three central squad leaders, there was seldom over twenty field snipers or ten two-man teams covering the entire regiment.

Statistics on the numbers of scout snipers that served during the Vietnam War are hard to come by. There were a maximum of ten sniper platoons, with one platoon assigned to each of the following units: 1st and 3rd Reconnaissance Battalions, the 1st, 3d, 4th, 5th, 7th, 9th, 26th and 27th Marine regiments, which equates to ten officers and approximately 340 field snipers.

Snipers with the 5th Regiment manned towers and lines for three major fire bases, as well as An Hoa and Liberty Bridge. Teams rotated through every company in the regiment, from Alpha to Zulu, worked with the local militia, and still managed to pull off the specialized assignments headquarters occasionally came up with.

Black, white, brown, and red, we came from all parts of the United States, yet our unique bond made us like one person. Our sergeant was a Filipino, whose accent made it nearly impossible to understand him when he got mad.

There was, of course, Chuck Mawhinney, my first and only team leader, and the legacy he left behind. Chuck, to my knowledge was probably responsible for more confirmed enemy dead (101) than any other single American during the entire war, one shot at a time.

We also had something unique, complete "free fire" in the bush. Snipers could shoot, anytime without clearance. We were the only ones permitted to fire without penalties from inside a perimeter over the heads of fellow Marines. A majority of the time, unless under fire, Marines had to get clearance from regimental command to return fire, and the time delay could be several minutes. Since we were part of regimental command, we had the authority to initiate engagement with the enemy. Needless to say, a lot of people wanted snipers, and we always seemed to be on a chopper or truck going from one assignment to another.

If someone requested us for a job that the skipper felt was unsuitable, as long as it wasn't from regimental HQ, all he had to do was say, "Sorry, all the teams are out right now," which was usually right. If the request did come from HQ, then the skipper was obliged to pull a team for the job.

Since we were scouts as well as snipers, we were expected to have a sixth sense of some kind. If a company set in for the night and we started digging a foxhole, pretty soon the whole company would be breaking out shovels. The grunts would say, "If the snipers dig in, everyone digs in." We were trained to be more aware of our surroundings, and after a day of looking for minute signs of enemy troops or sifting through the spartan remains of an abandoned enemy camp, we did get a reasonable idea of what might happen in the next few hours. Sometimes it was just a gut feeling.

I once figured out what I was getting paid for it all. Including hazardous duty pay and combat pay, I was earning 43 cents per hour.

★

Scout Snipers
An Hoa
October 11, 1969

Dear Mom,

I got a letter from you yesterday. As usual, I'm slow writing. When they send me back to the bush, I don't know whether I'll take writing gear, all I had got ruined last time. No matter what we do to prevent it, it gets wet anyway. I can see right now that the next three months are going to be miserable.

Yes, I've heard about R and R, and I didn't get it this month. I'm down again for it next month, still trying to go to Australia. We only get six days, and you're right, it isn't very long. The thing that makes me mad is that the guys in the bush who really need it have to fight to get one, while some of the guys in the rear can manage to get two or three.

Just got in from Arizona again and the weather hasn't slowed things down there at all. If anything, it's worse because it's one area that the monsoons don't completely flood.

Your snow storm seems like heaven to me. They always tell what the weather is in certain states and home is one.

I got the package you sent. I can never tell you how much those packages mean. Some of the guys never get any, so yours help fill the gap. The guys here think my people back home are okay!

I had better close for now. It sounds like everything is going well there. Tell Grams I got her letter and enjoyed it. You take care, Mom, and don't worry about me, I'm doing fine, just a little wet.

Love, Joseph

On October 4, Ron and I were with Charlie Company, setting in for the night after crossing the river into Arizona earlier. Nothing we had seen during the day indicated a possible attack that night, but I had a feeling one was coming.

We dug a shallow foxhole that could just hold the two of us if we lay head to toe. That type of foxhole made it more difficult to use our weapons, but was easier to dig than a deep hole and would afford nearly as much protection. Eleven o'clock that night brought an attack that was heavy, even for Arizona.

Without warning, we were taking well-placed rockets and mortars at the rate of two or three per second. It's difficult to think during the first terrifying seconds of a firefight, but one thing was obvious. It would take at least a company of very well-equipped NVA to put out that kind of fire.

Ron and I dove into the hole at the same time and ended up head-to-head, squeezed tightly together. I knew if it kept up, a barrage that heavy could quickly lead to an overrun, even for a tight outfit like Charlie Company.

One of us had to turn around so we would have our 360-degree field of view, but to do so would briefly expose either me or Ron to the fusillade of shrapnel that filled the air. A good team leader never asked his partner or any man under his control to do something he wouldn't do himself.

I moved to get up and was immediately knocked back down by a thumbnail-size piece of aluminum, probably from the tail fin of a rocket that had just gone off in a tree nearby. It hit me above my right eye, and when I reached up to pull it out, it was still hot. If it had been a quarter inch lower or steel shrapnel, it would have messed up my medical records but good. I wiped a trickle of blood from my eye and tried again. This time I made it, and as I lay there, the back of my hand accumulated red streaks, as I kept wiping the blood from my brow.

Dirt and pieces of trees were falling on us, as we watched for red flares and waited for a mortar to drop in our hole. After three minutes without a letup, it was becoming apparent that whatever had hit us was bigger than a company. My jaws were getting sore from clenching my teeth at every near miss that shook us.

In the confusion, the skipper managed to find some big guns at a fire base barely within range and called in textbook artillery strikes. Whoever was manning those guns was lobbing 175mm artillery rounds over our heads, directly on enemy positions, at a rate I didn't think possible. They had just evened up the odds, and the incoming was beginning to ease up. Charlie finally decided it wasn't worth it anymore and broke contact.

The company had held. As flares lit up the area, I saw what scant minutes ago was a company perimeter had been turned into a jumble of craters and shattered trees.

I took out my canteen and sat on the edge of the foxhole and started washing the blood from my eye. When Ron saw me, he said "I'll find a corpsman." I started to stop him and thought better of it. Even a minor scratch could become dangerously infected in the bush, and a corpsman could clean it properly.

As the doc put antiseptic and butterfly stitches on my eyebrow, he said, "I'm turning you in for a Heart." I objected. We had three dead Marines and seven wounded, and I didn't think it right to get a Purple Heart for such an insignificant thing.

When he walked away, I thought I heard him mutter under his breath something about turning me in anyway. Months later, I was unceremoniously handed a Purple Heart for the incident by an office clerk in Okinawa.

By early morning on October 6, Charlie Company had just moved into a large flat valley and set in three quarters of a mile from India Company 3/5, which was pinned down by an enemy sniper in a tree line one thousand yards from them. He had already shot five men, two fatally. I estimated our range to be two thousand yards from the tree line, technically over the limit for the bolt rifle. I asked the skipper if we could move closer.

"Permission denied."

"But, Skipper, he's got those guys pinned so tight they have to piss laying down. They need some relief!"

"Sorry, Ward, you'll have to do what you can from here. They've got air strikes on call as soon as the cloud cover breaks, and I don't want you out there." I briefly reflected back to a sniper duel in Arizona in mid-August which I barely came out on top of. Dave Sulley and I had just set in on a predawn

Four who joined the Marines together (left to right): Mike O'Grady, Dave Young, J.T. Ward, Nick Herrera. Summer 1968. *Doris Ward-Bayles*

J.T. Ward receives citation for Honor Man from Lieutenant Colonel Dallas Walker. Fall 1968. *Marine Corps Recruit Depot, San Diego*

J.T. Ward at an Hoa combat base with his first letter from home. Spring 1969.

An Hoa combat base seen from sniper tower. Summer 1969.

Weapons used by 5th Marine Regiment, Scout Snipers (Vietnam, 1969-1970)

Modified Remington 700 bolt-action rifle with free-floating medium-heavy barrel. Muzzle velocity: 2550 feet per second

M-14. Can be fitted with Starlight scope. Muzzle velocity: 2800 feet per second

M-16 with Starlight scope. Muzzle velocity: 3250 feet per second

NVA prisoner taken during ambush on Go Noi Island. 1969.

Company pinned down by enemy fire in the central
highlands, Quang Nam Province. Summer 1969.

Sniper tower on west side of An Hoa combat base.
Summer 1969.

Replacement troops board Sikorsky en route to Operation
Forsyth Grove. Summer 1969.

Scout Sniper "Bear" in front of team leaders' tent, An Hoa combat base. 1969.

J.T. Ward lunching with local militia on dog meat, rice, and a cabbage-like vegetable. Summer 1969.

Scout Sniper Dave Meeks weaving a warning trap in Quang Nam Province. 1969.

Two Sikorskys make emergency evacuation of remains of one Marine and one ARVN company in Arizona Territory. Fall 1969.

J.T. Ward with full field gear, ready to go on assignment, An Hoa combat base. Fall 1969.

Marine patrol cutting a path through thick undergrowth at base of central highlands. Spring 1970.

hunter-kill. We were watching a tree line seven hundred yards away when I saw a puff of smoke from a rifle. A split second later, a bullet hit two feet in front of me. I took a deep breath and fired back, hitting him in the face. It couldn't have been more than seven seconds between the two shots. When we checked the body we found an American M-1 carbine with a scope. I wondered what small mistake he'd made that caused him to miss me.

I pushed the memory out of my mind and asked the skipper if Ron and I could move to a firing point one hundred yards outside the lines.

"Okay, Ward, but stay close." The skipper had the final word and we would have to make do, but the spot I'd picked was actually two hundred yards out. Eighteen hundred yards was better than two thousand. I really wanted that guy.

Charlie Company was lobbing mortars into the tree line; India Company couldn't get up long enough to use their own. We passed a crew hurriedly unwrapping mortar rounds and dropping them down the tube, when they all shouted, "Short round!" By reflex, everyone hit the ground. A short round was a mortar shot that fell back on the unit firing it. It didn't happen often and usually wasn't the crew's fault. They were mainly caused when the propellant in the round burned improperly, and if it made it out of the tube at all, it could go anywhere.

I craned my neck and watched the mortar creep upward a hundred feet and arc back down. I tracked it until just before it hit thirty feet away, when I stuck my face in the mud and covered my head with both arms. The sound of shrapnel flying so close over us almost drowned out the noise of the explosion. No one was hurt, and the mortar crew would take some ribbing, but it was considered an occupational hazard, to be quickly dismissed. Ron and I got up. While we wiped the mud from our faces, a grunt yelled, "Hey, throw 'em a little harder, will ya?" followed by another voice, "Ya missed me, try again," a few cat calls, and that was it.

We jogged to the small rise in the ground I'd picked as a firing point. It wasn't a very good spot, but the skipper was right. We didn't want to get hung too far out if air strikes were already on call. We lay flat on the ground before I realized the terrain had played a trick on my distance judgment, and we were still two thousand yards from the trees. I had the scope set for fifteen hundred yards and couldn't remember the numbers to set it for two thousand. I dug through my pockets and came up with a soggy piece of paper that had all the settings. Ron watched the tree line with the field glasses while I redoped the rifle. After a couple minutes he said, ''I don't see him.'' Our own mortars were still going out, and I looked at India Company in the distance through the scope.

''They're still down.'' I said. ''He's there somewhere.'' I looked at the trees for a hint as to his location. A slight puff of smoke, maybe a muzzle flash, some movement—anything. After several minutes, I had to rest my eye from the scope. I looked at Ron who was rubbing his face.

''Ron, do you see anything?''

''Not a damn thing, and I've been watching for a solid five minutes.''

''Me, either.'' I asked Ron if he was up to trying to draw his fire, maybe we could see a muzzle flash if it was in our direction.

''Let's do it,'' he said. I had Ron load an M-14 magazine with tracers and fire them into the trees, which would leave no doubt as to our location. I watched through the scope for anything that would give him away, but saw nothing. I looked at the next firing point seven hundred yards further on. We had to get closer to find this guy, let alone make a shot. I checked the clouds and figured they might clear at any time. When I thought of the ass chewing I'd get from the skipper, I decided against it.

Over the next two hours we tried everything we could think of to draw his fire. At one point Ron stood up and jumped around, waving his T-shirt, but to no avail. He wouldn't take the bait. The skipper must have thought we had lost what little sense we had as he watched us carry on. During this time we didn't know it, but the enemy sniper had shot another man dead in India Company.

When the clouds began to clear and the first of three Phantoms came in to bomb the tree line, India 3/5 had been pinned down for over five hours. We had watched for two hours and hadn't seen the slightest hint as to the sniper's location. He's good, I thought, damn good. If Charlie had a classification of Sniper Expert, he was one, and I began to think like him. With the best Russian sniper rifle, I estimated he had a maximum range of 1,200 to 1,500 yards. With the bolt rifle, under the same conditions, my maximum range was a full-torso hit at two thousand yards. He knew not to give his location away and concentrated on shooting up the company he had in range.

The smoke from two loads of 750 pound bombs and a full drop of napalm blocked our vision completely, so Ron and I returned to the perimeter. When we got back, we listened to the command post radio as our sister company called for more air strikes. The sniper was alive and had wounded another man. I suspect the next sortie of jets bombed an empty grove of trees. He probably did what I would have done at that point and got the hell out of there.

While we cleaned our rifles, I thought what a day's worth one of Uncle Ho's best had given. One enemy sniper had killed three grunts, wounded four, tied up two companies and six fighter-bombers a good part of the day, and we hadn't seen any sign of him.

The next morning, India Company stirred to find a two-man listening post dead, their throats cut. I figured the sniper was indirectly responsible for their deaths, too; he had worn the company out so much during the day that they had fallen asleep on watch.

The weather over the next three days was terrible. Enemy contact dropped off considerably. We were bogged down, and so were they. The occasional incoming mortar was a minor inconvenience compared to the misery of being wet for days.

At sunrise on the ninth, the sky had cleared completely and I felt a warning in the calm, cool dawn air. We got the word later that morning to head into An Hoa ASAP. A typhoon was expected within forty-eight hours, and regiment was calling as many men into the rear as possible. All available choppers were tied up extracting troops too far out to walk in. We were looking at a 40-click forced march across terrain, turned to mush by days of torrential rains. To make it in time, we would have to ford the north fork of the Son River to get out of Arizona, cut through the middle of Go Noi Island, then ford the south fork of the Son to reach the road to An Hoa. A forced march meant only five-minute rest periods, and they would be few and far between. The men lightened up, discarding all nonessential items into the company fire. Every pound of gear carried would become critical.

We made fair time reaching the river, and once there it didn't look good. Normally the river was only waist deep, but it was swollen with rain and came up to our chins. The skipper called for the best swimmer in the company. A wiry redhead came running up and stripped. He tied a quarter-inch nylon rope around his waist and moved upstream to counter the cur-

rent and dived in. I didn't envy him his task. He had a grueling three-hundred-yard swim, and none of us really
believed he could do it. He made it across several anxious
minutes later, and after flopping on the bank long enough to
catch his breath, he tied the rope to the nearest tree. The
word went out, "If you want it dry, get it high," and we
started across. "Last in, first out," was a good rule of thumb
for Arizona, so Ron and I crossed with second squad. To
keep the bolt rifle out of the water, I had to loop my arm
around the rope and hold the rifle as high as I could with
both hands. As we crossed, I watched the man in front of me
to see if he stepped in a hole.

The first squad to reach the other side set up M-60 machine
guns to provide security for the rest of the company while
crossing. Some had taken off all their clothes and laid them out
in a futile attempt to dry them. By the time the last of 4th
Platoon was in the water, the front of the company was a
quarter of a mile into Go Noi, bogged down in sticky, knee-
deep mud. When the last squad was in the water, the enemy
sprang an ambush from downstream on the Arizona side. Three
grunts in the middle of the river were shot dead instantly, and
through the scope I watched a heroic effort to retrieve the
bodies while under fire. They were able to get two, but the
third body floated downriver toward the South China Sea.

I looked at the far bank and saw the smoke from two
AK-47s, not fifty yards from the point we had left Arizona. No
telling how long they had stalked us, waiting for this precise
moment.

I had a seven hundred yard shot if I was standing, which
wasn't bad, but I would be firing scant inches over the heads of
the men in the column behind me struggling to get through the
mud. I decided not to take the chance, and through the scope
I watched a tragic comedy played out. Most of 1st Squad was
naked, their clothes still laid out to dry. At one point, a machine gunner ran across a sandy stretch of bank, spraying the
opposite side with an M-60, wearing only two belts of ammo
hastily thrown over one shoulder.

It was a quick hit-and-run, but very effective. Fourth Platoon
had an added problem. The Marine Corps doesn't leave its
dead behind. If we had wounded, a medevac would have been
made available, even with choppers in short supply. The dead
would have been taken at the same time. But alone, the dead
had no priority.

Fourth Platoon wouldn't have to go it alone. Each man in the company, including the skipper, would have a turn holding one end of a poncho with a dead Marine in it. Go Noi Island had turned to soup. In places we had to literally pull each other through the mud by grabbing the hand or rifle strap of the man behind, using the weight of our upper bodies as we lay backward into the mud to pull him to the spot where we had just been standing.

When a poncho was handed to me and Ron, I had to get my mind off what we were carrying and the burning ache in my legs. I thought back to infantry training at Camp Pendleton. By chance the smallest guy in the whole company was in my platoon. He didn't weigh 130 pounds, and when the company went on a forced march the troop leader always handed the guy a fifty pound rock. He made it quite clear from the beginning that the rock had to get from point A to point B, or we'd have to do it all over again. That little guy labored to make a hundred yards the first time, but the rock still got from point A to point B.

That damn rock became a source of pride to our platoon. If a man fell while carrying it, we picked him and the rock up. If the men were slow to pick the rock up, I had to grab the rock and run it to the front of the platoon where it would start its bizarre journey from one man to the next as we made our way across the countryside. We could have handed the rock to the next platoon, but not my boys. No matter how tough it got we always carried it. When we finished ITR, our platoon number was painted on the rock and it lay in front of the barracks, silently awaiting the next group of trainees.

I began to think the "rock" too heavy this time. As my legs gave out completely, I remembered what was cradled in the poncho. The two bodies, like that rock, were passed through the company from front to rear where they were left. They were picked up again by the last platoon and passed to the front of the column by the time we reached the south fork of the Son River.

We used a regular crossing point to leave Go Noi Island. It was wider but shallower than most of the river and had ropes permanently strung across the water. Amphibious vehicles were always stationed on the far side to provide fire support and assist in getting dead and wounded out, particularly when the ropes were covered by water. We'd made it. Under terrible conditions, Charlie Company had made a march that should have taken thirty-six hours in less than twenty-four, and none too soon. The morning sky was turning an ominous dark purple, like an ugly bruise.

Ron and I rode across on an amphibious vehicle with part of the command post and two dead Marines. We detached ourselves from the company and began the long walk to An Hoa. We entered the village from the backside, and as much as I wanted to see Lee and Ann, I was too muddy and exhausted to stop. All I could think about was getting in, cleaned up, and off my feet. Ron and I were looking forward to being dry for a while, but the approaching storm had different plans in store for us.

As we walked through the village, I noticed the shopkeepers pulling down storm shutters and closing up, while most of the villagers carried valuables into their bunkers.

When we reached An Hoa, everyone was busy battening down the base, and the overflow of men had spread to our tents. There were ten or more people in each eight-man tent. Ron and I had to scramble to get space on the floor for the night. We were extremely closed-rank. Normally, to come into our area, an outsider would have to be escorted by a sniper, but these were unusual circumstances. Even the gunny and skipper had people in their tents.

There were several reasons for our closed-rank policy. The main one being that, as part of headquarters, we were privy to classified information. We also had expensive equipment. A bolt rifle would bring two or three thousand dollars on the black market, and one small Starlite scope for an M-14 or M-16 cost over eight thousand.

While in the rear we also tried to avoid the grunts, to lessen the requests from disgruntled Marines to shoot their skipper or gunny. At the front of our compound was a bright red sign, a friendly notice that they were entering sniper territory. At the back of the compound was a large, not so friendly, sign with our insignia, the Grim Reaper, on it. Our confirmed kills were posted there daily. Except for an occasional officer or friend of one of the snipers, I don't recall a single man coming into our area without approval.

The showers were left open to accommodate the flood of men coming in from the bush so Ron and I had to wait half an hour in a long line of men. Personnel permanently stationed in the rear didn't have a chance to get in. Compared to the rest of us, they were immaculate and were firmly and continuously pushed to the rear of the line until they finally gave up and returned to their units.

We walked into the showers fully clothed to get as much mud off our jungle utes and boots as possible, while we undressed under a stream of cold water. The showers were always cold. After a three-minute shower, we grabbed our wet uniforms and streaked back to our tent, where we changed into clean, dry fatigues.

We took our places on the floor to rest and bask in the luxury of being dry for the first time in days, cleaned our rifles, and went to sleep.

Late that afternoon, I stirred to the steadily increasing wind, soon to be accompanied by a torrent of rain. The winds were approaching hurricane force and it seemed to be raining up, down, and sideways. Our best efforts to secure the tent didn't work; the wind was blowing hard enough to force water under the tent flaps, where it swirled around inside. We were soon wet again, but the march in had been so demanding that the growing fury of the storm didn't prevent me from again sliding into a deep, yet troubled, sleep.

During the night the power went off. Someone had hung flashlights from a tent pole that cast ghostly shadows, gyrating with the motion of the tent, as the wind tried to pull it apart.

In my uneasy sleep, I became aware of a strange sensation. I opened my eyes to see a big, brown rat crouched neatly on my chest staring right back at me. I bolted upright, slapping the rat with one hand, while reaching for my battle-ax with the other. In the short time it took me to get to my feet, I must have used every expletive in my vast inventory. I took a step to go after the rat and fell over one man sleeping on the floor and landed on another. They both awoke with a yell, and heads began popping up all around me. The tent was crammed with men.

"Where the hell did all you fuckers come from?" I shouted.

Someone answered, "Our tent blew down."

I sat up the rest of the night, holding the ax on my lap, waiting for the rat to come back, but I knew that it wouldn't return. Was it because I was nervous at being closely confined with so many strangers?

By mid-morning of the next day, An Hoa was in the eye of the storm, and an eerie calm fell over the base, while in the distance all around us the clouds rolled and boiled in anger. It would be two hours before the other side of the storm reached us. We put up the tent flaps to dry the inside as much as possible and get the extra men out of our area; they had just enough time to repair their own tents.

Thirty percent of the tents had blown down, power and phone lines were hanging loose everywhere, and trash and debris littered the base. When the storm hit us again, it had lost most of its punch. The winds had dropped to fifty miles per hour, and most of the typhoon's energy was expended on the release of heavy rainfall.

I'd just gone through the equivalent of a hurricane and didn't consider it important enough to write home about. I was six months into my tour, and I didn't realize how jaded I'd become.

★

Scout Snipers
An Hoa
October 17, 1969

Dear Mom,

It's late, but will try to get this done tonight. We just got the word that we're supposed to get hit tonight, so we have the Starlites on our M-14s. Snipers are the only ones that can fire inside the perimeter. Usually when they pass word like that, there's about a 50 percent chance of it happening.

Sounds like winter has really struck there. No matter how bad it gets, enjoy it. I hear there's places where it never snows. Know what I mean?

Yes, the war has slowed some. The gooks can't get through this muck much better than we can. They usually take to the mountains this time of year to build up strength if they're planning an offensive in the spring.

How do we stay warm? We don't. We do have rubber rain suits we can wear over our jungle utes but it rains so hard we get wet anyway. The suit helps keep in a little body heat, that's all they're good for. As far as sleeping goes, we usually lay in the water. It's no big thing cuz we're usually wet anyway.

Humping through the mud does get tiring. When we came in from Go Noi Island, in some places it was knee deep. It does have it's compensations, I get a kick out of watching guys fall in the slop. I do my share of it, so I can afford to laugh at the others. It's easy to drown though, if someone falls into a bomb crater with all his gear on. The craters fill up with 20 or 30 feet of water, and we can't see them because the water is at least six inches deep everywhere.

I've got another partner. He's pretty new in-country and his name is Pat Zenishek. He learns quickly and I like him.

I got your letter with Laura's birthdate in it, and I just had time to read it once before we moved out and it got wet so I couldn't read it again. Would you please send it to me again? I don't know what's wrong with me. When I came into An Hoa, I needed something out of my sea bag and to save me I couldn't remember the combination to the lock. I had that same lock since boot camp and could open it with my eyes closed, but I ended up breaking it off. This place is definitely hard on a guy's mind.

Well, Mom, I don't think I'll stay up to watch the fireworks, it's already midnight so I had better crash. Pat and I are going with Delta Company early in the morning to Arizona. Now don't worry just because we're going to Arizona, it'll be my sixth time there and I have a feel for the place. Besides, there are fewer booby-traps there than most areas, and that's one of the things that scares me most. I just got the word a little while ago that something was going on there. Give Grams my love.

Love, Joseph

P.S. Oh, yeah, my squad leader went and got me a couple beers and then started hinting around for me to get a hair cut. I think they're getting desperate. It doesn't matter how long my hair is in the bush anyway.

At 6:00 A.M. on the eighteenth, the clouds cleared enough to chopper into Arizona, and as usual, we landed in a hot LZ. My partner this time was Pat Zenishek. Snipers changed partners frequently, because of wounds, illness, rotation or promotion to team leader. Pat was new in-country and was one of the best damn shots I ever saw. We were in Arizona to help an ARVN unit that had been in steady contact with Charlie for twenty-four hours. This would be the first and last time I'd fight with ARVNs.

When we landed, they were in near chaotic retreat from what we would consider relatively light contact. Delta's skipper was determined to make the ARVNs stand and fight. We began taking heavy fire, and it soon became obvious that the ARVNs were the bait and we the fish.

The skipper and gunny managed to regroup the ARVNs, while Delta fought to establish a perimeter. Twelve Chinook helicopters carried Delta Company into Arizona. Ten left. Two were shot up too badly to get off the ground, and through the smoke and confusion I glimpsed the crew of one chopper run to board another bird out.

Over the next few days, we seemed to be constantly carrying dead and wounded Marines and ARVNs to Army medevac choppers, coming in with their ramps already down. In and out in less than two minutes.

By the morning of the nineteenth, the ARVNs had set in, but wouldn't advance. We were taking heavy casualties. The skipper sent the gunny to keep them moving forward, as Delta began a head-to-head frontal assault, which was the only way to get out of the mess we were in. Between medevacs, artillery barrages would soften up enemy positions. We were making scant yards at a time. As the day wore on, it became obvious that we had locked horns with a battalion of aggressive NVA.

The frontal assault is the forte of the Marine Corps. First a heavy barrage of artillery, then an advance forward, no matter how slight. Delta was good at it, and with the prodding from the gunny, the ARVNs were moving in the right direction again. We would have to endure this special brand of hell for several hours before we were crawling over and past enemy bodies and knew we were getting the upper hand. We were out of range of any big guns, and it was still too overcast for air strikes, but precise and massive hits by 105mm and 155mm guns from small fire bases in our range were taking their toll on Charlie.

By noon, the company was running low on ammo, and the resupply choppers were dropping their slings from a hundred feet and taking withering fire to do even that. Only three choppers made it in with replacements, about ninety men altogether. One of the three Sikorsky choppers took a mortar round after unloading, and the crew had to wait for the next medevac to get out. We had not planned on being out long, so I had brought only eighty rounds of match ammo. I had lost track of the number of rounds I'd fired through the bolt rifle, and Pat had emptied all of his. I gave him twenty match rounds to fill one M-14 clip.

We were crawling through a bloodbath, and when we finally reached the position the ARVNs had abandoned, there were bodies and body parts everywhere. Mud, blood, sweat, and pieces of human flesh all mixed together in a hellish paste. I looked up to see a grunt with dysentery roll over, pull down his pants, and shit right there. Why not, I thought. Someone had to add the final touch.

Thanks to outstanding command, the dogged determination of Delta Company to never stop moving forward, and thousands of artillery rounds, by midafternoon we had pushed the enemy to the foot of the mountains on the far side of Arizona. They seemed to be in retreat and were surely exhausted—we were. To attempt escape up the steep hillsides, covered with dense jungle, would be suicide. They would head either north or south along the base of the mountains, but which direction they would go was anybody's guess. The skipper already had a plan, and he wasn't going to pull any punches, but first we had to get the hell out of there and fast. B-52s were on their way, and we were in the target zone. We immediately began running back across the ground we'd just fought so hard to take, slowing only to pick up the dead and wounded. The bombers would be dropping 500-, 750-, and 1,000-pound bombs.

The last medevac cleared the area and we managed to cover about one thousand yards when the word went out, "Dig in, we have two minutes!"

B-52s bombed by radar from 30,000 feet and were unfailingly accurate even at night and in bad weather. I wasn't worried about the bombs being off target, but the thousand pounders were definitely on my mind, and there was no time to dig in.

Charlie was about to get hit by the thing he feared the most, and we would be taking a healthy dose of it ourselves. Pat hadn't seen a B-52 bombing run yet, and I don't know what he thought when I told him to get behind a tree, hold onto the base, and keep his head down.

I'd witnessed many such bombings, and in my mind I always imagined that the planes flying high overhead were civilian jetliners coming to take us home. Always the illusion was broken as the first of hundreds of bombs whistled earthward. This time my illusion wouldn't be broken, it would be shattered. The first bombs hit five miles to the south of our last point of enemy contact and fell north for ten miles along the base of the mountains. Individual explosions blended into one continuous rumble that grew in intensity as the bombs fell closer and closer to our position. At their nearest point of impact, shrapnel from one-thousand-pound bombs was whirling over us with a hideous moan. Shock waves coming through the ground and air made it impossible to focus my eyes, and the landscape seemed to quiver like Jell-O. Only the devil knew what the enemy was going through.

The minute it was safe, the skipper had us up and moving again. With three hours of daylight left he wanted us three hours closer to getting out of Arizona. Pat's eyes betrayed his disbelief at what had just taken place, and he looked at me with the understanding that he was in deep. To be in Vietnam was to be in deep shit. As we moved out we walked past pieces of shrapnel, some over eight feet long, several inches wide, with razor-sharp edges.

The sun was setting when we rendezvoused with a supply chopper and set in for the night. Everyone got ammo but Pat and me. We used match ammo in the M-14 and bolt rifle. Each box of bullets and each bullet in a case of match ammunition had the same serial number, which meant it had been manufactured at the same factory on the same day and with the same batch of gun powder. Once we sighted in our rifles to a certain serial number, we had to stay with that lot of ammo until it ran out. When it did, we started on a new case, resighted the rifles to that lot number, and stayed with it until it ran out, and so on. Although the exact type of ammunition was not as critical in the spotter's M-14, which covered the range from five hundred yards to point-blank, it was quite another story for the bolt rifle. Under combat conditions, we were working the rifle in the range of five hundred to nearly two thousand yards. Even the slightest variance from one round to the next would make the accuracy of the rifle completely unacceptable.

Pat had used the twenty rounds I'd given him. That left sixty. I counted the rounds I still had, forty-nine. Suddenly the events of the day flashed through my mind. I realized I hadn't filled out a single kill sheet and never did. I figured the remaining forty-nine rounds would be plenty, since we were only supposed to be in Arizona long enough to get the ARVNs out. To be sure of getting more of the same lot number, we'd have to catch a bird into An Hoa and come back out. A sniper could forget the settings for his scope, the combinations to his padlock or even get so drunk he might not know his own name, but there were two things he never forgot: the lot number he was working with at the time and his medevac number, in that order. (The medevac number was the last three digits of a man's serial number, and was used to keep track of him as he passed through the medical system.)

We did have one thing in our favor. The bolt rifle, the M-14, and the M-60 machine gun fired the same basic round. Although much too inaccurate for the bolt rifle, in a pinch M-60 rounds worked fine in the M-14 for close-in protection. I dug us a foxhole while Pat emptied a belt of M-60 ammo to fill his magazines. I'm glad that at the time we didn't know Pat would have to do this two more times before we made it out of Arizona.

The B-52s had definitely caught someone's attention and I didn't know if they were mad or just taking advantage of the improved weather. We were hit that night, all the next day and night.

On the morning of the third day, the twentieth, we fought our way into a small village we'd just leveled with artillery fire, and one grunt literally fell through a hidden trap door into an NVA hospital bunker. A tunnel rat went in long enough to find three dead NVA and medical supplies. Charlie had been there just minutes before or the dead would have been taken. We had our hands too full to mess with blowing the bunker, so the skipper marked the spot on the map for penetration bombing later.

The enemy was forcing us to zigzag across Arizona, going sideways as much as forward, and not much of either. Medevacs were waiting in holding patterns, ready to rush in between artillery barrages to load casualties. One medevac and one Cobra gunship were shot down, killing the crews of both.

By the end of the fourth day, we were still two miles from the Son Thu. We never made it to the river. Even with reinforcements of ninety men, Delta was down to seventy-one. The ARVNs had about forty men left from a company of 240. We figured Charlie had lost at least 1,500 men. The toll on both sides for only four days was staggering. I'd lost several friends, and the remainder of us looked half dead. The skipper called for an emergency evacuation the next morning.

Just to make it possible to evacuate, jets dropped napalm for two solid hours around our perimeter. After the napalming, three Sikorsky helicopters started in under fire. One was hit and turned back. The other two made it in, and a mixture of ARVNs and Marines ran to board. Pat and I got on a chopper with fifty-two other men. Fifty-four of us were standing, squeezed together in a helicopter designed to carry thirty-five troops. Both door gunners were firing 50-caliber machine guns, and the noise was deafening, but it was soon drowned out as the pilots kept increasing the power and the pitch of the rotor blades. I had to cover my ears as the rotors clacked louder and the chopper began to vibrate. No way, I was thinking, we're way overweight. The twin turbines were screaming full blast, and I wondered how much more the rotors could take, when we slowly lifted off. We just cleared a line of trees ahead and gradually gained about eight hundred feet of altitude during the twenty-minute flight to An Hoa. Pat and I just stared at each other and wondered when one of the rotors would give out under the stress.

At An Hoa, we began what at first seemed to be a normal descent, but as we got closer to the LZ it became apparent that we weren't slowing down fast enough. The rotors were clacking even louder than when we left Arizona. The chopper hit the middle of the LZ hard enough to collapse the front landing gear, and slid off the LZ on its nose and rear wheels. Even with the damage to the chopper, that pilot had pulled off an amazing feat. Along with the other Americans on the chopper, Pat and I jumped off and kissed the ground. As we went to report in, I glanced back at the helicopter. It and the pilot had given their all to get us out. I found out later that the other chopper couldn't make it all the way and had to set down in the middle of Go Noi Island to split the load with another chopper. As a last thought, I checked to see how many rounds I had left. Four.

*

Scout Snipers
An Hoa
October 25, 1969

Dear Mom,

It's taken me a few days to get calmed down enough to write this. We had a bad time of it in Arizona this last time out. I'll be here until I see if my R and R comes through. I really need it. Pat went back out to Arizona with another team leader. I don't like changing partners, but I'm worried some pogue here in the rear will swipe my R and R. My feet are doing fine. The powder and socks you send help a lot.

Yes, I'm glad Nick may be getting out of here. I can't help thinking he'll be leaving just in time. I'm really fed up with US policies here. As soon as we pull out, the gooks are going to walk right through this country, which means 40,000 Americans have died for nothing. The people who demonstrate and have things like that moratorium disgust me. Anymore burning a US flag or a draft card is as common as spitting on a sidewalk, and most places they would do more to you if you did spit on a sidewalk. You don't realize what all this crap really looks like till you see it from the outside, like I'm doing now and like the people of other countries do. I don't know, I guess the reason I'm so upset now is that this last time out in Arizona, we found some more medical supplies in a bunker with a stamp that read, "Donated to the People's Republic from your friends at Berkeley College." I got sick to my stomach. Every time we pick up a *Stars and Stripes*, it's splattered all over it about peace demonstrations, and maybe you'll find a small clip buried in the rest of the garbage about a demonstration in support of the troops here. I don't even bother to pick up a paper anymore. The US is headed for a big kick in the teeth, and it's got it coming. I imagine you think I've gone berserk, but it doesn't help to talk to anyone around here cuz they can see it, too. I'll give you a break and stop here. I could use some more vitamins and a couple batteries for the radio as that kind are hard to get here.

Spring starts here about the end of February. I just hope the rains hold off till I have my R and R. When it rains hard, Liberty Bridge is under water and the only way out of here is by chopper. If it's raining very hard, they can't fly, and I'd hate to miss my R and R because of that.

When it was raining, it rained almost constantly, day and night for about three weeks. I guess the worst is yet to come. Well, Mom, I better close for now. Of course give Grams my love. You take care and be careful driving when the streets are slick. Bye for now.

Love, Joseph

After two days in An Hoa, it was obvious that my R and R wasn't going to come through at the last minute. Pat was with Whiskey 3/5 in Arizona. He was a good partner, so I caught a supply chopper to link up with him again and relieve the team leader he was with.

Pat was a superb shot, with steady nerves, and we got along so well that I wanted him back as my partner. This decision was nearly my undoing. I was combat weary, and voluntarily going back to Arizona bordered on the irrational.

Over the next few days, the weather was intermittently good and bad. We were able to alternate between air strikes and artillery to keep the enemy busy.

Pat and I were having good results. I'd logged one kill at 1,800 yards during a light drizzle, and ironically I did it while resting the rifle on top of a grave stone. When we checked the body we found a well-fed, well-equipped Vietcong. But for a bullet hole between his shoulder blades, he looked too good. His rifle and equipment were new, and we found a healing shrapnel wound on his leg that had been properly cared for.

It wasn't a good sign. I was so concerned over the discovery, when I filled out the kill sheet I wrote across the front in large letters, IMPORTANT, SEE DETAILS. I wanted my skipper in An Hoa to get the information ASAP. We normally turned our sheets in when we went into the rear, but I didn't know when that would be. I sent the sheet in with a door gunner on the next supply chopper. Something was out of balance; Charlie was looking better than he should have.

Midday of the thirtieth, Whiskey set in on a small rise with thick tree lines on two sides, six hundred yards away. We began taking light weapons fire from one section of trees. Whiskey was a good company, but someone got their wires crossed when the skipper called for an air strike.

When calling for air support, two conditions had to be met. The first and most important was that the jet not come in directly toward us. Jet fighters were so fast, once they initiated their bombing run, we only had five to fifteen seconds to correct the pilot, who wouldn't have to be much off target to drop his ordnance right in our lap. The other condition was that the plane not pass directly overhead from behind. Shell casings, streaming from the jet's 20mm cannons, traveled at four hundred miles per hour. More than one GI had been killed by the wrong end of a 20mm round.

The whole company watched as a Phantom streaked out of the sky toward us. He dropped a full load of one thousand pound bombs on target, but there was a hitch. All the bombs went off but one. The enemy fire stopped, but we were about to get a lesson on momentum, as the dud bomb skipped like a stone over water at first, then began to slide. It smashed through four rice-paddy dikes and slid into the company perimeter, where it came to rest on a grunt's pack. If that size bomb had gone off where it ended up, Whiskey Company would have ceased to exist. We all quietly moved away from the bomb like it was a huge smelly turd. After we were a safe distance away, the engineers asked the grunt if he wanted his pack, and if so, he'd have to go get it himself. That poor guy was about to lose all his personal gear, and he knew it. With a very forlorn look on his face he shook his head no. The engineers carefully approached the bomb and placed C-4 charges on it. They set the fuse, and before long, the bomb and pack were turned into a very big hole in the ground.

★

Scout Snipers
Da Nang Hospital
November 8, 1969

Dear Mom,

Well you probably know by now what happened. I wanted to get a letter off to you and let you know that I'm not hurt very bad. At 7:30 this morning, Pat and I both got hit. The shrapnel that hit us was from a grenade, so the pieces weren't too big. I got a piece in the right side, two pieces in my right thigh, and one in my right knee. No bones broken, just holes. Pat caught pieces in his forehead, one glanced off and the other stuck under the skin. He'll likely be going back to An Hoa in three or four days.

Like I said, we were hit at 7:30 A.M., and I was out of the operating room at 10:30 A.M. Pretty good service, huh? Right now I'm working on my third IV and Pat is in the bed next to me. He runs all my errands.

I hurt a lot and I'm going to have some dandy scars, but that's all, so please don't worry too much. They've got round-eyed nurses here and I'm checking them out, so you know I can't be hurt too badly.

I'll close now, Mom. I know it won't do any good to tell you not to worry too much. All I can say is that we could have been hurt a lot worse than we were. Will write again soon.

Love, Joseph

Address:
Lcpl Joseph T. Ward, 2452991
Box 4B NSA
Da Nang
FPO/San Francisco 96695

On the 2d, Whiskey Company was sloshing through a series of rice paddies in Arizona, when something in the water caught my eye. I stooped to get a better look. It was a bad idea to touch anything you weren't sure of in Vietnam, but it wasn't a booby trap. I plucked it out of the water and found I was looking at a beautiful piece of workmanship. I was holding a wicker tube, four inches in diameter and fifteen inches long. It was made from the finest slivers of reed, the weaving on one end and around the outside was just loose enough to allow water to pass through. The other end had the most delicate pieces of reed woven into a cone shape which came together near the center of the tube. I couldn't figure out what it was until I put my hand down the cone end and wasn't able to pull it back out. It was a fish trap to catch the small silver fish that inhabited the streams and rice paddies. I gently spread the reeds and pulled my hand out. I wanted to take it with me, but it was too fragile to get out of the bush. Besides, Pat and I would be hard put to get out of Arizona in one piece ourselves. Also, the trap might mean the difference between a family's having or not having some protein that day. I carefully placed it back in the water, and hurried to catch up with Pat.

The next day, I developed another problem with my feet. Actually the problem wasn't my feet, it was my boots. The aluminum plates in the soles, meant to prevent punji stakes from penetrating a man's foot, had worn through the insoles, and wearing them was like walking on flattened razor blades.

When the company reached a spot where it would set in for a few days, I asked the gunny to order me a new pair. I was barefoot at that point, as the old boots were doing more harm than good, and I threw them away.

The next morning, Pat rushed up to the supply chopper to see if my boots had come in. They hadn't. I asked the gunny, "What's wrong?"

"They didn't have your size at An Hoa, they'll have to come from Da Nang." He went on to say he'd reordered them with the evening resupply, but I wasn't really listening. My mind was calculating how many men in the Corps wore the same size twelve boots and the fact that we could deliver millions of dollars worth of ordnance in a day, but couldn't get a pair of boots to a guy in the bush. I actually went on a short patrol that day, barefoot. That night a pair did come on the evening resupply, but they were three sizes too small and my feet were swollen anyway.

The gunny was madder than I was. He got on the radio to An Hoa and told headquarters, "If the morning supply chopper doesn't have the right boots in it, I'm going to catch the same chopper back in and kick the ass of the first man I find with Ward's size, officer or private." The next morning's supply chopper not only set down a sling, but landed, too. After more

han two days of mud squishing between my toes, I had a keen
nterest in that helicopter. When the ramp lowered, a door
gunner got off, with a pair of boots slung over his shoulder. I
quickly went to greet him. He shouted over the noise of the
otors. "Are these yours?" I nodded and checked the size.
They were the right ones.

"Someone really raised hell about these," he said. I gave
him a thumbs-up and he ran back to the chopper. The boots
came just in time—Whiskey Company moved that day, and I
would have wrecked my feet making a company movement
barefoot.

We set in for the night on a large, gradually sloping hilltop.
The perimeter was more spread out than usual. I picked the
highest spot in the perimeter for Pat and me to set up. We could
fire safely over everyone's heads on three sides without moving. A small hollow in the ground, surrounded by tree trunks,
would serve as a good natural foxhole and firing point. Three
fair strides away were some bushes we could use to make a
low-profile poncho shelter.

I knew without a doubt from what we'd seen earlier that day
that we would get hit. As a last thought, I put our rifles and
ammo in the makeshift foxhole to save some of those precious
seconds when a firefight first breaks out. I even had a fairly
good idea where it would come from, and just after sunset it
did. Mostly small-arms fire and RPGs.

We took three crouching steps and dove into the hole so fast
that we slid into our rifles. Bullets were crackling closely overhead and hitting the tree trunks with a splintering *whack*. I
peeked over the logs. I was right. Charlie was in the trees,
three hundred yards away from us. This was Pat's job. He
could see things through the Starlite on the M-14 that no one
else could, and he didn't hesitate to expose himself to enemy
fire and get them in his sights. He looked at me for permission
to fire. I immediately slapped him on the ass as the familiar
roar of a firefight built up. He fired three rounds, the first one
a tracer followed by two match rounds. He paused briefly while
the scope recovered from the muzzle flash, then another tracer
and two more match rounds.

Our roles were reversed, and I was spotting for Pat. It wasn't
hard. Halfway through his first magazine, bullets were swarm-
ing at us, missing our heads by inches, but Pat kept at it. He
was screwing up Charlie's program.

By stretching and recompressing the spring very carefully,

we could fit twenty-one rounds in a twenty round M-14 magazine. Pat calmly worked his way through seven, three-round volleys and ducked down to change clips. As he started to take up his aiming position again, I pulled him back down. Twenty-one muzzles flashes and seven tracers had left little doubt as to our location, and we were taking heavy return fire. We'd have to lay low until another sector took some of the heat off of us before we dared stick our heads up again. As we lay there listening to a firefight we couldn't really see anymore, I thought I heard incoming artillery. I didn't have long to think about it as the first of our own 175mm rounds hit inside the perimeter, one hit close enough to bounce us off the ground.

"Friendly fire" was an all too common part of the Vietnam War, and civilians and Americans both suffered from misplaced air and artillery strikes. The reasons for such accidents were often complex and elusive.

One of the first things Chuck taught me was to forget what I'd been taught about calling for air and artillery support. The manual procedure was to give the coordinates of your own unit, as well as the enemy's. Given the fluidity of combat in Vietnam, there was rarely an established front line, and the front was wherever we happened to be at the time. In the confusion of battle, even the steadiest of men could transpose the two numbers, or in its rush to help, air control or a gun crew could make the same mistake. Snipers were often responsible for calling fire support. Chuck taught me to simply not give our coordinates. When pressed to do so by fire command, all we had to tell them was, "We're moving, please hit the coordinates given."

A company in the bush, by logistical necessity, had to continuously radio its location to regimental headquarters, which also included fire control. Whatever the reason, we quickly forgot about the enemy as we took fifteen Big Ones (175mm).

The wide spacing of the company that particular night, which at first seemed to be a disadvantage, was suddenly in our favor as round after round landed in the perimeter.

Pat and I curled tight in a fetal position, as the crack and thunder of each explosion made it nearly impossible to think.

Our own incoming and the firefight stopped at the same time. I pictured those gooks laughing their asses off all the way back to Hanoi. On the other hand, one dead and five wounded Marines left us little to be happy about. If not for the unusual spacing of the company, the results would have been much worse.

Pat and I returned to our shelter to find it gone, the ponchos blown away by a close hit. A piece of shrapnel had passed through Pat's pack, and my bush hat had two holes in the brim. A light drizzle started, and we rebuilt our shelter with poncho liners. We put our rain suits on and once again would be sleeping in the mud.

By sunrise on the eighth, the company was preparing to move when we heard four faint explosions in the distance. We hardly paid them any mind until we saw a large, black object tumbling over the treetops, where it plopped in the mud thirty-five feet from us. The enemy had dug shallow pits in the ground, taken four of our dud 155mm artillery rounds, put their warheads in the shells, and used charges of C-4 to accurately blow our own artillery back on us. Fortunately, the shell that landed near Pat and me was a dud. Had it exploded that close, it would have cut us in half. The other three did go off.

The grunts had a habit of placing their grenades around the edge of their foxholes for easy access. Two shells went off without any serious consequence, but an unoccupied hole took a direct hit. I watched as a gray streak flashed scant inches off the ground and hit between Pat and me. At first I thought it was a piece of shrapnel the size of a fist, but it landed five feet from us and exploded.

It was one of our own M-30 hand grenades, blown halfway across the perimeter. An M-30 is designed to kill everything down to the size of a rabbit over a fifteen-foot radius. My legs were pointing straight up when I hit the ground on my head and right shoulder. Pat was blown backward over his heels.

We were within arm's reach when the grenade went off, but ended up over thirty feet from each other. The pain started the instant I sat up to look for Pat. He was staggering to his feet, both hands covering his face. Blood was streaming from between his fingers. My God, I thought, he's lost his face.

I didn't know how badly I was hurt until I started to move toward Pat. I didn't get far. I yelled, "Corpsman up!" Then I realized the crotch of my pants was soaked with blood.

"No. Oh, no, not my balls," I exclaimed, as I used my good arm to frantically unfasten my rainsuit and pull my fatigues down. Two pieces of shrapnel had hit the inner thigh of my right leg, only two inches below my genitals. Shrapnel had hit my right knee. Another piece hit four inches below my right arm pit, glanced off a rib, and traveled toward my back. One piece had cut halfway through the femoral artery and was bleeding so heavily, I nearly forgot about Pat and my other wounds. A corpsman rushed up and, seeing me first, began to treat my thigh. I was in so much pain I couldn't talk, so I pointed at Pat, who was lying on the ground again. The doc left me a handful of battle dressings and went to check Pat. Another corpsman came to treat me.

By the time he gave me a shot of morphine and used his finger to paint a large M on my forehead with my blood, I had soaked four battle dressings from my thigh wound alone. The M would tell the doctors that I'd been given morphine in the bush. The corpsman took a three-by-eight-inch tag, tied it to my wrist, and again used my blood to write my medevac number on it.

The command post radioman was standing by, and the corpsman said, "Call an emergency medevac and no bullshit about it, Ward's bleeding badly."

If the morphine was working, I couldn't tell. I looked at Pat and saw he was sitting up. He'd been knocked goofy, but his wounds were superficial. His main problem was that because of his head wound he couldn't have morphine.

The call for an emergency medevac had been intercepted by a Huey gunship only five minutes away, and the corpsman barely had time to bandage my other wounds before it landed.

The morphine was starting to help a little, a very little. As several hands grabbed me and headed toward the chopper, I demanded that the bolt rifle be given to me. Unless a sniper was dead or unconscious, it was his duty to keep possession of the rifle. I took some comfort in hugging it as they carried me to the chopper.

We were put on an American helicopter, flown by a South Korean pilot and copilot, with an American adviser–door gunner.

Hueys are fast, but too small to lie down in so we had to sit up during the ride to Da Nang. I sat between Pat and the adviser. Pat kept passing out and slumping forward. I used the arm on my good side to hold him upright in the seat; we weren't even strapped in.

Thanks to the size of the chopper, I felt every air pocket we went through during our short, but seemingly endless, ride to the hospital. I would liken it to being suspended by a long rope

in a hard wind. The adviser kept talking about how fast we
were going. Hell, if we had been flying a thousand miles per
hour, it wouldn't have been fast enough for me. Between my
pain, bleeding, and the rough helicopter ride, I wasn't sure I
was going to make it.

When we landed on the huge asphalt LZ at the hospital,
several nurses and corpsmen began running toward us with
stretchers. I was in shock and didn't know how Pat planned to
get in, but I was determined to walk. When I got out of the
chopper, I took two steps and fell on my face. I would ride a
stretcher after all.

While I was carried to triage, a corpsman tried to take my
bolt rifle. "Weapons aren't permitted in the hospital." My grip
on the rifle tightened. "Get an officer," I said. "I can only
sign the rifle over to an officer." They set me down as a nurse
rushed off to find the nearest brass. My mind was getting
fuzzy. I was vaguely aware that another nurse was inserting an
IV in each arm. Someone else was using large shears to cut my
rain suit and jungle fatigues in half down both sides. Nothing
was spared, and when the guy reached my boots and kept
going, my head cleared.

"I just got those boots," I said adamantly.

"We'll get you more."

I looked around and noticed what an unusual place they'd
put me in. I saw row after row of wooden tables set in a cement
floor full of drain holes. There were sandbag walls on three
sides, and it was covered by a simple tin roof. I asked where
I was. I'm not sure who answered.

"The outside operating theater. We use it to handle the
overflow from a major battle." I shouldn't have asked the next
question.

"Why all the drain holes?"

"It makes it easier to hose the blood off of the tables."

"Oh, shit," I said and laid my head back down.

It wasn't hard to find officers in Da Nang, especially around
the hospital. The nurse returned in a couple of minutes with a
colonel. It was one of the few times I was glad to see some
brass.

"Sir, will you please make sure my rifle is checked into the
armory and the serial number recorded?"

"Yes, I will, Marine; now let go of the damn thing before
you bleed to death!" I was ready to.

When they picked me up again, I realized I didn't have a

stitch of clothing on. We moved inside the main building where
I was put on a cold, stainless-steel table. They were already
working on Pat at the table next to me.

"How ya feel?" he asked.

"Bad. You?"

"Bad."

Things were happening very fast. I was given a prep shot for
surgery while a doctor checked my wounds. A corpsman
shaved the right side of my body. It all went. Leg, pubic, and
arm hairs, everything. I was getting drowsy as the "I-don't-
give-a-shit-shot" started to take hold. The same corpsman began another bag of blood, slid me onto a gurney, and headed
to X-ray to find out where the shrapnel ended up.

Although I was twelve thousand miles from home, I was
about to be reminded of how much we had shrunk our world.
The X-ray technician matter-of-factly asked where I was from,
undoubtedly like he'd done with countless other men before
me. I told him. He asked what town, and I told him.

"No, shit!" he said. "My girlfriend lives there. Do you
know Linda Thomas?" Christ, I thought, between arguments
with Laura, I'd gotten acquainted with Linda a lot better than
I wanted the guy to know.

"Yeah, I went to high school with her."

"Well, I'll be damned. What a coincidence," he said. Great,
just what I needed. I tried to relax and put the pain out of my
mind while he X-rayed me, all the time jabbering on about
what a fluke it was that I knew his girlfriend. I thought about
the blood running from my thigh wounds onto the table and up
my back.

In a few minutes he was holding films of my entire body to
the light. I counted three bright shiny spots a half inch by a
quarter inch.

"Where's the fourth one?" I asked.

"Oh, they sometimes get behind a thick piece of bone and
don't show up well on X-rays." He laid the films on my chest
and began pushing me, almost at a run, toward surgery. I was
vaguely aware of a nurse prepping my wounds as we rolled
down the hallway.

I abruptly came out of the anesthesia while a nurse was
checking the dressings. I jerked upward and caught her in the
chest with my left forearm, knocking her onto the next bed.
Then it hit me, pain so intense I nearly blacked out. My whole
right side was immobile. She quickly recovered and helped me

slowly lie back down and catch my breath. As she wiped the sweat from my face, she kept saying over and over, "I'm so sorry, I should have known better." When I could see clearly, I noticed the oak leaf on her lapel, but hitting a major was the least of my worries.

"I'll get a shot," she said and turned to leave.

"Wait, Ma'am, how bad am I?"

"You'll be fine," she said and hurried away. Oh, man, you can't hurt like this and be fine, I thought, and looked at the bed on my left. A Vietnamese boy about eight years old lay there, staring at me. What little of his body that wasn't bandaged showed signs of napalm burns. He had to be in terrible pain, but his face was expressionless, and that look in his eyes—I had seen it before. Then it came to me. That captured NVA captain had the same haunting look.

The nurse returned with the biggest shot of Demerol they could give me. She injected it into my IV tube, and I felt myself slipping away again.

I came to in a ward with thirty-nine other men. Pat was in the bed to my right, a ROK lieutenant was in the bed to my left, and the rest of the men were Marines and sailors with various illnesses and wounds.

On the wall at one end of the ward was a stark, black-and-white sign that read, LEARN TO LIVE WITH IT. Unable to fully use my right hand, a nurse had to help me write my first letter home.

★

Scout Snipers
Da Nang Hospital
November 9, 1969

Dear Mom,

There isn't a whole lot to write about, but I will whenever I can so you'll know I'm okay. Today wasn't such a good day, but I can't expect too much. I guess this sort of thing takes awhile. Actually I'm not so bad off, there's a little Vietnamese boy here with burns all over him. I sure feel sorry for him.

They're sticking me with a lot of needles and poking pills down me. I'll hate to see this IV go cuz they can give me most of my shots through it.

It looks like Pat leaves tomorrow. It's going to be kind of lonesome without him. If it weren't for him all the time going to and from the head with my little can, I couldn't even go to the bathroom. When he's gone, I'm going to give these corpsmen a workout. They're coming around with the cart. I hope they don't change my bandages again. He just stuck a thermometer in my mouth. Oh, yeah, my R and R came through for this month and now I can't use it.

Well, Mom, take care and I'll write when I can.

Love, Joseph

I'd embarked on a six-day journey through pain that made a mockery of human endurance. Combat wounds are deep and dirty, and the threat of infection is ever present. The enemy would often smear water buffalo dung on punji stakes and bullets to increase the chances of infection. Shrapnel needed no help. Its sharp, jagged edges destroy large amounts of muscle, nerves, and bone as it spins through the body.

When the doctor came by to check me the morning after surgery, it seemed like he had to cut through an endless wrapping of gauze to expose the wounds. When he did, I didn't take much comfort in what I saw. There was a slit four inches long and bone deep just under my right knee, a hole four inches long and four inches deep in my inner thigh, and an eight-inch gash all the way to the ribs in my right side.

The doctor told me that he had cleaned a lot of rubber—material from my rain suit and fatigues—sand, and three pieces of shrapnel from the wounds.

"Three?" I asked.

"We couldn't find the one under your arm," he replied. "If it's still in there, it'll probably slowly move around inside your body. After about a year, it'll be covered with a gristly coating and won't cause any harm."

The wounds would have to be left open, cleaned with antiseptic, and rebandaged at least once and sometimes twice each day. I'd already seen the cleaning procedure done on other men on the ward, and I wondered how I was going to get through it. First a heavy shot of Demerol, then twenty to thirty minutes later the cleaning cart came. Men cried, screamed, and even crawled out of bed in a futile attempt to hide and keep from having their wounds cleaned. With a Korean Marine on one side and Pat on the other, I wasn't about to do any of these things.

Two hours after the doctor talked to me, I had my first experience with the cleaning cart. Even with a hefty dose of pain killer, I stopped the corpsman halfway through the procedure. It felt as though my brain was going to explode. I had to have something to get my mind off of the pain. I asked the corpsman to take the pillowcase from my pillow and roll it in a tube, I bit down and nodded for him to continue. I set my only thoughts on destroying that pillowcase as I bit, ripped, and tore at it with my teeth. Pillowcase number one didn't last two days before I'd chewed it to pieces.

I usually had the same corpsman, and we soon became friends. I had to have two cleanings the second day, and in the afternoon he handed me a new pillowcase and gently got me into a wheelchair. I'd just had my shot, so I asked where we were going.

"You'll see," he said. He wheeled me down a long corridor, stopped at a rarely used side door, and as he pushed me through it he said, "I think you need some fresh air." I was suddenly outside in a deserted part of the hospital grounds. He lit up a joint laced with opium and handed it to me.

"Maybe this will take some of the edge off."

"I'm sure it will. Thanks, Bill." We silently passed the joint back and forth, watching for any brass that might happen by.

When we had finished, he asked if I was ready. "Let's get it over with," I said, and then it was back to the ward. That little trip would become part of my daily routine. I knew the corpsmen and nurses often felt helpless to relieve the suffering that surrounded them daily, but at least one corpsman had come up with a partial solution. I was so stoned, I was seeing triple, and the afternoon cleaning went better, still nothing could stop the knife edge of pain from cutting to my very soul.

The cleaning the next morning didn't go well. When Bill pulled an egg-sized blood clot from my thigh, a small hole reopened in the femoral artery. Blood started to spray out of my leg, three feet in the air, as though someone was pumping the life out of me with a squirt gun.

I forgot the pain and watched in macabre fascination as Bill tried to stop the bleeding. Before long his face and uniform were covered with blood. It was all over the sheets and floor and not getting any better.

"Shit!" he said in frustration. "I'll be right back with a doctor, hang on." Hang on I thought, hang on to what? My blood was spraying this way and that, and all I could do was lie still and watch it happen. I didn't know it at the time, but someone else was intently watching the whole thing.

Not thinking to cover the wound with anything, I became

mesmerized with each squirt and tried to calculate how long
before I bled to death without a transfusion. When Bill returned, holding a bag of blood in one hand and pulling a doctor
down the hall by the sleeve with the other, I figured I had at
most thirty minutes left.

During the next twenty minutes, the surgeon wiped the blood
from his eyes with his sleeve at least a dozen times. The
bleeding stopped as quickly as it started. The surgeon said that
he was able to get a better hold with the stitches in the artery.

"How are you doing?"

"Okay, sir, I think."

I was given another pain shot and a few minutes to rest. The
bandages were cut away, and my side wound was cleaned.
Thus was the demise of pillowcase number two.

At 11:00 that night, I was resting fairly well, trying to fall
asleep, when I met the smallest member of the ward. A mouse
jumped from the Korean's table onto my shoulder, ran across
my chest onto my table, and disappeared. At first I was mad.
Rats and mice were so troublesome in Vietnam, I'd come to
dislike all rodents. When he did it again the next night and
every night afterward, I couldn't help but respect his audacity.
I could set my watch by him. It was as though he was making
rounds like the doctors. I reckon every man on the ward tried
to catch that mouse and never came close. What did they
expect, it was a Vietnamese mouse. I nicknamed him "Uncle
Ho," and when I was eventually moved to another ward, I left
some candy for him in a partly open drawer in my bedside
table.

*

Scout Snipers
Da Nang Hospital
November 10, 1969

Dear Mom,

I'm doing pretty well so far. They're taking good care of me.
Pat didn't leave today for which I'm glad. I don't think he
minds, either. I learned one thing last night. You've got to be
an expert to use a bed pan. Pat was funny, he said, "I don't
mind emptying your pee can, but the bed pan is going too far."
I got a corpsman to take care of it for me. His name is Bill. The
nurses are good people too.

Pat hung my state flag on the end of my bed. It's good for

conversation. I'll close for now and write to Laura. Will write again tomorrow.

Love, Joseph

I'd settled into a routine: a big shot of pain killer, followed by a wheelchair ride down the hallway, and back for another session with a pillowcase.

One morning, Bill and I were passing a joint back and forth, when he lightheartedly remarked, "You know we've had to increase our order for pillowcases." His voice turned serious, "You've gained a lot of respect around here, Joe."

I asked what he meant. "You have some of the worst wounds on the ward, but you don't scream when they're cleaned."

We finished the joint in silence. All Bill knew was that it had something to do with the pillowcases. He didn't ask how I did it, and I'm glad; I don't know if I had a decent answer myself.

One of the most motivating steps in my recovery was the incident with the bedpan. I swore I would make it to the head the next time. When that time came, I had Bill get me into a wheelchair and roll me to the head. He was a little hesitant.

"Are you sure you're up to this?"

"Yeah, just leave me next to the toilet." I spent most of two hours getting from the wheelchair onto the toilet seat and back again. Seemingly a small accomplishment, but I was up and moving on my own even if for only a couple feet. It was too much pain and effort to do it each time to pee, but I wasn't about to use a bedpan again.

*

Scout Snipers
Da Nang Hospital
November 11, 1969

Dear Mom,

A note to go with this film. I'm going to have Pat mail it for me. I think you'll find the photos real interesting. I hope they come out. I've got another roll to send.

Most of these pictures I took this last time in Arizona. By the way, that's where we got hit. There are a few pictures of a firefight. We finished off the roll in the hospital. I didn't have any flash cubes so I don't know if those will come out or not. Must close now.

Love, Joseph

I went through three cameras during my tour, and took pictures of everything, except bodies. My mind was quite capable of permanently forming images of the dead and wounded, besides Mom would see the prints. I sent dozens of rolls home to be developed. Mom had duplicates made. She kept one set there and sent me the other so I would be sure they were coming out.

I moved around so much and, like any sniper, was so active in the field that a diary would have been nearly impossible to keep. The combination of photos, letters home, and my mother's meticulous entries in her own diary helped make this writing possible.

★

Scout Snipers
Da Nang Hospital
November 12, 1969

Dear Mom,

See, I told you I would write every chance I get. I feel pretty good tonight. Some of the soreness is gone so I can work the muscles in my leg a little. They still have to clean the clotted blood out of the wounds. The doc says it'll still be two days before they can sew me up.

Pat's gone and just like a mother hen I gave him all sorts of instructions. He's going to try to send the mail I have at An Hoa to me.

My Korean friend helps me now. He doesn't know a single word of English and I sure don't know any Korean, but he always seems to know when I need something. I was asleep tonight when they brought chow and when he woke me up he had a tray piled high with food. Guess he figures a big guy like me eats a lot more than he does. I can just smile and nod my head and he knows I'm grateful.

Well, Mom, they'll be turning the lights out soon. I'm doing fine, so don't worry at all.

Love, Joseph

The Da Nang Hospital treated anyone who needed it, even if the rules had to be bent once and a while. North and South Vietnamese, Koreans, a few Australians, and an endless stream of sick and wounded Marines and navy personnel.

At times, the corpsmen and nurses were overloaded. If a man needed help and couldn't fend for himself, he had to rely on the buddy system. When Pat returned to An Hoa, I thought I'd lost my buddy, but I hadn't. Bill was right. I had gained respect by my methodical destruction of one pillowcase after another.

That someone who'd silently watched the bleeding episode and all the wound cleanings didn't hesitate to fill in for Pat. The Korean lieutenant paid me honor by waiting on me constantly. He was recovering from malaria and able to get around freely. Over the next few days, he emptied my piss can, brought chow, picked up things I dropped, and knew when to run down a corpsman to give me a pain shot. Not one word was spoken between us the whole time, but he had an uncanny ability to tell when I needed something. I liked our South Korean brothers immensely; my only regret was that I didn't serve side-by-side with them in actual combat.

★

Scout Snipers
Da Nang Hospital
November 13, 1969

Dear Mom,

Well, another day and I'm getting along. The doctor said they may sew me up this afternoon. That will sure be a relief. Dan came from An Hoa and brought the mail I had there.

Later—I just got back from getting stitched up. I don't feel so good now, but nothing the kid can't handle. At least they don't have to clean me out anymore. Must close. I'm doing FINE.

Love, Joseph

When Dan brought my mail from An Hoa, the first letter I read was very disturbing. It was from Laura and mostly about her attendance at a party and the good time she had with a friend of mine. There I lay, and a "Jody" was back home taking care of my girl. It couldn't have come at a worse time, and I decided to break my engagement to Laura when I returned to the World. I knew that neither of us would ever be the same again.

When a man went to be sewn up, there was an informal celebration on the ward. He wouldn't have to endure the wound cleaning anymore. My time came. With a sense of anticipation and apprehension and, of course, a trusty pillowcase, I was wheeled to a large room and put on another stainless steel table with a single, bright light overhead.

Seemingly from nowhere, a burly doctor leaned forward into the light and asked, "Where do you want me to start?" I told him, "Anywhere," and tried to figure out if having a choice about it made any difference.

He started on my knee with steel-wire sutures and it went okay. He did the thigh wound next and it went well. Two out of three, I figured no sweat, then there was the side wound. When he inserted the wire into my side, my stomach muscles tightened so hard my chest and legs snapped together, rattling my teeth. He pulled the wire out and my muscles slowly relaxed enough to lie back down.

"Hey, Doc, what the fuck was that?"

"Sorry, friend, there's some major nerves that help control the abdominal muscles in the way. I'll give it more local anesthetic, but I doubt that it'll help."

It didn't, and when the same thing happened again I had to call a halt. "Wait a minute, Doc, we gotta figure something out here. Another one of those might break my neck."

We decided to do it while I bent forward, since I was going to end up there anyway. It worked, but it would also be a week before I could fully straighten up again.

★

Scout Snipers
Da Nang Hospital
November 14, 1969

Dear Mom,

A quick note to let you know what's up. They're moving me to a different section. I'm able to walk around some now, so they'll be putting me in medical hold soon. I'll be here in Da Nang for at least another ten days and then I'll go to An Hoa to finish healing.

I'm not ready for any foot races, but I can walk if I take it easy. Doc says I'm getting along exceptionally well, no sweat. Take care and I'll write when I get moved.

Love, Joseph

As soon as I was able to limp around on my own, I went to the armory each day to check on my rifle. I know I drove that poor armorer crazy, but my pack and its contents were gone. My state flag, which I had wrapped around the rifle barrel to keep it dry, the bolt rifle, and five rounds of match ammo were all I had left. But he politely took it from the rack and showed it to me. He even cleaned it and oiled the stock with linseed oil.

I also started looking for a way to get off the hospital grounds and have some fun.

*

Scout Snipers
Da Nang Hospital
November 15, 1969

Dear Mom,

They still haven't moved me so I don't know what's up. I don't think they do, either. I've been walking all over the place. I even took a shower this morning, the first since I left An Hoa, much to the relief of everyone. I do feel like a walking junkyard though, they used steel sutures to sew me up. Shucks, I'll be back to work in no time.

I went to see *Gone With the Wind* last night. It sure was long, but it wasn't too bad for a thirty-year-old movie. I want you to do something for me. Take as much money out of my account as necessary and pay off Laura's ring as soon as possible.

I haven't had any mail except for what they brought down from An Hoa. None has come through to this address and it's been eight days, I'm kind of worried that it won't.

I'm doing well, which even surprises me. I'm glad cuz this hanging around gets on my nerves. They brought a friend of mine in from the 5th last night. He got shot in the back and it looks like he'll be going to Japan. I'm going to close now and go sit outside for a while. Take care.

Love, Joseph

The care at the hospital was outstanding, but I was bush-hardened and felt confined. I started pushing my daily walks, or should I say hobbles, farther and farther. The hospital complex was huge, and I was determined to see it all.

Returning to the ward from the chow hall one day, I noticed a big, three-story building, alone and separated from the main buildings. It was encircled by a ten-foot-high chain link fence, topped with barbed wire and flood lights. SPs were standing at precise intervals on a line painted fifty feet away from the fence all the way around the building. It would be a long painful trip, but my curiosity got the better of me and I set off.

I approached a shore patrol, and he immediately came to port arms. "Please state your name and business."

"What is this place?" I asked.

"The wounded POWs are kept here."

"Oh, yeah? Uh, why the painted line?"

"Anyone who crosses that line without clearance will be shot."

"I see. Thanks." I took a last glance at the stark building and its surroundings before limping back to the ward. I gave this building a nickname, Pandora's Box.

★

Scout Snipers
Da Nang Hospital
November 17, 1969

Dear Mom,

I'm still kicking around. I've got about another week here before they send me back to An Hoa. Sure wish I knew what was going on back there.

Some general came around and gave me my Purple Heart. That's one medal I didn't count on getting.

I'm going to medical hold this morning. The doc says I'm healing real well. This sort of life is starting to get on my nerves, so I won't mind going back and they won't have any trouble finding someone to fill my bed.

I've seen quite a few guys I went through boot camp and ITR with here. The ones that are here are better off than a lot of them I've heard about. A lot of my Stateside friends haven't made it through.

Mom, I'm healing like crazy, so there's no need for you to worry. I'm tougher than I thought.

I'll close now and get my meager belongings ready to move to another building. Tell all hi, take care.

Love, Joseph

During one of my walks around the hospital, I unknowingly entered the ward with mostly men who'd lost their genitals. The total silence struck me right away, no small talk and certainly no laughter. Blank stares met me from each bed, and I was halfway through the ward before I realized it. I felt terrible, as though I'd intruded on a special, personal brand of misery that my mind couldn't deal with.

I shuffled off the ward as fast as I could. When I leaned

against the wall to catch my breath, I shuddered at the thought of how close I'd come to being on that ward. I gave it a nickname, too, the Death-After-Life Ward.

When I returned to my bed, it had been changed and a clean gown placed neatly on top. They usually don't change them that early, then I noticed not all the beds had been made.

When Bill came with a pain shot, I asked, "What's up?"

"You're gonna get a medal this morning. After you've changed your gown, stick around the bed."

I was usually in quite a lot of pain after my walks, especially this time, thanks to my blunder onto the Death-After-Life Ward. I was quite content to relax and let the pain shot dull the pain and my thoughts.

A half hour later five of us were wheeled in our beds to a hallway nearby and set evenly apart along one wall. Almost immediately, a two-star general and his small entourage came into the hall. An aide read a short speech about wounds received during combat in the defense of the Republic of South Vietnam and something about the appreciation of the American people. At that point I quit listening.

My name was read, and the general came to my bedside. He asked how I was doing.

"Okay, sir."

"I hear you've been a little hard on our pillowcases."

"Yes, sir, I guess I have."

He leaned over and softly said, "Get well, Marine," and quite appropriately pinned a Purple Heart to my pillow.

Just before I was moved to medical hold, Bill brought me a new rolled-up pillowcase. "This is from the staff," he said. "What's inside is from me." I unrolled the pillowcase and found six joints laid end-to-end. All I could say was, "Thanks, man, I'll never forget you."

Going to medical hold was my chance to make a break for it if I could get my hands on a uniform. I still wasn't allowed a pass, but I was determined to get away from the hospital for a while. The opportunity came very unexpectedly on the eighteenth.

Medical hold was more like a large barracks, with cots instead of beds. My wounds were healing well, but I still had a painful limp from my knee, and even with a uniform, my awkward way of walking would tip off the shore patrol at the gate. As I lay there trying to figure a way out, I thought I saw a familiar face coming my way. It couldn't be, I thought. I rubbed my eyes and looked again. It was, sure enough, Dave Young. He was just getting over malaria and had found out I was in the hospital.

We were elated to see each other, and as we talked nonstop, Dave threw his pack on my cot and opened it. He pulled out a uniform and a pair of boots. "I thought you might have use for these, and I see I was right. You look like hell in pajamas."

"Yeah, and I feel like it, too. I've gotta get out of here. Say, how did you know my boot size?"

"I didn't, I just told the pogue at supply to give me a pair of big boots, and he said he had more of that size than any other." I thought briefly of the trouble I had getting them in the bush, and here in Da Nang they had a surplus of size twelve jungle boots.

I still had the problem of the limp, so while Dave tidied up the uniform, I scoured the ward for some extra pain pills. I came up with a handful of Darvon and swallowed them while I slowly got dressed. The pills helped, but I still had quite a limp. We decided that if Dave walked close on my right side, I could lean against him enough to disguise the fact. It worked. We walked right past the guards and caught the first bus to the beer gardens. We spent the day there, and the combination of pills and beer made mush out of my brains. I fell and reopened my knee wound.

When we got back to the ward, Dave used his pack for a pillow, stretched out on the floor, and was out for the night. There was a note on my cot which read, "Ward, where are you? Bill." As I changed into my hospital gown and robe, I wondered what he wanted; I'd been moved from his ward. It didn't matter, I had to have my knee checked, and I didn't need a doctor asking questions that I wouldn't want to answer.

Bill was off duty for the night, so I went to his room. He took one look at me and said, "You snuck out of the hospital, didn't you?"

"Yeah, and it wasn't easy."

"You damn jar heads. Why didn't you find me, I'd have gotten you a pass. Let me see that knee."

"Why were you looking for me?"

"I want you to meet someone. That hole isn't bad; I can close it with butterfly stitches, but you've got to be more careful. You're not healed yet."

"Okay, okay, but who did you want me to meet?" I watched him close and bandage an inch-long tear in my knee.

"You'll see," he replied without looking away from his work. One thing about it, Bill had a flair for the dramatic. Maybe that's why we got along so well from the start.

"There," he said, putting the final touches on his patch job. I asked again who he wanted me to meet. He looked at me, "You okay to walk or do you want me to get a wheelchair?"

The increasing pain in my wounds told me I was definitely getting sober. "I'll walk. Let's go."

He steadied me as we walked past the simple private rooms the corpsmen lived in. We rounded a corner, and at the end of the hallway was a scene that didn't fit at all with the hospital norm. The walls between two cubicles had been taken out and a large Vietnamese tapestry covered a twenty-foot entrance to something.

I gave Bill a perplexed look. He just smiled and said, "You're gonna meet a for-real Medal of Honor winner."

"No shit, how bad is he?"

"Oh, he's quite well, come on." My curiosity was tearing at me, as we pushed through the tapestry without even asking permission. Expecting a wounded man in bed with lavish surroundings, I wasn't prepared for what I saw. The room was stark and lit only by three candles. On the left was a regular canvas cot, a footlocker, and wardrobe. In the middle of the room was a table and stools made from empty grenade cases. The makeshift table was covered with a small tapestry. The medal lay casually next to a candle.

Behind the table sat a man with long hair. A corpsman was seated on each side of him. Bill introduced me to him. There was a little banter amongst the corpsmen as the man took a joint out of a breast pocket, lit it up, and we passed it around.

I don't know which fascinated me more, the medal or the man. Most Medals of Honor are awarded posthumously, but this guy didn't seem to have a thing wrong with him.

He saw how I looked back and forth from the medal to him over and over. How crazy this is, I thought, passing a joint around a Medal of Honor. When we'd finished the man told me, "Go ahead, pick it up."

My distress was obvious. Most people only see this medal behind a glass case. To actually touch one seemed a desecration somehow. The room was very quiet, and I was torn between the desire to do it and the feeling that I didn't have the right.

"Go on, look at it," he said. I hesitantly picked up the medal and leaned closer to the candle.

The medal is no larger than any other, and it takes close inspection of the inscription before it gives its identity away. The thing that sets the medal apart from all others is the way in which it's worn, around the neck by a wide, sky blue band.

The medal seemed secondary, as I felt the material of the band. It was slightly soiled from the hands of men trying to do what I was doing, figure out if it was the medal or the neck band that made it so special. I looked up in confusion.

"I suppose you're wondering how I got it." I nodded. I was at a loss for words.

"I pulled a couple wounded grunts out of the line of fire and jumped on a grenade." I looked at him in disbelief.

He smiled ever-so-slightly. "I had on a flak jacket and one handy that I threw under me when I jumped onto the grenade. I got off with some broken ribs and scratches."

He must have died in his own mind a thousand times in those brief moments before it went off. He knew full well that flak jackets weren't designed to take anywhere near that kind of abuse. He had earned the medal just as much as the man blown to bits by such an act. I felt the material one last time and laid the medal back on the table.

When I looked at Bill, the conversation began again. "Come on," he said. "You need some rest."

I shook the man's hand. "Take care," he said.

"You, too," I replied, and we left.

A short way down the hall Bill turned to me. "He can have anything he wants, you know."

"Why does he live like that?"

"It's his way of protesting the war."

I'd been treated to an unheard of chance to pay my personal respect to all the Medal of Honor recipients that didn't live to see their medals awarded.

★

Scout Snipers
Da Nang Hospital/An Hoa
November 28, 1969

Dear Mom,

I'll start by saying that I'm back in An Hoa. I got here late yesterday. I was released from the hospital on the 25th, that's the day they took my stitches out.

I was an out-patient from the 20th till the 25th, which meant I could go to the USOs and EM clubs during the day, but on the 18th who should come to see me but Dave Young. We were together till I came back yesterday. He's over his malaria and was going back to his unit today or tomorrow.

We also found two other guys from home that we knew, Randy Peterson and his brother Barry. It was just like old home week. We tried to call Mike, but couldn't get through. We checked the hospitals for Nick, but he wasn't at either of them.

There was a lot of mail for me here, and don't worry about that mail you sent to the hospital cuz most of it got through to An Hoa.

The last letter from you was dated November 18th, so I'm not too far behind. I knew you would be worried, so I made two MARS calls, but there was no answer. I'll try again here. If I don't get through here, I'll call on R and R. I'm down for January and I'm still going to Australia.

Mom, the only wound that's going to give me trouble is my knee. I can walk okay, but stairs and hills do hurt some. The doctor said I would have trouble with it the rest of my life. It's really more of an inconvenience than anything.

I'm not sure if I'm going back to the bush, but I imagine so. The other two wounds still act up some, but I think with some exercise they'll be okay.

Yesterday was Thanksgiving and they served turkey with all the trimmings.

Well, Mom, I've gone on long enough. I'm just as ornery as ever. Thanks for the package. Will write again soon.

Love, Joseph

I rarely slept past 4:00 A.M., but I had pushed it too hard the day and night before. I awoke at 8:00 A.M. on the nineteenth to the steady, monotone sound of someone repeatedly calling my name.

My eyes snapped open to see Bill standing there. "You alive?"

"Yeah, I think so." I slowly sat up. "Christ, I feel terrible."

"You should, you had quite a day yesterday. You're gonna do it anyway, you may as well save us all some headaches." He laid a new starched uniform on my cot, handed me a bottle of pain pills and a pass. Suddenly, I was fighting the tears I'd held back for so long.

"Ah, what are you going on about? Hell, they would have probably given you a pass in a couple days anyway."

I saw Bill one more time before returning to An Hoa, but on the day my orders came through to leave the hospital, he was away on liberty. I knew he had a girlfriend in Da Nang somewhere, yet his absence suspiciously coincided with my departure. Knowing Bill, saying good-bye would have seemed too final.

From the nineteenth to the twenty-fifth, I was seldom at the hospital, as Dave and I set out to really see Da Nang and look for guys we knew. A formidable task indeed.

We knew Nick had been wounded, and all we'd heard was that he wasn't hurt badly, so we checked the hospitals in Da Nang. When we didn't find him, we assumed he'd been sent back to his unit, while the whole time he was on the Hospital Ship *Repose* anchored in Da Nang harbor. Frustrated, we went to the beer gardens.

We spent a fruitless morning trying to get through on a field phone to Mike at Hill 37. Let down again, we went to the beer gardens.

A great USO show put on by the Australians with lots of rock and roll and pretty girls made us wish we were back in the World. Homesick, we went to the beer gardens. From the squalid refugee camps to the air-conditioned air force mess hall, we covered Da Nang.

On the twenty-fourth, a tedious search of the registry at the USO at China Beach revealed the names of two brothers we went to high school with, Randy and Barry Peterson. They were stationed together at the motor pool near the airport. We decided to try to find them the next day after my stitches were taken out and I was discharged from the hospital.

My orders were cut on the twenty-fifth, and naturally stated that I was to catch the first available helicopter to An Hoa. "Screw the orders," I told Dave, and we went to check out my bolt rifle. Dave stretched his stay in Da Nang with a sudden "mild relapse of malaria."

When we found Randy, he was, to say the least, surprised and sent a friend to get Barry. "We're going to the EM club. How'd you guys find me?"

"We followed the flies," Dave said.

When Barry entered the tent, we'd managed to get four friends from a middle-American town of fifteen thousand together at the same time. The odds of this happening in Vietnam were astronomical. I knew without a doubt that I would be later than usual getting back to An Hoa.

We had what seemed like a full lifetime of things to talk about as we walked to the EM club. Randy was the first to enter, and in his excitement at seeing us, he forgot to take his cover off. A bouncer the size of a water buffalo, standing just inside the door, snatched Randy's cover and slammed it into his stomach. We were pissed, but the club was full, and a fight would have shut it down and had everyone after us. We decided on a tactical retreat.

We all fell asleep in a foxhole, and pain woke me early the next morning. I hadn't slept on the ground since I was wounded, and I didn't need Bill nagging at me to take it easy for a while. I took some pills and got the others up so we could go to Randy's tent to get warm. I was in a lot of pain and really did have to take it easier than I had been.

The four of us passed the time drinking beer and talking about home. By noon, Randy was becoming worried about a man from his tent who had been gone since early the evening before and still hadn't returned. He went to find him and came back a half hour later, barely able to stop laughing long enough to get the story out.

The guy had gotten so loaded, he stole a truck from the motor pool and drove it full tilt down a runway of what at the time was the busiest airport in the world. Somehow he didn't get hit by an airplane, and—thoroughly convinced he could make a ten-ton truck fly—he ran off the end of the runway and crashed. But for a broken nose and some bruises, he was okay. The plane that took him back to the States for a possible section eight discharge flew much better than the truck did.

My time was running out. If I was more than two days late reporting in at An Hoa, the gunny would send my squad leader to look for me, more out of worry than concern for any regulations.

Dave was going to stay around Da Nang for a day or two before having a miraculous recovery from his "relapse" of malaria. I reluctantly said my good-byes and caught the late afternoon chopper to An Hoa. I gave the gunny my orders.

"Late again, huh, Ward?" Before I could come back with my usual response, he asked, "How are you?"

"I'm okay, Gunny, don't know if my knee is up to the bush right yet, but I don't want a desk job."

"Good, you can work the tower and lines while you heal."

"Fine with me, Gunny," I said as I got up to leave. At the door I couldn't resist the opportunity. I turned to him and said, "I had trouble catching a bird." With a twinkle in his eyes and a big grin, he came back with, "Get out of here, Ward."

I went to my tent and sat on my cot. I was home.

★

Scout Snipers
An Hoa
November 29, 1969

Dear Mom,

You wanted to know why I wanted that ring paid off. Well, here it is: I'm breaking my engagement to Laura. I should never have tried to tie her down while I was here. It's been a long haul. What can I say?

Mom, this is just a note to let you know that I'm doing fine. Don't worry about me, I don't think this war needs me much longer. I guess I'm just tired.

Thanks for the packages. How do I really say thanks for being the best mom in the world?

By the way, I've only got a hundred and twenty days at most, and the kid will be home soon. I better close and get some letters written. Take care.

Love, Joseph

I took the letter from Laura I received in the hospital as a Dear John. Of the two ways to handle a Dear John, I took the least final option by deciding to suck it up and get on. On the other hand, a few guys took their DJs too hard, and something inside them snapped. They would put a .45 caliber pistol to their heads and pull the trigger, or stand up in plain view during a firefight which was almost certain death.

Once I watched as a grunt stood up during a firefight and

started dancing. I don't know why he didn't get shot, bullets were hitting close to me, and I was flat on the ground. He was still dancing when the fight was over. Two days earlier, he'd gotten a Dear John letter from his wife. She'd found someone new and wanted a divorce. To him, he'd lost all reason for surviving the war. His fire team wrestled him to the ground, and when they carried him to the medevac, he was totally incoherent.

The first few days back at An Hoa I rested and spent most of my light duty at that bunker in no-man's-land. We had two new guys, and I took one or the other out with me as my partner. I felt it was a softer introduction to the war than the one I had.

On December 2, at 4:00 A.M. Private First Class Suther, in-country just four days, was on watch with the Starlite. He called my name. "I think I saw something," he said. After hours of looking through a Starlite scope, fatigue and nerves could cause a man to see things, especially a new guy. I rubbed my eyes and sat up.

"How sure are you?" I asked.

"Pretty."

"What sector?" He indicated a point about six hundred yards out. The visibility was good that night, but seeing anything other than a mirage over five hundred yards away with the Starlite was questionable. I looked and didn't see anything. I knew calling for an illumination round would tip Charlie off and he'd get away, if he was there in the first place.

Suther may have been a new guy, but he was my partner, and I gave him the benefit of the doubt. I called headquarters to be sure one of our own patrols wasn't coming back in through that sector. HQ's response was "Negative."

I switched to fire control, and a gunny in charge of a battery of 81mm mortars. I gave him the coordinates of an area three hundred yards from our bunker. "I need a five hundred yard wide dispersion of ground and aerial bursts, and walk 'em straight away from the base."

"How far?" he asked.

"I'll tell you. Oh, yeah, no flares until the first dozen have gone out."

"You'll have ordnance going over your heads in sixty seconds," and he hung up. After the first forty or fifty rounds, Suther looked at me with a mixture of disbelief.

After another seventy-five rounds, I called off the mortars. They had covered an area five hundred by one thousand yards.

Illumination rounds would keep our sector lit until daylight. If anyone was out there, they either didn't feel very good or they got out when they were spotted.

As usual, at first light I was back at the showers, and after cleaning up, I headed toward the mess hall. On the way, Suther ran up to me to say a search at dawn had turned up a satchel charge lying next to a large pool of blood eight hundred yards from our bunker.

"Why did you believe me? You didn't see anything. How'd you know?" I had to shut him up.

"Look," I said. "I didn't know for sure, but I'd be a damn poor team leader if I didn't listen to my partner, now wouldn't I? Come on, let's get some chow."

We usually got our trays and went back to our cots to eat alone. Not because we liked it, but being privy to classified information, chow hall gossip could be dangerous. It also helped snipers maintain a low profile while in the rear.

"What's your first name, Suther?"

"Call me Red."

"Okay, Red, let's eat in the NCO mess." The NCO mess hall was for lance corporals and above.

"How am I going to get in, I'm a PFC." I looked at him thinking, God, was I that naive when I got here? Probably so. I took the lance corporal bars off my collar and handed them to him.

"Put 'em on and give me yours. Now let's go."

As we walked to the chow hall, I told him that after he'd been there awhile, most everyone would know he was a sniper, and things would smooth out for him, but to watch out for the requests.

"What requests," he asked. When I explained, he became very quiet.

"Sergeants and lieutenants only rate a fragging," I added.

"What's a fragging?" I hesitated, he looked so young.

"How old are you?"

"Nineteen, why?" I didn't answer. I suddenly felt much older than my twenty years.

The NCO mess hall was nice, and after we sat down with our trays, there was table service for water, coffee, milk, and green Kool-Aid. A lot of the food in the Corps was green. Red ordered milk and was perplexed when I told him no. He changed his order to Kool-Aid.

"Why no milk?" he asked.

"You'll be going to the bush pretty soon and won't be able to get milk. If you're out for very long, you'll be craving it so bad when you come in that you'll drink milk until you're sick, really sick. You'll swell up like a balloon for two or three days, so try to break yourself now." Our conversation lightened as we ate.

"What's going on back in the World?"

"Are the gooks as good as I've heard?"

"Got a girl?"

"What's it like in the bush?"

"What series number are they on at boot camp?" and so on. After we'd finished eating, I told him I wanted his help.

"Yeah, sure. Anything," he replied. "What?"

"I need a pack mule." He looked at me in confusion. "Let's go; I'll tell you about it while I get my bolt rifle and go to ordnance." We talked as we walked.

"It's been awhile since I was in the village, and I gotta get there before they send me off somewhere. I want to take some weapons to the militia, and my knee isn't up to humping much weight."

"Where do we get a pass?" he asked. I grinned and held the bolt rifle up.

"Got it right here."

The sergeant who worked ordnance knew me well by then.

"What do you want this time, Sniper?"

"Uhh, let me think. Six claymores. Ah, a dozen grenades, six belts of M-60 ammo, and fifteen trip flares. Hmm, got anything new?"

"Yeah," he replied. "Some LAWs with flechette rounds."

"Okay, give me six."

"You know where to sign for this stuff," he chided as he started pulling everything on the counter. Since snipers had security clearance, we weren't required to show written orders to get supplies. He once asked me what I did with all that unsniperlike ordnance.

"We use it to keep people away from our tents," I said. We both laughed, and he never again questioned where all the stuff was going. I loaded Red down with as much as I thought he could carry and got the rest.

When we walked past the SPs at the gate without being stopped, Red said, "Damn, that was easy! They told me I had to have a pass to leave the base."

"If you get to be team leader, you'll understand."

"All those mortars last night, you called them in just like they were nothing."

"That wasn't piss. If you make team leader before you get your butt shot off, you'll be calling in air and artillery strikes a thousand times as heavy."

"Do you go to the village often?"

"Whenever I can. I have friends there."

The village was only a couple miles away, but we had to stop several times along the road. My knee was really raising hell. When we got there, some militiamen came to greet us. They'd already sent someone to find Lee Oot. We unloaded the gear and sat on a poncho liner, my knee kept me from squatting.

A militiaman brought us two bowls of rice wine. I thought about warning Red, but I'd found out the hard way and he could, too. When he took a big swallow and started choking, I probably laughed harder than the militiamen who loved to play that trick on the naive Americans. After a few minutes, Lee came jogging toward me.

"Joe, Joe, I hear you wounded. You okay?"

"Yeah, sure."

We hugged, and Lee couldn't keep from crying. Red surely thought it a strange spectacle. Lee looked at Red for the first time.

"Long rifle?"

"Yes, and he's okay. When the time comes, teach him what you've taught me. I also want him to take over the CAP work here." I pointed to the things we'd brought. "I wish it was more, Lee."

He gave me his customary nod, but kept looking at me like I was a ghost. Red was at a loss when Lee and I started talking to each other in a mixture of Vietnamese, French Vietnamese slang, and English. We began talking about things only Lee and I understood. Lee was a major source of intelligence information, and he had a lot to tell me.

"My knee is starting to feel better. How about another bowl of wine," I asked. Lee clapped his hands and another was brought. Red was gallantly working his way through the last of his wine, and I'm not certain, but I think I saw his eyes roll a couple times. Lee asked if I had seen Ann yet.

"No, I had enough trouble just getting here. As a matter of fact, maybe you could find us a ride back to the base."

"No sweat, Joe, no sweat."

"Lee, I've seen things since we were last together that have been bothering me. The NVA and VC are healthier and better equipped than when I arrived. Lee, it's mostly NVA down here now."

He looked at the ground. "Yes, the NVA come more and more, and the VC support them very much. They are getting very strong."

"Lee, let me get you and your family out of country." His blank stare told me he was finally thinking about it. After a couple silent minutes he half-heartedly declined my offer.

"Damn you, Lee," I snapped. Although his face showed no disappointment, I knew it was there. The discussion over, I changed the subject. "I've got to get back and get some sleep. I'm on lines tonight. How about that ride?"

"Sure thing, GI," and he smiled. He left and returned with two mopeds and two young women to drive them. In his own special way, Lee had a lot of class.

"Tell Ann hi." He nodded and waved as we took off. I had to keep my knee out to the side of the moped, but it sure beat walking. Red had a different problem. His first encounter with rice wine got him so drunk his head was wobbling. He didn't make fifty yards before he fell off the back of the bike. We had to employ a common method the Vietnamese used to get wounded people to a medical facility. We tied his hands together above the breasts of the girl driving. It worked like a charm.

At the gate, the SPs stopped us since we were bringing civilians into the base without clearance. One SP looked at Red.

"What's wrong with him?"

"He's in love."

"Looks drunk to me."

I unslung the bolt rifle from my shoulder and laid it across my lap. I had played my hand, and when they saw the rifle they didn't know what to do.

"Look, Sarge, we have lines tonight and all we want is to get some sleep. I'll vouch for the girls," I said.

"I don't know what you guys have been up to, but go on in, and I never seen you," replied the sergeant in charge, shaking his head.

The girls helped me put Red in his cot. I gave them each five dollars MPC (Military Payment Certificates), and they rode off.

I went to my cot and fell asleep hugging my rifle. At 6:30 P.M. my squad leader got me up for lines.

"Who you taking with you, Suther?"

"Yeah."

"What do you think of him?"

"He's smart, got eyes like a hawk, and if he can shoot, he'll be a good man."

I headed out for another night on the lines.

★

Scout Snipers
Liberty Bridge
December 6, 1969

Dear Mom,

I'm still around. Got a letter from you yesterday, and the card you sent. Sure was nice.

I'm at Liberty Bridge and about all we've been doing is standing tower watch and sometimes riding security on the road sweep. My knee gets in the way once in a while, but I'm learning to get along with it, other than that I'm fine. I'm down for another R and R next month. I hope nothing happens this time.

You said Nick was on a hospital ship at Da Nang. Dave and I were going to check them, but we figured he wouldn't be there. Sure wish we had now.

Well, I've got to try and get some more letters written. Take Care.

Love, Joseph

My first assignment out of the hospital was Liberty Bridge with Suther as my partner. Liberty Bridge, I thought, that's not bad duty. There's even a small EM club there. I grabbed my pack and gathered the rest of my gear together. It wasn't hard since everything was hooked to my web belt: my Turkish battle-ax, eighty rounds of match ammo, a first-aid kit, four canteens of water, and my bush hat. I carried my helmet and flak jacket to board the chopper. I stuffed my tactical maps in a thigh pocket and went to get Red. He was sick. I doubted that he'd ever been that drunk before.

"Saddle up, we're going out. The shape you're in, I don't think you're gonna enjoy this chopper ride. Meet me at the Seabees' bunker in twenty minutes."

The bunker the Seabees used was large and had two fans

going full blast at openings in the rear wall. The fans weren't for cooling, they were for sucking the pot smoke out. At any one time, ten to twenty guys would be in there smoking it up. Often the smoke was so thick it was hard to see the guy sitting by your side. There was always an ammo box full of joints near the entrance. I took one and sat next to Ron Willingham, an engineer I'd come to know well.

We talked a short while before a captain came in, took a joint out of the box, sat down across from us and lit up. It was like an underground club. Most everyone at the base knew about it, but nothing was ever done to shut it down. I looked up to see Red standing at the entrance.

"Come on in, Suther." He was hesitant. "That's an order, new guy." He reluctantly entered. "Hey, bring a couple joints with you," and I pointed to the ammo box. His eyes were still adjusting to the dark bunker. He took two joints from the box and started toward us, then he saw the captain. He came to a shaky attention and said, "Good morning, sir."

Oh, shit, I thought and grabbed him by his web belt and pulled him onto the bench beside me.

"Do you see that man in front of you now?"

"No, not very well now, but I think he's a cap—" I put my hand over his mouth.

"There's no rank in here, ever, do you understand?" He nodded. I took my hand away and told him to light one up.

"Light what up?"

"One of those joints you just picked up."

"But I've never smoked this stuff." I took him by the collar and pulled him close.

"Look, FNG, I don't want my partner puking on the chopper because he's hung over. Have you ever seen anyone puke in a helicopter?" He slowly shook his head. "Well it ain't a pretty sight. It's so windy you don't just throw up on yourself, but on everyone, and I won't allow you to disgrace the snipers like that. Now light up."

Forty-five minutes later, with a little assistance from me, Red boarded the chopper with the biggest, dumbest grin I'd ever seen plastered on his face. I threw his flak jacket on the bench and sat him on it opposite me. I had to smile as I watched him close one eye then abruptly open it while the other eyelid slowly slid shut. He was about to have his first real chopper ride.

We relieved the team already at the bridge, so we were kept

busy on tower watch and security for road sweeps. Road
sweeps were done in one of two ways. Two grunts would walk
the road in front of a tank, using metal detectors. Always
behind the tank was a truck with a .50-caliber machine gun
mounted on the roof, half a dozen grunts, an engineer, a corpsman, and sometimes a sniper team. The other method was to
attach a mine detonator to the front of the tank. The snout on
the detonator was twenty feet long and dragged heavy chains
over the road to set off the mines a safe distance away. Unfortunately, Charlie often countered this procedure by using
delay fuses. Sometimes the delay caught the truck behind the
tank. Another road sweep would leave An Hoa at the same
time we left, so the two sweeps would meet about midway
between the bases.

On the twelfth, we reached the usual meeting point, and the
other sweep wasn't there; the tank commander with the opposite sweep radioed that they had hit a mine. When we were in
sight of the other sweep, the tank was okay, but the truck
behind it was completely destroyed.

I thought I was hardened against the brutality of Vietnam by
then, but what I saw made me want to die. A delay fuse on a
two hundred pound box mine had exploded exactly beneath the
center of the truck. Pieces of the truck and men in it were
scattered over a hundred-yard radius. The first thought I had
was whether or not there was a sniper team aboard, although
the only reason for the other team to accompany a sweep would
be to get to an assignment elsewhere.

I ran up to the tank commander and asked if there had been
any snipers in the truck. He was visibly shaken, and his face
was pale. His voice quavered as he answered.

"I don't think so."

We still had to check, so Red and I began a grisly search of
the rubble.

I felt bad for Red as I heard him retch several times, and he
wasn't alone—a member of a tank crew vomited behind me. I
was nearly overcome by the heavy smell of burnt flesh myself.

We didn't find anything to indicate that a team was on the
truck, but something was bothering me more than usual at the
sight of such carnage. It was one of the bodies. Everything
from the waist down was gone, and the remains were charred.
Still, there was something about him. I went back to look at his
dog tags. They were scorched and partly melted into his chest.

Pieces of blackened flesh stuck to them as I pulled the tags away. When I read the name Lopez, I realized he was a friend from my platoon in ITR. I kept seeing his face as I remembered it in training. I don't know how long I knelt there, trying to will him to look that way again. My mind was like a broken record stuck in a nightmare groove.

Red must have sensed some of what I was going through because he gently put his hand on my shoulder. I stood and faced him, "Jesus Christ, Red, Jesus. Let's get the fuck outta here!"

I took the dog tags to the tank commander of their sweep and told him I knew Lopez. "He was a good man," I said bitterly. I started walking back to the bridge. One of the men from our truck shouted, "Don't you guys want a ride back?" I didn't answer; I just walked faster. We returned via a shortcut through the rice paddies and open fields, which cut the distance from eight miles to nearly four. It still took us most of the rest of the morning to reach the bridge. I had to stop often to rest my knee.

We were scheduled for the sweep the next morning, and I thought seriously about canceling us out, but after some soul-searching, I decided we'd go. I realized that to not get back in the saddle as it were, would be to give in to my fears. Fear and ignorance were killers in Vietnam.

I tried to be optimistic as we set out with the road sweep at dawn, the same as we had the day before. About three miles from the bridge we watched a jet streak low over a small tree line a half a mile away and drop a load of five-hundred-pound bombs. We were only mildly interested since we were outside the danger zone for such a strike, but something strange happened. A piece of shrapnel the size and shape of a grapefruit skipped across an open field heading straight for us. I figured, surely it would expend its energy before it got close. I didn't know if it was part of a bomb or what, but its size and shape kept it coming.

It was about a hundred yards away when three of us shouted "duck!" I grabbed Red by the arm and pulled him down. It hit the heavy tailgate hard enough to put an eighteen-inch-deep dent in it and send a stinging shudder through the entire truck.

That did it. We weren't getting any results on the sweeps as snipers, and just to have us along to give the tank free-fire clearance wasn't worth the risk. I pulled us off the sweeps and confined our duties to tower watch, lines, and a few short patrols.

On the thirteenth, we got the word that we were wanted at Hill 65. On the fourteenth another team relieved us, and we caught a chopper to the hill.

Chapter IV ★ One Hundred Days and Counting

★

Scout Snipers
Hill 65/An Hoa
December 19, 1969

Dear Mom,

A lot has happened in the last few days. I've gone from the bridge to Hill 65 and now back here to An Hoa. I'll tell you the story of the last few days when I get home. You won't believe it.

Well, the word is that the 5th is supposed to pull out in February, so I may get stuck going home on a ship. They've canceled all R and R's after January, so I'm not sure whether mine will come through or not. It's possible I may still get it, but I'm expecting not to. You can start looking for me anytime after February.

You remember Pat, my partner who was hit the same time I was? Well, he got hit again and was sent home. I guess he's going to be okay, but that poor guy sure had a rough tour. He'd only been in-country a little over two months.

Have you heard any more about Nick? Is he back in the States or what? Well, Mom, I better close. Take care and I'll write again soon.

Love, Joseph

P.S. I am enclosing my short timer's calendar. When you get it, color in a block each day starting with 100 and by the time you get to one, I should be home.

Pat was wounded the second time by an RPG while I was still on light duty. He caught shrapnel in both legs and one arm. It was his ticket home, and when he wrote me that he knew how I felt when I was wounded, I believed him totally. When I heard he'd been sent to Japan, I knew he was on his way back to the World.

Hill 65 was a major fire base with all the amenities: a PX, EM club, and old movies that were shown in the chow hall three nights a week.

There were two and a half sniper teams at the hill, because a team leader who was also the field squad leader had rotated home. I had seniority, so I automatically became the new squad leader. The only other man with any time in-country to speak of was Ron Saunders, who had three months. I teamed him up with Red.

Except for having to be field squad leader, it was good duty, that is until the night of the seventeenth. We'd taken a few rockets and mortars over the previous couple days, but otherwise it had been fairly quiet.

I'd been nursing my sore knee and a bottle of gook rum until about 9:30 P.M., when I went to the tower to check up on the sniper team. I'd put Red and Ron on the first watch of the night. Suddenly, a firefight started outside the lines, eight hundred yards away.

A company of Marines was returning to the base, when they were ambushed by a company of NVA. From my vantage point with the Big Eye, I had an amazing view of an intense firefight. It wasn't hard to tell who was who. We used red tracers; Charlie used green—as though the politicians had color-coded their pawns.

I'd spent too much time in the bush, and when I gave Ron the range and told him to fire, he looked at me with surprise. "Aren't you going to call for clearance?"

"Take too long. Fire!"

He aimed his M-14 and quickly capped a tracer and two match rounds. "Down a hair and walk right." That gave Ron the go-ahead and he fired another tracer and two match rounds.

"You're right on target, faster!" Shell casings were bouncing around inside of the tower as he emptied the first magazine. Red handed him another one. I told Ron to do the same thing, but faster. I knew the scope would streak out soon, and it would take time for it to recover. The effect of the bright tracers temporarily ruined the scope's capability. Red handed him another magazine. He had a rhythm going, and clip number two didn't last thirty seconds. Just then a bullet hit the tower.

"What was that?" Red asked.

"Hell, Red, they're shooting back at us. What did you expect?" In fact, bullets were hitting the tower with some regularity. Ron went through another magazine, and I snatched the scope from its mount, and we got down behind the sandbag liner of the tower. Ron and I talked while he reloaded. Red muttered a different swear word each time a bullet hit the tower.

"Looks like they got a machine gun on us," I said. Ron agreed.

"Well, it sure ain't safe to leave the tower now, even if we jump. What do we do?" he asked.

"Shoot the bastard," I said. "I'll see if I can find him." The scope was nearly recovered when I rested it on a sandbag. I immediately got back down.

"Shit, Ron, he's just outside the perimeter and about fifty yards to the right of their main unit. Look, I can't ask you to get up again, we're too hot. Why don't you give me the rifle?"

"No way, man, me shooter, you spotter." Since this was Red's first time under fire, I told him to stay down and feed Ron clips like he'd been doing. We got back up, and Ron unloaded another magazine. He threw it on the floor as we ducked down again.

"Ron, he moved. Did you notice a pause?"

"No."

"Red, did you?"

"No."

"We must have missed it. Let's wait and see if he breaks to move. He's too hard to hit when he's in position. Listen, Ron, if he stops, start firing ten feet to the right of that last spot and keep going."

We waited, and sure enough the bullets stopped hitting the tower.

"Now," I shouted, and we got up again. Ron fired another magazine, and we ducked down. The seconds passed slowly—nothing. Pretty soon, we looked at each other and busted out laughing.

"I think we got him," said Ron with a satisfied grin.

"Yeah, I think so. Give Red the rifle and let him work on Charlie before the firefight's over." The Starlite was streaked out from the tracers and muzzle flashes. Ron and I watched Red empty one clip and start a second before the firefight stopped.

I sat down and looked at the floor of the tower. It was a mess with shell casings, empty magazines, dirt from sandbags, and wood splinters.

"Man, was that a rush or what? All those tracers," Ron exclaimed.

It was a cool night, but I was drenched with sweat. Before long, I heard someone calling in a stern voice from the ground. I went to the edge of the tower and looked over. "Who's in charge up there?"

"Me."

"Who's me?"

"Lance Corporal Ward."

"Okay, Ward, the base commander wants to see you, now!" I started down the ladder, and near the middle, I stepped on a rung that had been peppered with bullets, and it gave way. I fell the last ten feet to the ground, landing in a dusty heap at the feet of a first lieutenant. The shock to my knee doubled me up with pain. The lieutenant bent over and asked me if I was all right.

"I think so; I'll need something to use for a cane though."

"Here, use my rifle. I'll give you a hand." We went straight to the officers' tent. The lieutenant sat me on a cot. "I'll get a corpsman to look at that leg. Don't leave, the commander will be here any time."

Everything began to hit me all at once: fatigue, rum and an adrenaline high. My vision was blurry, but I could tell that there were several officers present. A corpsman came in and checked my knee.

"There's nothing broken, but that's a nasty scar you got there, pal. All I can do is wrap it with an Ace bandage."

Before the doc was finished, the base commander entered the tent. Everyone, except me and the corpsman, came to attention. He sat on the cot across from me.

"You know why you're here don't you, Lance Corporal Ward?"

"No."

"You fired from inside the perimeter without clearance."

"So what?"

"It's against regulations."

"Fuck the regulations and fuck you."

"Do you know who you're talking to?"

I had to lean close to his lapel to see the eagle. "Yeah, you're a colonel. So what?"

"I run this base!"

"Oh? Well you don't run it very good, so fuck you." I was vaguely aware that the officers were intently listening in.

"You're making one hell of a lot of trouble for yourself, boy."

"Boy? Why, you son of a bitch. We'll see who's the boy here if I get my hands on you, you asshole!" I reached for the colonel. Several hands rather gently pulled me back to the cot. The lieutenant stepped in at that point and suggested to the colonel that they let me sleep it off.

"I'll keep him here with me, sir."

"Yeah, good idea there, Lieutenant. Uhh, what's your name?" I laid back and was soon out for the rest of the night.

At 5:00 A.M. of the eighteenth, the lieutenant was standing a few feet from me with a flashlight. "Ward, wake up."

I jerked forward. "Where am I?"

"Officers' quarters. Listen, and listen good, I only have time to go through this once. You really pissed the old man off."

"How bad?"

"A few fuck-you's."

"Oh, shit! What now?"

"He wrote you up; you have to be in An Hoa by noon."

"When's the first chopper?"

"Not soon enough. If the colonel even sees you again, he'll hang you on the spot. You better take the mine sweep. It leaves in thirty minutes. Here are your orders. Let's get your gear. I have to stay with you until you leave."

As we walked to the gate where the sweep was forming, I told the lieutenant, "I think I'd rather hang than ride a truck all the way to An Hoa."

"Be glad he didn't arrest you."

"Why didn't he?"

"I took responsibility for you, besides you were out of it, and I figured you couldn't make much more trouble for yourself than you already had."

"Thanks."

"Don't thank me, you're part of regimental headquarters. You'll have to answer to someone higher up than the old man here. You kind of had one on him, which doesn't happen very often. I think all the officers enjoyed the show."

"What's your name?"

"That doesn't matter, just get on that truck and get the hell out of here. I have enough problems."

"Uh, Lieutenant, would you tell PFC Saunders to take over for me here?"

"Yes, yes. Now go."

The trip to An Hoa was all I expected it to be. The only thing that took my mind off the rough, dusty ride and the pain in my knee was the thought of the brig at Da Nang.

My central squad leader met me as soon as I got off the truck.

"Ward, what the hell is going on? The gunny wants to see you ASAP!"

"I'll tell you what I know on the way."

I knocked on the gunny's door and was immediately summoned with, "Come in, Ward." How did he know it was me, I wondered. Things were moving faster than I could keep up with. I entered his tent. He was serious, and he started talking before I sat down. "Do you know a Lieutenant Merkel?"

"I'm not sure, Gunny."

"Well, he sure knows you. He called last night. Said you had some problems at 65."

"Does the skipper know yet?"

"Oh, yeah. In fact, I have one hour to get you ready to stand tall in front of the man. Your squad leader is rounding up a new uniform and boots right now, you gotta look good."

I glanced at my jungle fatigues and boots. Pretty ragged I thought. I'm a bush Marine. What the hell was I doing in this mess?

"I'll open the showers so you can clean up and shave everything that don't get hard when you think about it."

"Jeez, Gunny, how much trouble am I in?"

"I don't know. It could be simple office hours or high mast. Only the skipper knows. First things first. When you enter his tent, no matter how long it takes, stay at attention. Don't look at the captain, stare at the curtain behind his desk, and speak only when spoken to, just like in boot camp. I can't go in with you, but I'll be waiting outside. Now let's get you ready."

The walk to the skipper's tent seemed very short indeed. At the door I started to knock, and as a last thought I wiped the dust off my boots on the back of my trouser legs. I looked at the gunny, he just nodded. I rapped on the door three times.

"Sir, Lance Corporal Ward reporting as ordered, sir!"

"Enter!" I came to attention staring at the curtain. I wanted to look at the skipper, but Fergie was clear about that. Captain Hudson began.

"You made quite a stir at Hill 65 last night."

"Yes, sir."

"There's several things here: firing from inside of a fire base without clearance, insubordination, even a physical attack against a superior officer, and there's more. Do I need to go on, Ward?"

"No, sir."

"These are all serious charges. I've never seen anything like it, Ward, and I've seen some weird shit."

"Yes, sir."

"I just had breakfast with Captain Burns, who flew in earlier this morning from the hill. He's the skipper of the company that got hit last night. You knew you were up for promotion."

"No, sir, I didn't."

"Well anyway, back to Captain Burns. While we ate he told me what happened. They found twenty-one bodies at daybreak and I'll be damned if he isn't giving you half the kills."

I couldn't keep from looking at him. My mind was racing, and I wondered which half of the twenty-first man we'd killed.

"I also received a personal call from a Lieutenant, ah, Merkel, I believe his name is. He wanted me to know that the tower was shot up pretty bad. It seems you had Charlie in a heavy enough cross fire that they had to take a machine gun away from the firefight to devote to you. They also found one NVA machine gunner and his ammo feeder just outside of the perimeter, shot to pieces. Does this all sound correct, Ward?"

"Yes, sir."

"As usual, we take care of our own, and I don't see any reason for it to go to HQ. On one hand I have a captain that thinks you should receive a commendation and on the other a colonel that would like to see you shot. Stand at ease, Ward."

It was very quiet, except for the sound of the skipper lightly tapping his pen on the desk.

"What do you think I should do with you, Ward?"

My thoughts instantly went to boot camp. The most often asked question had to be, "What do you think your punishment should be, Recruit?" If a man set it too low, the DI would really pile it on. If he set it too high, he'd be punishing himself unnecessarily and look like a hotdogger to the other men. I wasn't in training anymore. I'd just been asked the question for real. I had to give the skipper an answer—and no time to think. What would Sergeant Graves do? No, what would he say? I blurted it out.

"Give me a medal, then shoot me, sir?"

A thin smile creased the skipper's lips. "You're close, Ward. You've been a corporal on paper for two months now. That stands, but I'm going to bust you back to lance corporal so I have something to send to Hill 65. Are you keeping up with me, here, Ward?"

"Yes, sir."

"Okay, now, I'm giving you a field promotion back to corporal. Congratulations. Dismissed." I came to attention, but didn't turn to leave. Hudson looked up from the papers on his desk.

"Anything else, Ward?"

"Uh, yes, sir. There were two other men in the tower."

"I don't fucking believe you, Ward. Stretching things a little, aren't you?"

"I guess so, sir."

"All right, give me their names, they'll be promoted, too. It doesn't mean I condone your actions at 65. You understand, Ward?"

"Yes, sir. Private First Class Suther and Private First Class Saunders, sir."

"Anything else, Ward?"

"Oh, no, sir."

"Good. Now get the hell out of here and do us all a favor. Stay out of trouble."

"Yes, sir!" I turned and marched out the door. The gunny had worn a small strip in the dirt near the skipper's tent. He was still pacing back and forth when he saw me leave. He rushed up to my side.

"What happened?"

"Gunny, you ain't going to believe this. He promoted me, busted me, and repromoted me just like that," I said, snapping my fingers.

"You fell in the shit and came out smelling like a rose, didn't you, Ward? I guess we better get you some corporal stripes. Just one thing Ward, I want to be the first one to pin 'em on."

"Yeah, sure, Gunny, no sweat." I was still trying to absorb the last ten minutes.

"We'll wait till the first of the month to do it so as many teams as possible are in the rear."

"Thanks a lot, Gunny."

Pinning on the stripes is an honor and ordeal at the same

time. The man with new rank has to walk between two lines made up of the men in his unit of equal or higher rank, and each one hits him on the upper arm. There happened to be four corporals and four sergeants in the rear to pin my stripes on. Although I think the gunny pulled his punch a little, the rest of them spit on their knuckles and wound back like they were going to throw a fast ball. At the end of the line, it felt as though my arms had been cut off at the shoulder. Sergeant Pule decided the stripes hadn't stuck, so I had to go back through the line.

I pushed the tent flaps open with my head. Two days later, I could hold a dinner tray and didn't have to send a new guy to the chow hall to get one for me. In a week, I could salute properly.

Shortly after my promotion to corporal, a small controversy touched the platoon. In late December, a newly appointed team leader in Sergeant Pule's squad received a package from his father.

As usual, interest in packages from home was high. The few of us in An Hoa at the time gathered around for the ritual, anticipating some treats. He opened the parcel to reveal several boxes of hand-loaded, silver tip bullets. Immediately the atmosphere in the tent became tense. The new team leader's enthusiasm faded quickly when someone sternly asked, "Are you going to use those?"

"Yeah, sure. Why not?" By then men were beginning to wander off. I waited until everyone was gone and said, "You know those are against the Geneva Convention." He knew as well as anyone the reason why they were banned. Silver tip bullets are designed to allow the soft bullet to mushroom upon impact, punching a very large hole through the body.

"The gooks don't give a shit about the Geneva Convention," he snapped. I didn't answer and just walked away.

During the following week he was treated rather coolly by the other snipers, at which point he took the bullets to the armory to be disposed of.

*

Scout Snipers
An Hoa
December 28, 1969

Dear Mom,

I'm still kicking. They just walked in with mail, good timing. Sure enjoyed those pictures. Everyone looks healthy. You all look great. I don't even know my own family anymore.

Well, this Christmas will be one to remember. I spent X-mas Eve on lines here at An Hoa. It was quite a show. As soon as it got dark, everyone started popping flares, red and green star clusters. It made the 4th of July back home look kind of sick. I figure it cost the US about fifty thousand dollars for An Hoa to celebrate Christmas and I felt better after I'd popped off my share of government money. Oh, yeah, they had a Santa Claus at the EM club and he looked just like the ones back in the States, only he had on a helmet and flack jacket.

About that truck, there were five guys killed and one was a guy I'd known since ITR. It happens so fast, you just never know.

Well my R and R didn't come through for January. I may still be able to get it in February. I'm just about out of hope. Nine months in this country and it's starting to show. Maybe I've got short timer's nerves. I feel lonely, I don't know why, I just do.

I work with counterintelligence which is part of the CIA. Not all the time, just once in a while. It's really not as glamorous as it sounds, but it beats working in an office which is what they wanted me to do at first.

I'll be picking up my corporal stripes pretty soon. It's another part of the chain of events that started when I was at Hill 65.

I got a letter from Pat. He was in Japan and on his way home. At least he'll be home and with his wife. Encouragement is the biggest part of healing from something like that.

It's been rainy and cold. This cold gets to me. The monsoons shouldn't last much longer, so they say.

I may be leaving An Hoa tomorrow or the next day. I know you have a hard time keeping up with where I'm at, I move around so much. I think I've flown more miles in helicopters than I have airliners.

No, I haven't been hearing from Laura. Probably just as well, I doubt if she'd care for this ole bag of scars anyway.

I just found out I don't have lines tonight which is a relief. I've been on every night since I came back from Da Nang.

No, the 5th won't get pulled out. I think they're waiting till after Tet to turn this base over to the ARVNs. There's been a lot of new guys from the States coming in lately, which I can't figure out.

The weather sounds better there. What I wouldn't give to be sitting in front of that fireplace right now.

Take care and I'll write again soon.

Love, Joseph

On December 25, I took Red to the safest bunker on the lines to spend Christmas. When we got there, the party had already started.

One of the grunts had a Clorox bottle with vodka in it, and after my first taste, I asked the guy if he'd rinsed out the bottle. "Nah, what for?" I couldn't come up with an answer that would make any difference, so we drank the foulest tasting vodka and smoked pot.

When it was dark enough, it was a signal to celebrate Christmas. I had never needed to pop flares, but on that night I couldn't get my hands on enough of them. The sky lit up over An Hoa with a dazzling display of red, white, blue, and green flares. The regimental commander made his displeasure known the next day. No one really cared, and I don't think the commander was all that concerned. It was probably the safest way for the men to blow off steam at not being home for Christmas.

On the twenty-ninth, Red and I were socializing at a bunker in no-man's-land. After midnight the field phone rang. I couldn't believe, they were calling us in.

The narrow trail that led to the bunker was half-a-mile walk that wound and twisted through rows of barbed wire, steep trenches, and gullies. It was overcast, and except for the light from an occasional flare in the distance, the one flashlight we had was almost useless in that kind of dark. I saddled Red up, and we started back. He had an M-16, and I had an M-14, both with Starlites.

I knew the path well, but given the conditions, even I had trouble getting in. Red, an FNG, was another story altogether. I couldn't keep from laughing as he fell or got hooked on the barbed wire about every twenty feet, destroying the Starlite scope in the process.

When we did get back, Red was truly a sight. His fatigues were ripped up, and he was covered with mud. When Sergeant Pule saw him, he had a fit. He was going to have to explain to the gunny what had happened to a very expensive scope. The gunny would then have to explain it to the captain. I was team leader and should have been catching his wrath. I stared in disbelief while Pule swore at everything in the tent. The walls, tent poles, tables, even our sacred little refrigerator. I'd never seen him so mad. I couldn't understand a tenth of what he was saying. I did know it wasn't stuff a guy would say to his mother. When he'd exhausted himself, his face froze in a most perplexed stare. I had to help him out.

"Combat-loss, Sarge, just write it off as combat-loss," I said.

"Yeah, yeah, that's what I'll do," he mumbled to himself and left.

I put Red's arm around my shoulder and struggled to get him to sick bay. The corpsman gave me a strange look as he led Red to a spot where he could strip him and get the mud off. I sat down to wait and fell asleep.

The doc woke me an hour later. "Your friend's ready to go. I know you guys are nuts, but he had scratches and bruises all over his body. What did he do, fall off a mountain?"

"Nah, he's a damn good shot, he just ain't learned how to walk yet."

The corpsman just shook his head, there seems to be a lot of head shaking in a war. Too often words just didn't fit the situation.

My first assignment with counterintelligence came the next day when my squad leader told me to pick another team leader that I got along with well.

"Another team leader, why?"

"That's the word. You'll both be using M-16s with Starlites. No packs, leave all personal gear here. Carry only your Geneva Convention card and K rations for twenty-four hours."

"Wait a minute, what's this all about?"

"There's a briefing in the command bunker in one hour. They'll tell you then. Sorry, Ward, I don't know any more than that."

Ron Feekes was in the rear. He was one of the first of my partners to make team leader. I was proud of the way he'd come along, and I liked the way he worked, so I picked him. I had a feeling his sense of humor would be an asset when we did whatever it was that we were going to do.

Except for a bright light that shone on a huge tactical map of Southeast Asia, the bunker was dark and cool. We were a couple minutes late, and when we arrived, several officers were seated in the bleacherlike benches around the map. A colonel was standing beside the map holding a long pointer and talking to the men already present.

When we came in he looked at us. "Ah, good. I see we have snipers with us tonight. Would you please come forward where everyone can see you and introduce yourselves." We walked closer to the light.

"Corporal J. T. Ward." I waited for Ron to say something and when he didn't, I nudged him.

"Uh, Lance Corporal Feekes, sir."

"Thank you, gentlemen. Please be seated."

We climbed to our usual corner of the bleachers, as far away from the rest of the men as possible. We sat down, and Ron leaned over to whisper, "What's up?"

"I don't know, but I don't like it already. The colonel is being a little too nice. And check that, there's two ARVN officers here."

The colonel turned back to the other men and said, "The snipers will be providing night protection for the chopper upon landing." No big deal, I thought. We'd done that before, but when he moved his pointer to a colored pin stuck in the map, Ron and I looked at each other and at the same time mouthed the words "Oh, Fuck!"

The pin the colonel had indicated was across the Vietnamese border in Laos. I leaned close to Ron, "You ever been in Laos?"

"No."

"Me, neither, but we're going tonight."

When the colonel began talking again, it didn't take long to surmise that this was an assassination squad. After the meeting, we were the first to leave. We talked on the way back to our tent.

At first we kept the conversation on a technical level. We decided Ron would carry four grenades and a .38-caliber pistol his father had sent him. I would carry extra K rations, dried soup, battle dressings, and ammo. We walked solemnly the rest of the way to our tent and sat on a cot, side-by-side. I broke the silence. "Look, Ron, I didn't know what this was."

"Ah, that's okay. You need someone to keep you from hurting yourself."

We laughed, shallow laughter admittedly, but laughter none the less. I took out my maps to see what it would take to get back if the chopper did get messed up. It wasn't encouraging, about sixteen miles of Laos and most of Arizona Territory to cross. We plotted three routes around Arizona and two through it. It all boiled down to pretty much the same thing, a forty to seventy mile trek through mostly unsecured areas without a radio.

We had four hours to get ready, and it would take most of it. We kept the conversation light while we cleaned and oiled our rifles, put new batteries in the Starlites, taped all gear, and meticulously applied camouflage grease paint to each other's faces.

At one point, Ron asked, "How are we going to handle it?"

"What do ya mean?"

"Up here." He pointed to his head. Our eyes locked in a silent stare.

I broke eye contact and went back to what I was doing. "The colonel said we were to provide protection for the chopper, so that's exactly what we'll do. What those guys do in the village isn't our concern. Concentrate on the bird, it's everyone's ticket back here."

When we reached the LZ, a Huey gunship was already warming up. Two counterintelligence agents got on first, then the ARVN officers. Ron and I were last on and would be first off. No one said a word as we made the longest and most uneasy chopper ride I'd experienced. As I watched the others, my mind drifted to the briefing. I had no illusions that prisoners would be taken. I concentrated on the task at hand.

The insertion was as unusual as the mission. A strobe light was thrown out of the chopper so the pilot could get a fix on the altitude. A single, dim red light in the cockpit served to make the mission all the more ominous. As the chopper descended, the pilot switched to "whisper mode," which was a tactic used to land undetected. The pilot disengaged the engines from the rotors at low altitude and allowed the airfoil effect of the blades to maintain lift while the chopper landed.

We came in hard and fast. As soon as we touched down, Ron and I jumped out on opposite sides. We ran about thirty feet out and took kneeling positions. The counterintelligence agents and the ARVNs, armed only with .45s and bowie knives, disappeared into the village.

I wondered if Ron was thinking what I was, that counterintelligence had to have the best. They had to have snipers to guard that helicopter. The next thirty minutes were extremely tense. The only sound was the *woosh* of the chopper's slowly turning rotors.

On the seven "night flights," as I came to call them, we ran into trouble only once. Two VC saw or heard us coming and started taking potshots at the chopper after we'd landed. They were on my partner's side and he returned fire. With the Starlite it only took three rounds to make the night quiet again, but our element of surprise was gone. The counterintelligence team didn't make it to the village, and as the pilot revved up for take off, we all ran back to the chopper. When we landed at An Hoa, an inspection of the helicopter revealed two bullet holes distressingly close to a major oil line to the engine.

Years later, I learned that I had participated in a specialized part of the Phoenix Program. It is estimated that only a dozen scout snipers were involved in the project.

*

Scout Snipers
An Hoa
January 11, 1970

Dear Mom,

I know I've been terrible about writing and I'm sorry. They're running me into the ground.

I've had lines every night and the gooks have stepped up their activity, so every night we're on 100% alert which means no sleep at night for a week.

Tet's almost here. All the defenses have been doubled and in some places tripled, so I guess they're expecting a big push this year.

You wanted to know what lines are. Lines are the first line of defense around An Hoa. Any snipers that are in the rear go out to one of the bunkers and keep watch with a Starlite scope, and we're the only ones that can open fire without clearance, so all the sectors want us. They keep us busy, for sure.

I had a good time on my in-country R and R, but of course it was always on my mind that I was still in Vietnam. I spent a couple days with Randy Peterson, then I came back. It was just a short break from everything.

When I got back I found out my out-of-country R and R hadn't come through, and I got so mad I went to the gunny and told him if they didn't get me an R and R that I was going to the chaplain and make sure I got one. I did and it's for Sydney from the 6th–13th of February. Nothing is going to keep me from going this time. I'll call when I get there.

I got my promotion. It's retroactive to the 1st of November, so I've been a corporal for over two months, which is okay. It's fifty dollars more per month.

Well, Mom. I've talked long enough. Take care and thanks for being so good to write.

Love, Joseph

Most of the month of January was a nerve-racking stream of incoming rockets, mortars, and enemy probes of An Hoa's perimeter.

With almost constant tower watch, lines, and an occasional night flight, I was becoming exhausted. When I heard Delta company was pulling into Da Nang for a three-day, in-country R and R at China Beach, I wasted no time asking the gunny if I could be assigned to them. He looked at me with a sly grin, and before I could say my nerves were bad, he was cutting orders for me to hook up with them.

When a company took an in-country R and R, it was something to witness. The bush-weary men would be brought into An Hoa, issued new fatigues, and choppered to Da Nang where they were trucked to a small military resort at China Beach.

Our weapons were checked at the armory just outside the gate. MPs and SPs were everywhere around the fenced compound. Whatever happened on China Beach during the next seventy-two hours was going to happen, and command didn't want it spilling over into the city.

The men were unloaded, and as soon as the trucks pulled out, two giant forklifts rolled onto the beach, one with a ten-by-ten-foot pallet of beer, the other soda pop. They set the pallets down, quickly backed out of the compound, and the gate was locked.

Over a hundred and fifty Marines descended on the pallets, yelling and shouting. After I was accidentally elbowed in the throat at my first attempt to get some beer, I decided to wait.

I watched as case after case of beer and soda pop was ripped and torn from the pallets. Ron Willingham had also managed to join the company for the R and R. He walked up beside me, held out a pair of wire cutters and said, "The skipper asked me to cut the bands on those pallets, but I can't even get close."

I didn't look at him. I was fascinated by what I was watching. All I could do was rub my throat and say, "Delta Company."

Corpsmen were treating men who'd cut themselves on the sharp metal bands that held the pallets together, but they kept at it. Before long, enough beer had been removed that the bands went slack and fell off. Ron and I were eventually able to get some and we sat under a palm tree to talk.

Within seventy-two hours, hundreds of cases of beer disappeared, most of it pissed or puked into the South China Sea. Before long the goodies the men brought with them started to emerge—hard liquor, pot, opium, speed, and heroin if a guy was that far gone.

During the next three days, I watched as the contents of the pallets melted away like icebergs in the sun. The only time the gate was opened was to take out an overdosed or beat-up Marine. By the time R and R was over, the beer was gone and the soda pop down by two thirds. A sorry looking bunch of Marines was loaded on trucks again to go back to An Hoa. Back to the war.

I checked out my bolt rifle and set out to visit some people in Da Nang. I liked Da Nang, I guess because it was a city with paved streets, cars, nightclubs, and people dressed in civilian clothes. I could reassure myself that colors other than camouflage green existed. Gunny Fergie knew I would be late getting back anyway.

I headed for the motor pool to see Randy Peterson.

"How do you get here so often?" Randy asked. I held up the bolt rifle and smiled. Randy had enough rank by then to pull a two-day liberty with no problem. Barry would have to stay on duty.

I emptied the pockets in my trousers and came up with ten warm, shook-up beers I'd squirreled away at the beach. We sprayed each other with beer and for a few brief seconds forgot where we were. We exchanged information about friends in the war, then the talk got serious. It was time to party.

The next day we set out to really see Da Nang. "I know a place where we can rent a sailboat," Randy said. That got my attention.

"Wheels?" I asked.

"No problem, we'll take a jeep from motor pool."

"That simple?"

"That simple," he said.

"Well, what the hell are we hanging around here for? Let's go." The jeep Randy picked had a major's insignia on it.

"Randy, you gotta be shitting!"

"Nah. We fixed it, so we're gonna take it out and make sure it's okay. Right?"

"Yeah, right." I got in and for some reason one of Fergie's constant "stay out of trouble"'s ran through my mind. We drove to the PX and bought a couple cases of beer, then I asked Randy to take me to the ROK camp.

The rumors were true. There wasn't any kind of fence or barbed wire around the compound, only a low wall made from grenade cases filled with sand. The gate to the entrance was oriental in design, made from heavy, brightly painted timbers. A guard stood motionless on each side of the gate, with rows of tents behind them.

"Stop," I told Randy. He looked at me funny, but pulled up to the gate. I took out a case of beer, carried it to one of the guards, and handed it to him. He took it with that quick, expressionless bow and laid it on the ground behind the wall. I nodded and went back to the jeep.

"What was that all about?"

"I owe 'em," I said and changed the subject. "How about that sailboat?"

We drove to a spot not far from China Beach and rented a small sailboat. We had both sailed the lakes back home, and we looked forward to taking on the South China Sea, our only provisions being three six packs of beer.

We sailed around a small peninsula into Da Nang harbor, where we were met by an awesome sight. Ships of every description filled the huge bay, merchant marine vessels, troop ships, oil tankers, and two hospital ships. Ships waiting to get to the docks stretched over the horizon. A destroyer sat ominously at the entrance to the harbor.

The water in the harbor was smooth as silk, and the sailboat handled beautifully. We drank another six pack, as we wove our way between one steel mountain after another.

With our courage bolstered by plenty of beer, we decided to check out the destroyer. Its sheer size deceived us as to its distance, and it took half an hour to tack to her stern. The hull was only forty feet away as we headed toward her bow, in awe at all the guns and with a serious respect for what the ship was capable of.

Marines guard navy vessels, and about halfway to the bow,

one spotted us. He leaned over the rail with a megaphone. "You are in a restricted area. Move one hundred and fifty feet away from the ship immediately."

"Ah, screw him," Randy said.

We continued our course. In thirty seconds the guard was back on the megaphone, rifle unstrapped.

"Repeat, you are in a free-fire zone, move one hundred and fifty feet away from the ship immediately!"

"He means it, Randy."

"Yeah, right, let's head in." We had the wind going back, and it wasn't long before we tied up at the dock.

Randy and I slept well that night. In the morning we got the word that the Australians were putting on a USO show at the EM club around noon. I looked at myself in the mirror while I brushed my teeth. I hadn't shaved in four days, my hair was too long, and I had on a bright blue T-shirt. I didn't exactly meet the daily dress code for Da Nang. I checked on my bolt rifle Randy was keeping locked in his wardrobe.

Barry told Randy that the major had asked how soon his jeep would be ready. Randy said, "Clean it up, especially look for beer cans and send it to him. I'll get another one."

We went to a different maintenance building, and inside, Randy took a clipboard from a nail on the wall. His finger traced a line down a list of vehicles and their present condition. He stopped and his hand moved across the paper. "Ah," he said and hung the board back on the nail. With a casual gesture he motioned for me to follow. We walked between rows of trucks and jeeps in different stages of repair. He zeroed in on a colonel's and got in.

"Let's go."

"Randy, are you nuts? A colonel's jeep? Why not a general's?"

"Too obvious."

"Too obvious?" I was trying to think of what the skipper would say if he found out I'd stolen a colonel's jeep.

Our first stop was at the air force mess hall for a good breakfast then to the EM club. The club wouldn't open until 10:00 A.M., so we had forty-five minutes to sit and watch a crowd of Marines grow in front of the club.

"Watch this," Randy said. "If they don't open the club right on time they'll bust the doors down."

I looked at him and smiled. "They bust up the whole club at An Hoa even if it is open." The doors opened on time, and a swarm of men rushed in. We elbowed our way to the bar, bought a couple beers, and scrambled for an empty table. We hadn't finished our second beer, when a fight broke out at the table next to us and in seconds a man was on the floor, curled up in agony. A half a dozen men jumped on the grunt who'd just buried a bayonet to the hilt in the guy's belly.

Just as I turned to Randy, the smell of warm human blood hit me. "Randy, let's go outside and wait."

It was hotter outside, but the smell of blood, like so many other sights, sounds, and smells of war, triggered instant responses, like incoming mortars and booby traps. We moved to the theater while the two Marines were hauled away, one to the hospital, the other to the brig.

It filled quickly, and we didn't have long to wait before a chopper landed on the stage and an all-girl rock band got off. Four hundred Marines thoroughly enjoyed the next two hours, and when the show was over, we hurried to the jeep.

Barry was about to go off duty, so we stopped at the PX for more beer on the way back to the motor pool. Barry climbed in and we set out in that jeep to cruise Da Nang like we owned it. Somehow we eluded detection for nearly three hours before the MPs pulled us over.

It was probably my fault since my cover had blown off, and the blue T-shirt didn't help. We were drinking beer and having a real good time, but the MPs weren't amused.

"Follow us," one of them growled. Randy seemed a little too calm as we closely followed their jeep. Since we were all Marines, they took us to shore patrol headquarters, and turned us over to the SPs. When they asked what units we belonged to we were immediately separated. Randy and Barry were taken to a bench at the rear of the room. I was told to stand by the field phone near the entrance, while a lieutenant spent forty-five minutes getting through to my skipper in An Hoa. He talked briefly, hung up the phone, went into a back room and returned with a cover and green T-shirt.

"You're to catch the next chopper to An Hoa. I'll have someone drive you to the nearest LZ."

"Lieutenant, I need to talk to Lance Corporal Peterson for just a minute."

"Okay, but make it fast."

"Say, lieutenant, I need a pencil and paper."

"Jesus! Anything else, sniper?"

I hurried to Randy and knelt down. "I need the combination

to your wardrobe to get my rifle. I have to be back in An Hoa ASAP.'' I wrote down the numbers and asked Randy if they were going to be okay.

"Sure, we get caught all the time."

"Thanks for telling me, and Randy, thanks for the good time. What will they do to you guys?"

"Ehhh, they'll make us sit on this frigging bench a couple more hours, then we'll have to deliver the jeep to the colonel. No sweat."

"I'm getting short, Randy, and if I can't get back to see you here, I'll see ya at home. You, too, Barry."

"Stay alive."

"Same to you guys."

I changed my T-shirt and went with an SP for a short ride to the LZ. The sergeant in charge told me that according to my orders I was late returning to my unit and I would have to burn shitters the rest of the day. I laid the bolt rifle on his desk. "You'll take real good care of this, won't you, Sarge?" I got the look I expected when I used the rifle to get someone to thinking.

I went to a grunt standing by a fifty-five gallon oil drum, cut in half and two-thirds full of shit, piss, and diesel fuel. We put a two-by-four through the holes cut in each side and carried it down the hill a ways and set it on fire. We just stood there and watched the black heavy smoke and flames come from the barrel.

Before the shitter was half burnt, the sergeant came to me with my rifle. He held it out, as though he might catch something terminal from it. "There'll be a chopper that makes two stops before it goes to An Hoa. It leaves in fifteen minutes." I took the rifle; he abruptly turned and walked quickly back to the bunker.

At An Hoa, Fergie and I exchanged greetings, and he leaned over his table and looked me square in the eyes. "The old man is getting tired of these phone calls from all over hell and back about you in trouble somewhere. I'm surprised he didn't bust you."

I knew I didn't get away with it clean, so I asked, "What is he going to do?"

"It's worse than getting busted, he's sending you to Hill 65."

"Oh, no, Gunny, tell me you're joking."

"No joke. Two teams are there, and you'll be in charge of

'em. There's been quite a bit of enemy activity in the area. Work it any way you see fit—and this isn't an order, but I suggest you stay out of the colonel's way.''

I leaned back in the chair and rubbed my temples. The gunny just looked at me with a big, wicked smile.

*

Scout Snipers
An Hoa/Hill 65
January 18, 1970

Dear Mom,

Will be going to Hill 65 tomorrow. I don't know how long I'll be there, probably till the 6th and I'll come here before my R and R.

Word is that everyone who is to go home in March, April, and May will have their RTDs (rotation dates) set up one month ahead and will go by ship as part of this pull out. This doesn't mean I'll be home any sooner. When I find out for sure I'll let you know.

I'm going to try to draw all the money I have on the books next month and send it home. That way I won't have to pay tax on it.

Better close now, have to get up early. Be careful on those icy streets. Will write again soon.

Love, Joseph

P.S. Am sending a couple rolls of film.

The gunny really didn't have to warn me to stay away from the colonel, but the only sure way to do that was to stay in the bush as much as possible. I left a team leader, Corporal Davis, and his partner, Lance Corporal Martinez, on the hill full-time, and I took most of the field assignments as a three-man team with Private First Class McDonald and Lance Corporal Lightfoot. I kept in touch with Davis by radio.

If there was a problem or a briefing at the hill I had to be at, I could catch the next chopper in and still leave a full team in the bush. As a three-man team in the bush, we would cover more assignments with more versatility. It made communications between the three central squad leaders at An Hoa and their teams better, and worked so well that the floating squad leader soon became standard procedure at Hill 65 when enough snipers were available.

The gunny was right. Enemy activity was heavy in the central highlands where the first and largest finger of the Ho Chi Minh Trail emptied onto the coastal lowlands, through Arizona Territory, and, in a winding pattern, between fire bases toward Da Nang.

According to the information from snipers working the area, Charlie had committed portions of three divisions to the task. Field units from the 5th and 7th Marine Regiments were being beefed up.

If I had five more teams, it would have been easier to have kept them busy. That many men was a tremendous number of troops, but locating them was still a problem. Three mornings out with Alpha 1/5, we found them big time.

I left McDonald with the company to give them free-fire capability and took Lightfoot out on a predawn hunter-kill. I knew the area well, and some months earlier I had caught a column of NVA at the same spot Lightfoot and I set in to await the first light of dawn. It had taken three and a half hours of moving silently in the dark to get there, and we were edgy, our nerves thin. I wanted to see how good Charlie's memory was.

Waiting for first light, I rubbed my knee, I was surprised at the amount of pain I was in and wondered if I really would be able to stay in the field after all.

At the earliest hint of sunlight, we were watching the same tree line where I had previously caught that company of NVA attempting to cross a three-thousand-yard open stretch of fields and rice paddies.

Charlie you're not perfect, I thought, as one carefully snuck out of the trees and ran to a rice-paddy dike, 1,200 yards from our position. He was quickly followed by a full squad, with a platoon setting in at the edge of the trees. Lightfoot looked at me in surprise. "I don't like this Ward. What do you want to do? Hit 'em with artillery and book? We can use the big guns at the hill."

"We'd better hit them harder than that. As many men as they've set in to cover their crossing of that open area, there must be a battalion back in the trees. Get air control on the radio." Lightfoot gave me the handset. "Air control, this is Long Rifle." I gave them Charlie's coordinates. "Do you have anything heavy that can make it to those coordinates in no more than ten minutes?"

"Hold on, Long Rifle, I'll check." He went off the air for what seemed a very long time, but in reality was only a few seconds. He came back with good news. "Long Rifle, I have two F-4s with napalm and five-hundred pounders on an aborted mission, seven minutes from your target. Do you want them?''

"Roger. The sooner the better." I had just set in motion the biggest single hit of my tour. Charlie was in a hurry to get somewhere. I later found out that they had hit An Hoa during the night, and we happened to catch them on the move.

Air control came back, "I'm handing you over to Major Holmes, call name Big Ten. Do you copy? Over.''

"Roger.''

Lightfoot nudged me, "Ward, check this out. They're starting across, and shit man, they're headed right for us.''

I got on the radio. "Big Ten, this is Long Rifle. We just lost two minutes. If you can't get here in five minutes, we'll be in a world of hurt! Over.''

"Long Rifle, this is Big Ten and my wing man, Hitter. I think we can make that, but everyone will know we're coming, over.''

"That's okay, Big Ten. Target from the edge of the trees and go north. Big Ten, you won't hear anymore from Long Rifle if your final approach is in the pike. Long Rifle Out.''

"Ward, we don't have five minutes; the gooks will be close enough to nail us. They've already set up two machine guns and two mortars.''

"We'll have to slow 'em down some.''

"Ward, you are as crazy as I've heard.''

"We can do it if you can keep those fuckers behind the dike from flanking us, or getting closer than seven hundred yards. I'll take out the mortars and the guns. Don't fire till they're seven hundred yards away unless I say so.''

Lightfoot shook his head. "I hope you know what you're doing Ward.''

"No sweat," I told him, while inside I had my own doubts. The whole thing depended on split-second timing between us and two jets still miles away.

Lightfoot was laying M-14 magazines in front of him so he could get to them more easily. I was heartened to see that he had the instinct to know we were about to get into an out-and-out shooting match. He'd never tangled head-on with that many enemy troops; neither had I. They could overwhelm us by sheer numbers, but we had the element of surprise, marksmanship, and concealment on our side. I looked at my watch with one eye and at Charlie with the other through the rifle scope. They had started moving, and the lead man would be within

Lightfoot's seven hundred-yard limit in less than sixty seconds. He looked anxiously at me. I gave him the hand signal to wait.

I looked at my watch and back at Charlie. The lead man was six hundred yards away. Lightfoot whispered as loud as he dared, "Ward!"

"Shuu!" I was listening for something, and just then I heard it; we all heard it—a sound like distant thunder. Charlie stopped and started looking skyward. They knew something was up but weren't sure what.

"Now!" I shouted at Lightfoot. He began firing, and at the same moment, I shot a machine gunner between the eyes. Lightfoot hit the three lead men before they could all take cover. My next shot took out the second machine gunner. My third hit a mortar man in the neck.

Shot four hit the second mortar man; just as he dropped a round down the tube, he fell over like a rag doll and the result of his last act as a soldier was a misplaced mortar that landed among his own people who Lightfoot had pinned down, killing two of them. They thought it was from us and that we'd hit them with mortars, too. When they moved, Lightfoot dropped two more.

My fifth shot hit the ammo man starting to take over the first machine gun. There were a lot of AK rounds randomly hitting the hillside. They hadn't located us, but if the machine guns and mortars were allowed to work steadily they would eventually find us.

Lightfoot was doing a number one job of pinning down what was left of the forward squad. They weren't able to get into the fight at all, and I could, for the time being, forget about them.

I looked back at the second gun. It was momentarily out of action. I moved the scope back to the first machine gun just as it began to belch smoke. I had to get back on the radio to listen for Big Ten in case his final approach was off target. In my haste I missed the man on the gun with my sixth shot.

"Son of a bitch," I yelled as I picked up the handset with one hand and began to reload with the other. Come on Big Ten, I thought while I chambered a round and put the first of five rounds into the magazine.

Lightfoot was methodically, calmly, firing at the men trapped in the rice paddy. I was glad I wasn't one of them. He wiped sweat from his eyes and swore once when a bullet hit close enough to kick dirt in his face. Other than that he said nothing.

Charlie had both guns going and was raking the side of our hill with unnerving precision. I watched as tracers ricocheted in increasing numbers nearer and nearer to our position and wondered if I had cut it too close.

I'd just put in round number four when I heard the voice of an angel over the radio.

"Long Rifle, this is Big Ten. I'm on final approach. Over and out."

I looked through the scope in the direction I expected Big Ten to be coming from. He was barely visible, but right on the money. Twenty more seconds, that's all we needed. I put in the last round and switched back to the trees and shot a third machine gunner brought into action.

Charlie was making too much noise trying to find us to hear Big Ten coming, and the jets were almost on them. I had time for one more shot and took out a mortar man, when the rockets and guns on Big Ten got Charlie's attention. Seconds later the tree line erupted in flames and black smoke. All enemy fire in our direction stopped, the only sounds were from Lightfoot, still working over those poor bastards in the rice field, and the faint roar of napalm devouring trees and humans.

Seconds later, Hitter was on the radio. "Long Rifle, this is Hitter on final. Over." I checked. He was right on the mark, too, but he wouldn't make a run. I looked back at the trees and saw an incredible sight. Charlie knew there was another jet on its way, and from a huge area of the trees behind the first strike, green tracers by the hundreds were streaking straight up. There had to be two dozen large-caliber machine guns putting out fire. I was right, it would take a battalion to have that kind of fire power.

"Oh, shit! Hitter, this is Long Rifle. Go around, heavy ground fire. Repeat, go around. Do you copy?"

"Roger, Long Rifle, I have a no-go."

I watched as Hitter made a sharp turn to the south and flew over us. I let out a sigh and wiped sweat from my face. I had come within seconds of getting a plane shot down, and it scared the hell out of me. It was time for us all to get out of there.

Lightfoot had nearly quit firing, and when I looked at the rice paddy, I was surprised at the damage he'd inflicted. I counted nine bodies on the dike or in the paddy itself.

I looked at Lightfoot. He paid me no attention, all his concentration was focused on the task that I had assigned him.

I got back on the radio. "Hitter, this is Long Rifle, come in."

"This is Hitter. What's the situation down there?"

"No good, Hitter. If you'll clear the area, I'll turn this over to artillery. Please acknowledge."

"Roger, Long Rifle. Big Ten and I are out of here."

I switched to fire control at An Hoa and got three batteries of 175mm guns and seven 155mms at Hill 65. I ordered up a ground-and-aerial-burst mix to cover the whole tree line. "Fire for effect." When they asked me how heavy, I told them to flatten the whole damn place.

"Lightfoot. Lightfoot!"

"Yeah, what?" He still didn't look at me.

"As soon as we see that the artillery is on target, we sky for a big man's ass."

"I'm all for that!"

The first artillery rounds rumbled overhead, and the resulting explosions above and in the trees satisfied me. We started back, constantly checking to be sure we hadn't been flanked. We also had to stop periodically to rest my knee. I was getting mad at the fact that I was slowing us down and vowed to do something about it when we got back to the company. We were two-thirds of the way there before the artillery stopped going out. They must have pumped a couple thousand rounds onto the target.

The company sent a reconnaissance team out to assess the results of our strike, and even I was surprised. They found forty-seven "crispy critters" in the trees, and ten bodies in the rice field. It would be safe to assume Charlie had carried off many more dead.

Upon reaching the company, I made a beeline for a corpsman I knew.

"Doc, I need to talk to you in private." We walked a short distance from everyone.

"What is it, Ward."

"I need some pain pills."

"Why?"

"My knee is raising holy hell. I barely made it back in today."

"Let me take a look at it." I rolled up my pant leg. "When did this happen?"

"About two months ago."

"Let me see the bottom of your boot." He took hold of my

leg and lifted it to where he could see the sole of my right boot.

"That wound is throwing your stride off. You're wearing the wrong side of the sole out. What the fuck are you doing in the bush?"

"I'm in the bush because I need to be. Now how about those pills?"

"Okay, but I could get in a shitload of trouble for this." He reached into his bag and threw me a bottle of morphine tablets.

"Write it off as combat loss, Doc."

"Yeah. That'll work, but I don't understand you, Ward. You could have a cush job in the rear or even go home. A lot of guys would give their left nut to have a million-dollar wound like that."

"Thanks, Doc." How could I explain it to him? I couldn't. Other snipers were the same way. Chuck Mawhinney certainly was. Aubrey, Franks, Garcia, they all were. I doubt if they could have explained it either.

I went to Lightfoot and sat down. "I just thought, Lightfoot, I don't know your first name."

"Terry. Call me Lightfoot. My friends do."

"That was some real nice shooting. Fill out a kill sheet, and I'll sign it. The reconnaissance patrol did a body search for us. All my kills were fried, and kills from a strike don't count any way." Terry nodded his head, but didn't reply.

"Ward, there's something that's been bothering me. How did you know when to open fire? I know it wasn't just because that lead gook was getting close."

"I heard them coming; we all did, including Charlie."

"What do you mean?"

"Remember that sound like thunder?"

"Yeah, the gooks were looking all around, but it just sounded like a plane had dropped a bomb a long way off."

"It wasn't, it was the sonic boom from those jets, they were hauling ass, and I knew they'd have to slow down to make a bombing run, so the sonic boom got to us a little before the planes did."

"Damn, there's so much shit I don't know, I'll never make team leader."

"I wouldn't be so sure of that if I were you. Actually, I'm making you team leader right now."

"No, you're shitting."

"Hardly." I handed him my rifle with the same words Chuck said when he gave it to me, "Take care of my baby. You can sight it in from that point on the west side of the perimeter, I'll spot for you, but not now. I've got to stay off this leg for a while."

He was speechless, as though I'd handed him something sacred.

"I'm going to the skipper and tell him what went on out there. After all, we did leave a hell of a mess. I want you to get started on the bolt rifle now. Keep it until I get back from R and R, if I get it." Terry Lightfoot was an outstanding shot, calm under fire and smart, just the qualities necessary in a team leader. My days in the bush were numbered, and I wanted the rifle to go to someone special.

I spent most of the next two weeks as Terry's spotter, teaching him as much as I could in a short time and, the way Chuck did me, I backed him up with his M-14. I saw a lot of myself in Terry. He logged twelve kills with the bolt rifle before I called Martinez out from the hill to be his partner. I left to check in at An Hoa about my R and R.

During the chopper ride from the hill to An Hoa, I thought about the new guy who'd be Davis's partner. The last thing I remember before falling asleep was that I couldn't think of the man's name. I was completely exhausted, mentally and physically. I didn't know we had landed until a door gunner awoke me.

"Ride's over, man."

"Yeah, what?"

"Said, we're in An Hoa. You going to get off or you planning to ride this bird all day?"

I didn't answer, I just got my gear and shuffled off toward regimental headquarters. If I didn't look eighty years old at that point, I sure felt like it.

I asked the clerk at HQ if my R and R had come through. While he thumbed through a stack of papers, I was prepared to swear in resignation and leave, then he said, "Yeah, yeah, here it is. It shows you down for Sydney on February 6." I'd all but given up hope after so many failed attempts.

"You're kidding."

"Nope, got it right here. Sign the bottom line, and I'll start processing your papers, then all you have to do is pass the medical and you're gone."

He handed me a paper with a long check list of diseases, most of which a guy could catch just by stepping off the plane in Vietnam. Not surprisingly, venereal diseases headed the list and there was a bunch of them. The clerk had gone back to his paperwork when I sarcastically said to him, "I guess they don't have the "drippy dobber" in Australia."

"What? Did you say something?"

"I said, I guess they—ah forget it. I'll bring this back as soon as I can." I went to check in with the gunny. His greeting was typically Fergie.

"Funny thing about you, Ward—you usually make it in here on pay day, but at the other times you don't do for shit."

"I never really thought about it that way, Gunny."

"I know your R and R came through. I took the papers to the skipper myself. I'm worried about you, Ward. You've been in the bush while Davis covered your ass at the hill."

If anyone else had made that statement, I'd have been surprised, but Fergie didn't miss much. He probably knew what was up when he read the first report in Davis's handwriting with my signature at the bottom.

"You look like hell, Ward, and I can't afford to have you go off the deep end on me now. Take R and R, forget about this place for a few days. Get laid, get drunk, get in trouble in another country for a change, I don't care what you do, just come back. We lost a team leader two days ago and including a couple replacements due in today, the platoon's down to fourteen men, mostly FNGs."

"Who got it, Gunny? Is he dead?"

"Beal, and no, he's alive, but he doesn't have a left kneecap now. A VC pulled an AK-47 out of the water in a paddy and shot him. A young bitch, and she singled him out of a whole company."

The noise from a brief barrage of out-going artillery was a welcome interruption of what had become a depressing conversation. Before the guns fell silent again, I had time to smoke a couple cigarettes and think. I was the first to speak after we'd savored a few seconds of total quiet.

"So what's the bottom line, Gunny?"

"I don't think there is one yet. The skipper was in Da Nang last week trying to speed up some replacements. He's also put out some standing orders."

"Written or verbal?"

"Verbal, so far, but you ain't going to like 'em." I shrugged, and Fergie went on. "Remember now, Ward, the old man is just being extra cautious for a while. The bounty has gotten pretty high on some of you guys. There's people out there willing to die so their families can collect the money. Starting today there'll be an MP on twenty-four hour watch around our compound." I thought about that for a moment and started to laugh. "Come on, Ward—this is serious."

"Okay, Gunny, but an army dog guarding us?"

"Funny or not, that's how it's going to be for a while. He'll be checking everybody entering the compound, and if you're challenged, don't get pissed off and do something stupid. Now remember, this is from the old man, and he wouldn't take kindly to it. Next, requalification is canceled, as far as we're concerned, until we have more people. You had more men at Hill 65 than we've had here, and we're spread thin. I'm not counting you or Zamora since you're going on R and R. Zamora, well, he isn't fit for duty right now."

"Who's Zamora, and why isn't he fit for duty?"

"Beal's partner. He was cherry until he blew that gook away. The whole thing was a bad deal, him being new, and his first kill just had to be a woman at close range. Anyway, he's got some real stuff going on inside. I've tried talking to him, so has the skipper and the chaplain, but we didn't get far. The skipper said if Zamora doesn't come around soon, he'll send him down."

"Mind if I take a quick look at his records, Gunny?"

"Nah. Hell, if you think you can do any good, you're more than welcome to try. He's got a good record, and we need him now."

Fergie opened a desk drawer, took out Zamora's file, and slid it across the desk top. I read his full name on the cover, and thumbed through the file, noting that his sniper school scores were average.

The only thing I thought strange was that he had dropped out of college with slightly less than a year to graduate and a B plus average. He wouldn't have been drafted, yet it seemed as though he had joined the Corps and worked with a vengeance to get through sniper school. I paused for a moment, wondering why the word vengeance came to mind.

I opened his S-2 file (the class 2 security clearance file). The first page was the usual personal information the FBI liked to gather about people. Near the bottom of the second page, I found what I didn't even know I was looking for.

Zamora's cousin had been killed in an ambush on August

9, 1967, near the DMZ. Zamora had come to Vietnam out of a feeling of guilt or revenge, and straight away got hit in the face with a shit pie. I closed the file and handed it back to Fergie.

"Well?"

"I don't know, Gunny. I'll talk to him, maybe someone closer to his rank will help. Any more good news before I drop my gear and get some hot chow?"

"Yeah, and I saved the best for last. The village is off limits to all sniper personnel until further notice."

"Ah come on, Gunny. Damn, who's gonna look in on the militia, and what about Lee? You know I get more information about Charlie from Lee in two hours than HQ gets in two weeks." Fergie shut me up with a wave of his hand.

"Ward, I understand what you're saying, and yes we get a lot of good leads from Oot. I know it's your pet project, and you've worked hard at it. I'm also not so dumb as to think you won't still go to the village. Just remember, if you get caught, the skipper will be real pissed. Christ, Ward, I'm surprised a gook hasn't already blown you away there. Anyway, I've passed the orders on. How you handle them is up to you, but for my sake, at least try to stay out of trouble. You have one point with the skipper for that strike by the hill, don't use it up."

"No sweat, Gunny. Is that all?"

"One last thing. Bear is going home soon and I need a central squad leader, and—"

I interrupted him. "Gunny, I haven't turned down extra responsibility yet, but I feel I would be more effective in the bush breaking guys in. Thanks anyway."

I detected a slight gruffness in his voice as he said, "Go get some beans and shower, you smell bad."

I got up to leave. "Oh, yeah, where's this Zamora dude?"

"The last time I saw him, he was in tent number three."

"See you later, Gunny." I headed toward the tent. Fergie was right, I would find a way around the orders not to go to the village. I was also heartened to know that someone higher up than me recognized the value of the contributions Lee made and that my CAP work had been effective.

When I first saw Zamora, he was leaning against his pack on a corner cot, eyes fixed straight ahead. Only a week in the bush and he already seemed to have the thousand yard stare. I momentarily wondered why I'd taken on this added problem. I feigned surprise as I entered the tent. "Oh, hey, hi, man. I thought this tent was empty."

He glanced at me briefly, but didn't reply. I sat down on the nearest cot. "I'm Corporal Ward. Call me J.T. or just Ward, and you?"

"Zamora."

"Could you speak up a little, my ears ring some."

"Zamora! PFC Zamora!"

"Okay, new guy, you don't have to shout. I'm not completely deaf. How long have you been in-country?"

"Two and a half weeks."

"You here for tower watch or what?"

"No."

"Why you in then?"

"My team leader was wounded."

"The central squad leaders are out trying to deliver pay and mail, so you and I must be the only ones in the rear right now?"

"I guess."

"I'll split tower duty with you till I leave. I'll take the day shift—no offense; privilege of rank. You had figured to stand tower, hadn't you?" He didn't answer. At least the tower at An Hoa should be manned if possible, and the two of us could do that much. I was beginning to see why the gunny and skipper were frustrated with him.

"Well I sure can't do it alone, now can I?" He still didn't answer, and I started to get mad. He had to carry his weight or hit the road.

I decided to hell with being tactful. "All right, Zamora, I'll get to the point. I'm a team leader and field squad leader. I know about the gook, and I know about your cousin."

He looked at me with contempt.

"We all agree, you've had a bad start, but if every sniper was here now they would all tell you to pull yourself together and get back to work. The skipper is going to send you down if you don't snap out of it."

"What do you mean, send me down?"

"Put you in a grunt outfit, then you'll be up to your ass in it. You've seen what they go through, humping extra mortars and gun ammo, walking point, standing lines, not to mention the fact that you won't have any say as to what you do."

"All right, Ward. Listen, I thought I was right in coming here. Now I don't know."

"Put that gook bitch behind you. Beal's alive and you're alive, thanks to your quick action. I'd take you as a partner anytime."

"Really?"

"Sure, as soon as you get rid of that hard-on you're carrying about your cousin. I take it you and your cousin were pretty close?"

"Yeah, like brothers."

"Well, it seems to me, the best way to get even is to earn a bolt rifle and kick some ass. You'd best think of the other snipers as brothers, too." He nodded, yet I still wasn't convinced he would be able to put it all together. He wouldn't be the first sniper to wash out, but my instincts told me the guy was worth some extra effort.

"Why don't we go to the NCO mess and eat before I make it over to sick bay and get cleared for R and R."

"I wasn't figuring on eating."

"I don't want to make it an order, Zamora, but I'm going to tell the gunny you're ready to go back out, and you better get in the habit of eating good chow when it's available, which isn't very often. Besides I would like to talk to someone fresh from the World."

"Okay."

We exchanged the usual chitchat while we ate. When we had finished, it was time to cut to the chase.

"Okay, Zamora, what's it going to be? Are you ready to go back to work? I can get you sent to Hill 65. There's plenty to do."

"Yeah, I'll go back out."

"Good. You'll be working with a guy named Lance Corporal Terry Lightfoot. He's good, and he needs a sharp partner right now. Do you think you can be a good partner, Zamora?"

"Yes. I know I can."

"Great. I want to send a couple messages with you. Tell Davis to stay in charge of the program at the hill and also tell him that Charlie has upped the bounty on us, he'll know what to do. Be saddled up and at the main LZ by oh-five-hundred. Any questions?"

"Not really, but I still feel sick inside, Ward. That woman couldn't have been more than twenty-five years old."

"That sort of thing is going to happen once in a while, Zamora. If you hadn't been quick on the trigger, you and Beal would both be dead. Get back out there and stay busy. That's the best cure for what you got. I'll see you later."

I was about to leave the mess hall, when Zamora said, "Thanks."

"Don't thank me till you find out what I've gotten you into. There's a lot of experienced NVA near the hill right now."

During my last visit to the hospital, I ran into Ron Willingham. He was there for the same reason, he was going on R and R to Sydney, and we had the same flight. We were about to be party partners again.

While waiting to have the last section of my medical checked off, I halfway listened in on a conversation between a grunt getting his medical for R and R and corpsman. The corpsman really caught my attention when he gave the grunt a bottle of pills and told him, "These are peter-harder pills. Take one each day and you'll have a hard-on the whole time you're on R and R."

The grunt asked with real enthusiasm. "No shit, Doc?"

"No shit."

"Wow, Doc, thanks." He finished dressing and left.

I caught the corpsman's arm as he started past me. "Hey, Doc, I'm no expert on the subject, but since when did they invent a peter-harder pill?"

"Since never."

"But you just gave that guy some pills and—"

"Just vitamins, but as long as he thinks they'll work, they'll work. It's all in the mind."

In very few words that corpsman had summed up the whole war. It was all in the mind.

Three replacements instead of two came that afternoon, and the gunny was elated that Zamora would be going out. Things were cracking my way. Maybe, just maybe, this R and R was going to come about.

Chapter V ⋆ Getting Short

On February 5, Ron and I sprinted like hell to be sure we were in front of twenty guys scrambling to catch a thirteen-man helicopter for the ride to Da Nang.

I felt uncomfortable waiting around with a bunch of other GIs to board a plane. I nervously fingered a roll of nine one-hundred-dollar bills in my pocket and wondered what Australia was like.

I resisted three offers to double my money on the black market. I knew that within hours the greenbacks could be in enemy hands. It was a temptation too many men couldn't resist. My thoughts were interrupted by a captain on a small podium.

"Everyone, give me your attention please. I want three lines in front of the booths to your right." I looked to see three small cubicles with GI blankets covering the entrance to each. Standing on the other side of the cubicles were dog handlers and three very big, unfriendly looking German Shepherds.

"One man at a time will enter the booths and discard any illicit drugs in the containers provided. This will be your last chance, people; if the dogs catch you with any drugs on your person, they get to take them off of you."

When I went into the booth, an ammo can on a small shelf was quickly filling up with all manner of contraband. I tossed in a party pack of joints and chalked one up for the dogs. They weren't bluffing, either—each of us had to let a dog sniff him over before we could board.

Ron and I took a seat and let the 707 take us away from it all, for a while anyway. We made a short stop in Saigon to let people off and take on some, then it flew straight to Sydney—a five and a half hour flight. I saw the opera house from the plane window and knew I had finally made it.

When I actually set foot on the pavement, I said to Ron, "This is one small step for J.T. Ward, and one giant leap for the women of Sydney."

There was one small hitch. Where were we going to find them? We didn't know anything about Australia and Sydney was a very big city.

As fortune would have it, I needed a new camera. My last one bit the big one thanks to the monsoons. We had reservations at the most expensive hotel in the King's Cross district of town, and when we taxied there, I spotted a camera shop nearby.

We left our suitcases in our rooms and went straight to the camera shop. Ron bought an Instamatic, and I got an expensive Polaroid, but we got more for our money than the cameras, we got information. When I paid for my camera I asked the shop owner, "Where's a good place to find girls and cold beer?"

"Well, mate, there's two places where the birds go quite a bit to hook up with Yanks, the Motor Club and the Texas Tavern."

"Texas Tavern?" I asked, a little confused about that one.

"Right. A cabbie will know the way. Did you want anything besides the camera and film?"

"No, thanks."

Outside, Ron and I talked about whether or not the guy was on the level or giving us the same line he gave every GI who came into his store. We had to start somewhere. The Texas Tavern was our next stop. I don't know why they called it the Texas Tavern. The decor wasn't very Texan, but then we were a long way from Texas. The band was playing a song with the lyrics "nice to be here," and after my eyes adjusted to the darkness I agreed. It was a very big nightclub and full of people, with at least three women to each guy. The man at the camera store wasn't just jerking our cords.

We ordered drinks and sat at one of the few tables not occupied. In less than a minute, two young ladies sat down and started a conversation. I leaned over to whisper in Ron's ear.

"Not really my type, how about you?"

"No. Maybe if we ignore them, they'll go away."

We did and in a few minutes they left. It was that simple. We continued to nurse our drinks while two girls at a time came to our table. If one didn't meet with our approval, they moved on. They weren't hookers either, just working girls looking to party and have a good time with a GI and that wad of money they knew we all had. We had surely died and gone to heaven, surrounded by round-eyed women wanting to be that one in three picked.

In the middle of our second drink, the two we'd been waiting for sat down. A striking brunette I took to right away and an attractive blond Ron couldn't take his eyes off of. The course of the night was set.

We finished our drinks, and Ron suggested we get a couple of bottles and go back to our hotel rooms.

There weren't a lot of formalities at the hotel. We went to our own rooms and proceeded to party. It had been nearly a year since I'd been with a round-eyed woman like Cheryl and without a doubt, the war was the furthest thing from my mind.

I decided to spend the rest of my R and R with Cheryl. She treated me to an exciting look at Sydney from the Down under to the suburbs, and we became very good friends.

Ron pretty much went his own way, and I occasionally met him in the hallway at the hotel. He never really said much about it, but he did end up with a lot of pictures of the Sydney Zoo. On the plane ride back to Vietnam he kept gagging and sticking his finger in his mouth.

"Ron, what in the hell is wrong with you?"

He leaned over and softly whispered, "I got a pubic hair stuck in my throat."

"What's the problem, Ron?"

He looked at me in irritation. "I got a pubic hair caught in my throat."

"Oohh." The next time a stewardess came by I stopped her.

"I'm sorry to bother you ma'am, but Lance Corporal Willingham here has a pubic hair caught in his throat, and we thought that maybe some crackers and a soda might wash it down."

What a poised lady. She was the only one within earshot who didn't blush. Two men lightly rubbed their throats, while Ron went into shock.

She smiled and said, "I think I can find something," and went to the galley.

I'd never seen anyone paler when Ron looked at me. "Man, I don't believe you said that."

I winked at him. "No problem, Ron. What are pals for?"

"Ward, there's no way I'd go on another R and R with you. If I'm dying, I don't even want to be medevaced with you."

The closer we got to Vietnam, the quieter the passengers became. I'm sure it was just my imagination, but I thought I caught a whiff of Cheryl's perfume just before they opened the doors of the plane at Da Nang.

The oppressive midday heat and humidity of Vietnam assaulted me when I stepped out. I tried in vain to not think that only hours ago I was in the arms of a beautiful woman, in a country where everyone and everything wasn't trying to kill me.

Without the bolt rifle, I would actually have to catch the next bird to An Hoa. I looked forward to telling the gunny.

I rapped on the door and stuck my head in to say, "Hey, Gunny, guess who caught—" A master gunnery sergeant walked around the blankets that separated the office from the living quarters, but it wasn't Fergie.

"Excuse me, Gunny, but is Gunny Ferguson around?"

"Who the hell are you?"

"Corporal Ward. Begging your pardon, Gunny, but is . . ."

"So, you're Ward huh? I was told not to expect you for another day or two. Well, since you're here, we may as well get acquainted. I'm Master Gunnery Sergeant Berger, and this is my house now. Sit down."

I eased myself into that familiar old wooden chair that didn't seem quite so familiar anymore. "Excuse me, Gunny, did something happen to Sergeant Ferguson?"

"You might say that. He rotated home."

"Home?" I had never given any thought to the fact that Fergie's tour would end before mine.

"He left two days ago. He wanted me to give you this." He handed me a manila envelope. I looked at him. "Go on, open it. I won't be able to get your attention until you do."

Inside was a short handwritten letter.

Ward, take over second squad for Bear, he's out of here today, too. It's time to come in, Ward. Charlie knows you in three provinces. I didn't tell you about squad leader before you went on R and R 'cuz I didn't want to hassle with you about it.

Gunny Berger is okay, just cherry. I expect you and the rest of
the men to make his orientation as easy as possible.

Gunny Fergie

P.S. I didn't have any trouble at all catching a bird.

As saddened as I was that Fergie was gone, I was also glad
he got out okay, and I had to smile at the postscript. Fergie had
gotten in the last word and given it some teeth. Central squad
leader, the very thing I didn't want. He was right though, I
would have argued about it.

"Corporal Ward. Corporal Ward!"

"Uh, yes, Gunny Berger. Excuse me, but I just found out
I've got second squad to look after and well, I'm a little surprised that Gunny Fergie, I mean Ferguson is gone."

"Take it easy, Ward. Last time I checked, we were still on
the same side. This is all new to me, too, so I need as much
cooperation as I can get—from everyone, especially people
like you."

I was still going to try to get off the hook. "I've never turned
down extra work, Gunny, but I think Corporal Chesko would
be very good with second squad, and I feel I have more to offer
in the bush." I shut up when he shook his head no.

He leaned back in his chair, seemingly satisfied that he was
more than one step ahead of me. "Sergeant Ferguson said you
might try something like this. I don't know the why of it and
don't want to. He told me to tell you, and I quote, 'It's either
central squad leader or permanent assignment to Hill 65,' end
quote." He just stared at me.

"No problem, Gunny Berger. I'll get on second squad right
away."

"Good. Since I've inherited the best sniper platoon in this
country, I doubt that I'll have any problems."

I tried to pay attention to him as he talked, but my mind was
drifting. It's not that Gunny Berger wasn't an okay guy, but I
was sure going to miss Fergie. Suddenly it dawned on me that
the skipper was also there when I arrived, and I interrupted
Gunny Berger again.

"Excuse me, Gunny, but is the skipper still here?"

"Yes, Ward, Captain Hudson is here. He signed on for six
more months, and I understand he'll be going on a thirty-day
leave."

Great, I thought. The skipper shipped for six, which helped

take some of the pain out of losing Fergie. I answered Berger's questions for the next twenty minutes, and as we talked, I figured I could get along with him just fine. I made sure by asking him if he knew how hard it was to catch a bird sometimes, and he replied, "I'm sure it is."

I was grateful to some out-going artillery that ended the conversation. I moved my gear from the team leader's tent to the squad leader's tent. There was plenty of room since there were only the three of us: Staff Sergeant Rogers, first squad; Sergeant Talley, who'd taken over third squad when Sergeant Pule rotated home; and me.

I wasn't used to such luxury. The tent was divided into living quarters by blankets. There was a bigger refrigerator than the one in the team leaders' tent, and it usually had beer or soda in it. Rogers had a nice reel-to-reel stereo and the cots had rubber bitches (inflatable air mattress).

I had one small problem though; I was the lowest ranking central squad leader. Fortunately, I knew Rogers and Talley well, and the only hitch I saw coming was that I was last in line for replacements.

I threw my gear on Bear's cot and took the clipboard hanging from the tent pole. I looked over the list of names and where each team was.

I had inherited four teams. They were listed by team leader, spotter, and location: Mendoza and Laird—Liberty Bridge, Feekes and Wunnicke—Ass. C.H. (on assignment in central highlands); Suther and Holder—India 2/5, AZ (Arizona); Craig and Lightfoot—Ass. AZ. I already had a problem. Two of my teams were in Arizona, and I was certain the two other squad leaders didn't have the same number of men there. Before I could do anything about it, I had to find out why both teams were there.

Talley and Rogers weren't in the tent so I checked their clipboards. Just what I figured, neither had a team in Arizona. It didn't take me long to figure out a way to even things out, but I needed both of them together. Suppertime would be good.

I went to go to the command bunker to be sure of what my teams were doing. I didn't like the command bunker, even though it was air-conditioned. It was dark and depressing. As central squad leader, I'd be spending too much time there and often contemplated going on medical hold just to get away from the frustration I felt. CI's information was often dated and the special assignments were getting riskier, not to mention the night flights. As far as my morale was concerned, central squad leader was the low point of my tour.

I had to show my Geneva Convention card (which passed for a military ID in a Combat zone) to get in, and it had to match up with a list of about forty people permitted ready access to the briefing room. Clipboards and tactical maps covered two walls. I went to the board with the assignments for HQ company.

McClain and Wright were listed as on assignment near An Hoa, which was good, they'd be in soon. Lola and Kilmnput were after a colonel just north of Arizona. That was an open-ended assignment, no time limit. Logan and Payne were more or less floaters, and I set my sights on them. They were in Rogers's squad and that was also a plus.

As it turned out, Talley was the one to lose one good team to me: McClain and Wright. Craig was getting short, and I wanted to get him out of Arizona. McClain and Wright were due back anytime, and when they came in Talley had to give them the bad news. They were going out to replace Craig and Lightfoot.

I ended up with four good teams, and it looked like things were going as well as possible until part of my plan to keep Craig out of Arizona backfired on me.

On the twentieth, Craig and Lightfoot were still in the rear awaiting an assignment coming up in the central highlands, but counterintelligence came up with a night flight before I could get them assigned out. Lance Corporal Moore's partner had been wounded, and Moore was in the rear waiting for a new spotter. I had the only other team leader in, and I couldn't bring myself to send Craig on a night flight; he had just over a week to go before rotating home. I decided to take his place. I knew that what I was doing was against regulations, but night flights were just too risky to send a guy that short on.

There were no problems with the mission. The problems began when I got back. Gunny Berger met the chopper when it landed, and I knew I'd been caught when I saw him.

"What the fuck do you think you're doing, Ward?"

"Working, Gunny."

"Well, nice work, the skipper wants to see you ASAP!"

"Do I have time to clean up?"

"No."

Damn, I thought, here I go again. I had camouflage paint on

when I entered the skipper's tent. It was nearly midnight, but he was still in his uniform.

"Sit down, Ward." I did and waited for him to start the conversation.

"It looks like you've been out tonight."

"Yes, sir."

"Have you been in South Vietnam all night?" He was getting right to the point.

"No, sir."

"No, shit! Did Gunny Berger or I know where you were going?"

"No, sir, I don't think so."

"No, shit. Three no shits and you're in trouble, Ward; that's two. I've got some rebellious fuckers in this outfit, but you beat anyone in second place, Ward. We do have a chain of command in case you've forgotten. Guess who I found out from."

"I don't know, sir."

"Does the name Colonel Webster ring a bell?"

"Yes, sir."

"Yeah, well, I saw your name on the roster of men he gave me who went on that assignment. You're a central squad leader, Ward. I don't need your ass hung out lost somewhere. Especially with a new gunny aboard. It's time to come in from the bush, Ward. What am I going to do with you?"

There it was, the question I was waiting for and dreading, but I had to have some kind of answer. By that point in my tour I'd become pretty cynical, and the only thing I could think to say was, "Send me to Vietnam, sir?"

"Not funny, Ward. I'm about to go on a thirty-day leave, and I'd appreciate not having to worry about my people while I'm laid up with my wife. Is that too much to ask, Ward?"

"No, sir."

He sat down, his face seemingly more relaxed than his words. He opened a drawer and took out a bottle of Chivas Regal and two coffee mugs.

"You drink Scotch, don't you, Ward?"

"Sir?"

"Do you drink Scotch?"

"Yes, sir."

An Hoa was unusually quiet, no outgoing artillery, no incoming rockets, just a faint background of stereos and the sound of Scotch pouring into a coffee mug. He slid a cup across the desk to me. I picked it up, took two hefty swallows, and relaxed back in my chair with a sigh. Along with our varied duties, the night flights had taken their toll on me and the team leaders. I didn't remember Scotch tasting so good.

"I understand your intentions, Ward, I really do. And I respect that, but you're not in the bush anymore. I need you here. Gunny Berger needs you, so do Talley, Rogers, and the rest of the men. I nearly canceled my R and R when I found out Berger was cherry. I still may. Ward, tell me no more stunts and I'll go."

"No more stunts, sir, I mean it."

"I think I've been here too long, I actually believe you. You'll rotate home while I'm on leave, is that right?"

"Yes, sir."

"You thinking of staying in?"

"No, sir."

"Sorry to hear that. It's been a stupendous pain in the ass and a pleasure serving with you, Ward."

"You, too, sir." We toasted. He turned to other business.

"I want a team ready by 0530 to go to Fox 2/5, right here." He pointed to a circled spot on a map on the desk. It looked to be about five miles northeast of Ben Dau. "They're having trouble with a gook sniper. He's bagged four men and wounded ten. They can't find him, and they can't shake him. Forty-eight hours, Ward, I want it taken care of in forty-eight hours."

"You got it, Skipper." I emptied my cup, set it down, and left to clean up. I fell asleep with my paint still on.

That built-in alarm clock I had woke me at 0400. As I wearily walked to the team leader's tent, I pondered the fact that Vietnam was a very transient place. Nearly the whole platoon had been replaced since I'd joined it. The skipper was probably right. It was time to come in from the bush and maybe even think about going home; after all, I was getting short myself.

Feekes and Wunnicke had just come into the rear, and I was already waking Ron up to go on another assignment, a dangerous assignment. I called Ron's name. He immediately sat up in his cot.

"Who the fuck is it?"

"Take it easy, Ron, it's Ward. I'll start some coffee while you go get Wunnicke. I have a job for you."

With the coffee made and the light of the burning C-4 replaced by the light of a flashlight, Ron was the first to speak. "Okay, ole partner, what is it this time?"

"Remember that day in Arizona when the captain wouldn't let us go after the sniper who raised so much hell?"

"Yeah, so?"

"Here's your chance to get even. Fox 2/5 has one screwing up their program, at least they think there's only one. He hits a man or two and disappears. I know you guys need some rest, but you're in the slot."

Ron let out a sigh. "Well, there ain't no other fuckers around here just like us fuckers, so we must be the fuckers. When do we leave?"

"The bird you want leaves at oh-five-thirty. The skipper wants him taken out in forty-eight hours, but take as long as you need, and track him down." I got up to leave.

"Anything else, Joe?"

"Yeah, be careful, Ron. He's four and ten."

"No sweat. See you in a couple days." He sat back down to fix another cup of coffee. There was no hurry. We were always packed, always dressed, always ready to go.

I went back to my cot, but I couldn't sleep. I was growing tired of sending my best friends out and never knowing if I would see them again.

*

Scout Snipers
Australia/An Hoa
February 17, 1970

Dear Mom,

Well, I got back to An Hoa okay. While I was gone they made me central squad leader which means I'll be around most of the time. I sure don't like sending the guys out.

There was a bunch of letters and cards from you here when I returned. I hope I answered most of your questions. It was really great talking to you. I kept telling myself that it won't be much longer until I'm out of this country.

I had a wonderful time in Sydney. There were plenty of round-eyed girls and entertainment. The people were just great. It was hard to leave. I'll tell you about it when I get home, which won't be too long.

Now, Mom, I want you to be ready on short notice to stop everyone from writing to me. I'll really be in a tizzy when my orders come through. As of this letter, don't send any more packages.

I'm enclosing a tax return, so would you take care of it for me? Mom, I'll close now and write more when I have time. Take special care.

Love, Joseph

I was getting so short, I didn't think I'd be spending another night in the bush, but I was wrong.

On the twenty-fifth, Gunny Berger gave me some bad news. Wunnicke's father had died, and I had to get the word to him as quickly as possible.

That sort of problem had a pretty high priority, and I was able to get a Huey to take me out just before dark. Wunnicke and Feekes were with Hotel 1/5 about two miles north of Arizona. I had intended to get a hold of them and catch the same bird back. Unfortunately, I had missed them. They were out on a hunter-kill and probably wouldn't be back for several hours.

I found the skipper and told him I'd have to pull the team and why. The company had changed skippers since I last worked with them. Captain Dale understood, even though he really wanted and needed a team. He told me they were crossing the river into Arizona in two days to hook up with three other companies and act as a blocking force for Alpha and Bravo 2/5 working with a battalion of ROKs.

"ROKs, huh, skipper?"

"Yes."

"Well, you guys probably won't even have to clean your rifles, except to knock off a little rust. If there's a team available when I get back, I'll send them out to you. Speaking of getting back in, when is your next resupply?"

"Oh-eight-hundred."

I got up to leave. "I'll be seeing you around, Skipper." He nodded, and I walked to the spot where Feekes and Wunnicke had put up a shelter for the night.

While awaiting their return, I grabbed a can of C Rations from Ron's pack, but I didn't have much of an appetite. I was worried about how I was going to give the word to Wunnicke; I was also fighting the urge to stay out as Feekes's partner until a replacement could be found. I had to put that idea out of my head. I'd promised the skipper. With him gone on leave and Gunny Berger being new, it was a bad time to make waves.

I didn't know Wunnicke well, only that he and Ron had been together since I took over second squad and they made a first-rate team. When I last saw Ron about a week and half earlier, he told me Wunnicke would be ready for a bolt rifle in five weeks and that he was coming along fine.

It was dark, the only illumination came from flares where the sweeping force several miles in the distance was meeting light enemy resistance.

The team returned to the company at 9:15 P.M. and as soon as they saw me they knew something was probably wrong. Except for occasional mail and pay, central squad leaders rarely brought good news.

Ron spoke first. "What's going on, Ward?"

I'd decided to be formal and to the point, at least at first. I turned to face Wunnicke. "Mike, I'm very sorry to tell you this, but your father died late yesterday." The look on his face told me he was hoping there had been a mistake.

"What?"

"I think you heard me, Mike."

"My old man's as strong as a bull. How could he just up and die?"

"I don't know Mike, but I read the dispatch myself. It came out of San Francisco. I'm really sorry, man."

I hadn't just told Wunnicke, but I'd told the other half of his very being, Feekes. As friends and partners they would both grieve the rest of the night together.

The next morning, the resupply chopper was right on time. When we boarded, Wunnicke had started the process that would have him home within forty-eight hours. I wondered what kind of sniper he would be when he came back. Would he come back? I would never know.

The following day, Gunny Berger and the three squad leaders were called into the gunny's tent. With the skipper gone, the gunny was in charge. I tried to shake off a feeling of foreboding as we all stood at attention.

"Sit down men. I've just received word from Colonel Webster that a sniper in this platoon is suspected of murdering a civilian. The name of the dead man is Truong Nguyen, and he lived near the village of Ben Dau. Talley, the sniper in question is in your squad. I have no intention of involving civilian or military authorities in this matter until we know what happened. Get to the bottom of this matter and do it posthaste. Do I make myself clear?"

"Yes, sir."

"Good. Now, acquaint yourselves with the report. I expect an answer within the week." The gunny handed each of us a manila envelope.

We went to our tent and discussed the contents of the file. According to the report, Truong Nguyen's body was found along a trail leading to the village. He had been shot in the chest and the bullet, having passed through the body, was lost. A witness had stated he saw an American sniper shoot Truong Nguyen. His description fit that of one of the men.

It was decided that we would question the sniper and his partner separately. That way neither would know why they had been called in or have a chance to discuss the incident. We returned to our tent and began.

The team admitted to being near the village on the day of the murder while with a company on a hunter-kill, but denied any knowledge of the incident. When the sniper found out what he was suspected of doing, he was terrified. He lacked a motive for the killing, and he was a good sniper. Talley, Rogers, and I felt the team was telling the truth. Still, we had a dead man, a witness, and spotty details. I decided to ask Lee if he could gather the missing information.

Lee had already heard about Truong Nguyen's death, but hadn't pursued it any further. In just two days he had the details we needed. The witness turned out to be a relative of the dead man and, according to Lee, a feud had existed between the two men for quite some time. By talking to family members on both sides, Lee was able to piece together a reasonable scenario.

In less than a week we gave the gunny his report. The sniper was cleared of any wrongdoing, and the information Lee had gathered was turned over to the civilian authorities.

*

Scout Snipers
An Hoa
February 27, 1970

Dear Mom,

I'll make this short as I have a few to write tonight. I'm sure you'll be pleased to know I'm coming home, so stop all mail. I leave the 3d of March, which means they gave me a thirty day huss. I'll be home within two weeks.

Now don't be surprised if mail from people you've never heard of starts arriving at the house for me. Maybe even from girls.

I'll call from California as soon as I get there.

As I expected, things are moving pretty fast right now. I better close cuz I have so much to do. You better warn everyone, I'm coming home.

Love, Joseph

By the twenty-eighth, I was down to two teams. Mendoza was out with shrapnel wounds and Lightfoot had malaria. Both would probably be back before long, but the squads were down in strength. I was right about being last in line for replacements, until Rogers rotated home on the first of March. There was a partial squad left that Talley and I could pick men from and another opening for a central squad leader.

The gunny left it up to us to choose Rogers's replacement. I wanted McClain, he'd proved himself to me. He was also getting short and didn't take shit from anyone. Talley wanted Airs, a man in his squad and the only other sergeant in the platoon. I couldn't believe it, but Talley was willing to flip coins, two out of three, to decide who would fill the spot. Corporal McClain became the new central squad leader. He had one team to start building a new squad with, but replacements were trickling in. I did make a concession though, I told Talley that Sergeant Airs would be my recommendation to the gunny for my spot when I left.

I pulled Dean Suther into An Hoa long enough to get him started with Lee Oot. When Dean and I went to see Lee on March 3d, he was yelling at some of the militiamen, but stopped when he saw us coming. He rushed up to me saying, "Joe, Joe, you must help me tell the men to no shoot at every noise."

"Whoa, slow down, Lee. What's the matter?"

"Joe, men blow eight claymores last night and kill water bull just because they hear noise." I was a little angry.

"Lee, I told you how hard claymores are to get right now."

"I know, Joe, I know, but you must help them understand."

"I'm afraid not, Lee. Dean is taking my place here. I won't be coming back out." Lee got that look on his face that always melted my heart. He nodded.

"Maybe you come back someday and see Lee?"

"Maybe, Lee." We hugged.

"Dean, get the men together and show them how to set those claymores, and give 'em hell for wasting this stuff."

I swore not to look back when I left, but I'm glad I did. Lee was pulling Dean by the sleeve and shouting for the militia to gather round. That was the last time I saw Lee Oot, my friend.

I stopped at Ann's, but didn't stay long. She had decided to go to Da Nang in hopes of finding a GI to marry and get out of Vietnam. Given the direction the war was going, it was the best course of action for her. No doubt she succeeded. I kissed her tear-streaked cheek and that was my good-bye to Ann Bae, friend and lover.

★

Scout Snipers
An Hoa
March 3, 1970

Dear Mom,

This will be my last letter from here. Wanted you to know they moved my flight date to the 9th which will mean only a few extra days.

Everything is going okay. I sent home a check today in the amount of $955.00.

I got a letter today from Randy Peterson and he said that Dave was on hold in Okinawa, so it looks like I'll beat him home.

I was at Hill 37 the other day and talked to Mike. He said he may get out sometime this month.

Not much else to say so I'll get for now. Will send a Mars-O-Gram when I get to Da Nang. Bye.

Love, Joseph

With my orders pushed back to the ninth, I had a few extra days in An Hoa to tie up loose ends. I used it to get out to check on my teams one last time, take them mail, and say good-bye.

The morning sun on the fifth greeted an usually peaceful Vietnam. I'd taken the last chopper from Liberty Bridge and partied all night with the Seabees. I was sitting alone on an empty bunker with my orders in my hand. They stated I was to catch an afternoon chopper to Da Nang and process home the ninth. Those few papers I held were what it was all about, or were they? I was mildly amused at how the government thought it could take the last year of my life and reduce it to one manilla envelope. No I wasn't tired that day, I was never more alive.

I saw Gunny Berger near the chow hall, and he suggested we eat in the NCO mess. As we sat down at a private table, I reflected on how rarely I'd taken advantage of those comforts.

"God, Ward, you look like hell. Where you been the last thirty-six hours? No forget it, I don't want to know."

"I wouldn't want to bore you, Gunny."

"I doubt if you would. You're out of here today."

"Right, I catch a bird this afternoon."

"Did Captain Mills see you yet?"

"Mills, who's Mills? What's he want me for? I swear, Gunny, I haven't done anything."

"Relax, he just wants to give you a re-up talk. You have to see him and get his signature on your orders before you can leave."

"Oh, yeah, shit, I forgot about that. I'll get over there after breakfast. Are there any messages you want to send with me back to the World, Gunny?"

"Nah, I'm afraid if I had you stop and tell my wife I was okay, you'd probably try to screw her." He held up his coffee cup. "Here's to you, Ward."

"Thanks Gunny. By the way, I'd like to be the one to post the kills today."

"Sure. Come by after you've seen Mills."

I went straight from the mess hall to Captain Mills's tent. I didn't give any thought to how I looked and I wasn't a pretty sight. I hadn't shaved in two days. I was wearing my trusty blue T-shirt and had a match bullet hanging from love beads around my neck. Of course my hair was too long. I knocked on his tent door and he told me to enter. I stepped in.

"Corporal Ward reporting as ordered, sir." I didn't wait for him to tell me to sit down, I just did. He looked at me for a moment and rubbed his forehead.

"You don't want to re-up, do you?"

"No, sir."

"Well I'm gonna tell you this anyway." He thumbed through some papers on his desk. "Ward, yeah, here you are. Ah, let's see. I can offer you three thousand dollars and staff sergeant if you ship for six months. Six thousand and sergeant if you go for a year." He looked at me.

"No thanks, sir."

"Okay. You've got four more months left in your enlistment. How about this. You ship for two months to make it an even six, and you get the three grand, staff, and trainer at sniper school Stateside.'' He looked at me this time with a slightly raised eyebrow.

I didn't answer. Damn, I thought, that wasn't fair. He nearly had me, and he knew it. We were both quiet for a minute. I liked the idea that I could train snipers and maybe, just maybe make a real difference. The next few seconds were the hardest of my life.

"I'm sorry, sir. I've given the Corps everything I've got. I'm empty now. I appreciate the offer, but I'll have to turn it down.''

"That's too bad, Ward. You've got a good record, and the Corps needs people like you. Well, I'll put you down for an early out, and you'll be a civilian in a week, but if you change your mind the offer stands. Whatever you do, I wish you the best.''

"Thank you, sir.''

I left Captain Mills's tent with a great sense of loss. I still felt an obligation to the Corps, but I meant what I said about being empty. Through obstacles that might have stopped other men, I had seen my tour to the end, and to do it took all I had to give. By staying in the bush, I had wrecked my knee and would need to have more surgery later at a VA hospital. I didn't get a partner killed and never shot the wrong person. I'd set the moral standards for the 5th Regiment's involvement with night flights, and had passed on a solid legacy of CAP work. Above all, I'd met and served with people who would have a positive influence on me the rest of my life. I could leave with pride.

I still had the Corps in my blood. "Once a Marine, always a Marine,'' and that's something no one could ever take away from me. That was the day I really said good-bye to the Corps, not a few days later in California.

I cleaned up and went to the gunny's tent to get the tally of confirms from the previous day. I hadn't posted the kills since I was made central squad leader and turned in my 63d and final kill sheet, but it was different this time. It was my way of saying good-bye to the platoon. I looked at the total, reflecting briefly on how it had grown and would continue to grow after I left, right up to the day this honorable group of men pulled out of Vietnam.

I didn't bother with lunch, I was making final preparations to leave. I double-checked my paper work and clipboard to be sure they were up-to-date and accurate. Sergeant Airs should be able to move into my position with no problems hanging loose.

With that completed, I packed the few personal belongings I had and went to say my final good-byes. It didn't take long with only three snipers and Gunny Berger in the rear.

I walked the path to the LZ for the last time, and when I got there two Chinooks were landing, their sole purpose was to transport to Da Nang men who were rotating home.

When we boarded, the word was passed that the pilots were going to make our last helicopter ride one to remember and they sure as hell did.

I had no doubts about the pilot's skill, but they kept my heart in my throat as they flew at high speed, scant feet above the rice-paddy dikes. Suddenly our chopper would rise and the other bird would slip underneath and end up on the opposite side, rotors nearly touching. They were swinging from side to side and doing maneuvers that would please a crowd at an air show, but not the guys riding along, only wanting to get to Da Nang alive. I let out a sigh of relief when we landed.

Processing out of Da Nang was more akin to the procedure a person would go through if he had been contaminated, and I suppose in many ways we had been. My pride took several blows as my jungle utilities and boots were disposed of and I was issued new ones. A doctor's examination was followed by a three-day informal quarantine.

On the morning of the ninth, I was dressed in freshly starched utilities and ready for inspection. After passing inspection, I went through the same dog-sniffing routine they pulled going on R and R.

I stepped onto the tarmac, and there it was—my freedom bird. Not just any freedom bird, but mine. All was quiet as we taxied to the runway and began our take-off. The instant the wheels cleared the runway, a window-rattling cheer filled the cabin, and the stewardess joined in.

Landing in Okinawa was another three days of processing, medical and dental exams, and a move up to dress uniforms. I was unhappy at having to pay a civilian a full box of Hershey bars to sew on my corporal stripes to pass final inspection in California. In Vietnam I could have gotten a mama-san to sew those stripes on for a box of C rations.

Not much had changed in Okinawa. I spent my spare time at

the NCO club, drinking Singapore slings, playing the slot machines, watching the B-52s take off, and not answering questions about the war from men on their way to Vietnam.

The flight to El Toro Marine Air Station in California was torturously long. There was another cheer when we landed, followed by the voice of the pilot over the intercom: "Gentlemen, we have just landed in the United States of America." We taxied to an area three hundred yards from the main terminal. "Due to conditions at the terminal, we regret that you must disembark here and follow the officer waiting outside."

We could see what the problem was—war protesters, about fifty of them gathered near the entrance to the terminal.

At the door to the ramp, a Marine captain with a clipboard was checking names and muttering a greeting of sorts that for some reason sounded familiar.

It came my turn to stand in front of him and I understood him say "Ward?" I nodded. Then he mumbled something, something that sounded like, "Welcome to the War-ld Ward."

Where had I heard this all before?

Epilogue

The four of us who joined the Marine Corps together returned and settled within a fifty-mile radius of our home town. Between us, we share six Purple Hearts.

Mike O'Grady works as a dispatcher for a concrete company.

Nick Herrera is a Class-A welder with a well known brewery.

Dave Young was a foreman with a large construction company.*

Joseph Ward is, well, sitting here writing this.

The dollar bill we tore in fourths to be taped back together to buy a beer and toast our safe return remains in four pieces twenty-two years later.

---

*David L. Young, born March 15, 1949, died June 9, 1991. Dave's request to be buried on the Manshantuket Pequot Indian Reservation was honored by the tribal council. He is the first nontribal member to be buried there.

About the Author

Joseph T. Ward was born in 1949 and grew up in New Raymer, Colorado, population one hundred, in the heart of the Pawnee National Grasslands, He began target shooting with a Remington single shot .22 caliber rifle at age five, under the supervision of his mother Doris and older brother Larry. His family moved to Longmont, Colorado, in 1961. He was honorably discharged from the United States Marine Corps in 1970.

In intervening years he has worked numerous jobs from grave digger to engineer in the oil business. J.T. began writing *Dear Mom: A Sniper's Vietnam* in 1979. Currently he resides near Longmont with his wife Rita and faithful dog, Seltzer.

"Morning was always a welcome sight to us. It meant two things. The first was that we were still alive. . . ."

A SNIPER IN THE ARIZONA
2nd Battalion, 5th Marines, in the Arizona Territory, 1967

by John J. Culbertson
Author of *Operation Tuscaloosa*

In 1967, death was the constant companion of the Marines of Hotel Company, 2/5, as they patrolled the paddy dikes, mud, and mountains of the Arizona Territory southwest of Da Nang. This riveting, bloody first-person account offers a stark testimony to the stuff U.S. Marines are made of.

Published by Ivy Books.
Available in your local bookstore in March 1999.

INSIDE THE CROSSHAIRS
Snipers in Vietnam

By Michael Lee Lanning

At the start of the war in Vietnam, the United States had no snipers; by the end of the war, Marine and army precision marksmen had killed more than 10,000 NVA and VC soldiers—the equivalent of an entire division—at the cost of under 20,000 bullets. Now noted military historian Michael Lee Lanning shows how U.S. snipers in Vietnam—combining modern technology in weapons, ammunition, and telescopes—used the experience and traditions of centuries of expert shooters to perfect their craft.

Lanning interviewed men with combat trigger time, as well as their instructors, the founders of the Marine and U.S. Army sniper programs, and the generals to whom they reported. The author demonstrates how the skills of these one-shot killers honed in the jungles of Vietnam provided an indelible legacy that helped save American lives in Grenada, the Gulf War, Somalia, and Bosnia.

Published by Ivy Books.
Available at bookstores everywhere.